A THEOLOGY OF
CHRISTIAN SPIRITUALITY

A THEOLOGY OF CHRISTIAN SPIRITUALITY

SAMUEL M. POWELL

Abingdon Press
Nashville

A THEOLOGY OF CHRISTIAN SPIRITUALITY

Copyright © 2005 by Abingdon Press

This book is printed on acid-free paper.

Library of Congress Cataloging-in-Publication Data

Powell, Samuel M.
  A theology of Christian spirituality / Samuel M. Powell.
     p. cm.
  Includes index.
  ISBN 0-687-49333-1 (binding: perfect, adhesive : alk. paper)
  1. Bible. N.T.—Introductions. 2. Spirituality. I. Title.

BS2330.3.P68 2005
248—dc22

                                                                                            2005000969

05 06 07 08 09 10 11 12 13 14—10 9 8 7 6 5 4 3 2 1

MANUFACTURED IN THE UNITED STATES OF AMERICA

CONTENTS

ACKNOWLEDGMENTS

Gratitude is due to my wife, Terrie, for years of unfailing support and love, without which I could not have written this book. Thanks are due to: Point Loma Nazarene University's Wesleyan Center for Twenty-first Century Studies for support in the writing of this book; Kathy Armistead of Abingdon Press, for the original conception of this book and for encouragement and ideas along the way; and to my colleagues in the School of Theology and Christian Ministry at Point Loma Nazarene University for helpful dialogue.

CHAPTER ONE

A PRELUDE TO CHRISTIAN SPIRITUALITY

Christian theology is the attempt to state clearly truths that cannot be lived easily. It is the task of the pastor—by reproof, rebuke, and exhortation—to help Christians with that life. By seeking clarity of understanding, theology contributes to the pastoral task and, indirectly, contributes to that life. The purpose of this book is to describe as clearly as possible the theology and some leading practices of Christian spirituality as they have been expounded in the Christian tradition. As such, this book is intended for students of the Christian faith, especially those who have special responsibility for the well-being of the church and its members.

A few prefatory words may be useful in conveying what is meant by a theological study of Christian spirituality. This book is neither a work of historiography nor a sociological snapshot of Christians' spirituality today. A theology cannot be a simple historical narrative of past practices, because Christians in the past have individually and collectively done a great many things contrary to authentic spirituality. It would be highly unedifying to identify the essence of Christian spirituality with the sum total of practices in the past. Consequently, we must exercise theological judgment in appropriating Christian history. At the same time, the theologian must respect the tradition of Christian spirituality and attend closely to practices that have become normative. To do otherwise would be to claim that we have nothing to learn from the past. This book is also not a social scientific description of what Christians are doing now. Although the theologian must be aware of the forms that Christian spirituality currently is taking, such a snapshot does not tell us what form Christian spirituality today *should* take. As long as the church exists in the midst of a fallen world, we cannot assume that what Christians actually are doing is just what they should be doing.

If a theological account of spirituality is neither historiography nor sociological description, what is it? It is a theological description and analysis of those aspects of the Christian life that, in the collective and cumulative wisdom of the church, have been recognized as normative and essential for our well-being as disciples. Its subject is those beliefs and practices that the church believes ought to characterize the life of every Christian and without which we are not faithful servants of God.

The fact that theology deals with the essential and normative features of spirituality means additionally that it has the task of helping the pastor and church leaders discriminate the good from the bad. Those with special responsibility for the well-being of the church must, in each generation, survey the religious landscape and determine the extent to which prevailing Christian practices conform to the classic and essential features articulated by theology. They must also take note of contemporary cultural practices that may have an influence on the church's practices. In the cultural context that this book presupposes (the United States of the early twenty-first century), there are three realities that make an articulation of a distinctively *Christian* spirituality a matter of urgent need.

First, we live in a culture that is, increasingly, religiously pluralistic. With the Christian church no longer enjoying a monopoly on the religious life of America, it is good for the church's leaders to know and to be able to articulate what makes Christian spirituality *Christian*. Whatever view we take on the question of the validity of and the truth in other religions, nothing is to be gained from allowing the common opinion to go unchallenged that all religions are, ultimately, the same. Regardless of whatever validity other religions may possess, the Christian church has the task of bearing witness to the gospel and living according to it. For this task, a clear knowledge of the distinctive features of Christian spirituality is needed.

Second, we live in a post-Christian America. By this I mean not only that America today is religiously pluralistic, but also that we can no longer take for granted any significant degree of knowledge about the Bible and the Christian faith on the part of the American public. There was a time when American culture was saturated with knowledge of the Bible. It may have been casual knowledge, and misunderstanding may have abounded, but even those who had no liking for Christianity nonetheless had some knowledge of biblical teachings. Revivalistic preaching and public moral exhortation, accordingly, could presuppose a widespread acquaintance with the elements of the Christian faith. Today the situation is quite different. Today we can presuppose no significant degree of biblical knowledge either among Americans in general or even in the church. Many of those in the church have not been schooled in the rudiments of the Christian faith as previous generations were schooled. For this reason, the church has an important educational task, both for its members (catechesis) and for those outside the church (evangelism). An articulation of the distinctive features of Christian spirituality is required for this task.

Third, the fact that our culture is post-Christian means that there is a residual tendency to identify the American ethos and the Christian ethos. Although there are probably few (in America) who still assume that one is a Christian precisely and only because he or she is an American, there is still a widespread impression that there is a high degree of harmony between Christian values and American values. We should subject this impression to critical and theological scrutiny. Although there is nothing to be gained from drawing the distinction between church and nation to the point of caricature by demonizing American culture, it is a valuable service for the theologian to explain, in practical terms, the important differences between the Christian life and the American life.

A Few Definitions

A few preliminary semantic points may provide a helpful orientation to our subject. First, it is valuable to note the difference between the *unique* features of Christian spirituality and its *distinctive* features. The *unique* features of Christian spirituality are those that only Christianity and no other religion or community exhibits. The *distinctive* features are the recurrent and enduring beliefs and practices of the Christian life that the church collectively endorses. A theological account should focus on

3

the distinctive features, not the unique features. A book about the unique aspects of the Christian life might be an important contribution, but it would also be a very slim volume, for many Christian practices (such as prayer, fasting, and acts of compassion) are mirrored in other religions. These practices are not unique to Christianity, although they are distinctive because they are recurrent and enduring. Of course, there are uniquely Christian elements in these practices (for example, the fact that Christians pray in the name of Jesus), but studying only the unique elements would mean missing much that is important. It would mean abstracting from the totality of the Christian life only those aspects that have no parallel in other religions and cultures.

Second, it may be helpful to distinguish *spirituality* from related terms in the Christian vocabulary. I am thinking here especially of *holiness, righteousness,* and *virtue.*

Holiness and righteousness are easily confused because, in some parts of the Bible, they are distinct, while in others their meanings converge. In many passages of the Old Testament, holiness designates that which is devoted to God's service, especially for use in the temple and which is thus free from impurity. Righteousness characterizes those who obey God's will and are thus free from guilt. The distinction between holiness and righteousness is evident if we consider utensils employed in the temple. They are holy because they are devoted to God's service but could never be considered righteous. But the distinction is less clear with human beings, for, as the Old Testament preaches, Israel's holiness implied the necessity of practicing righteousness. This connection between holiness and righteousness comes to be strengthened in the biblical tradition, so that in the New Testament there is little difference between the two. Yet neither holiness nor righteousness exhausts the meaning of spirituality. Both are necessary aspects of it, but it is more extensive than being devoted to God's service and obeying God's will. It goes beyond freedom from impurity and guilt. It may seem odd to say that there is more to the Christian life than devotion and obedience; but spirituality, in common use, includes devotional practices and subjective attitudes not strictly encompassed by devotion and obedience.

It is similar with virtue and spirituality. The latter certainly embraces the developing of a virtuous Christian character. Although spirituality has the closest of connections to the practices that result in a virtuous character, it is not equivalent to such a character. At least as traditionally portrayed, virtue is a matter of being disposed to act in appropriate ways as the situation demands. The connection to Christian spirituality is obvious, for we can hardly be considered spiritual Christians if we are not disposed to act appropriately. Nonetheless, the language of virtue does not say everything about spirituality that we want to say. Spirituality is about not only acting, but also reverence toward and fear of God as well as hope, compassion, and other states that are not simply dispositions to act. No doubt authentic reverence, fear, hope, and compassion will issue forth in concrete acts. But they are not simply reducible to certain acts.

The term that comes closest to describing spirituality is *piety*. Unfortunately, this term is particularly ill-suited in our day. In common use it suggests either an excessively moralistic view of the Christian life or an attitude of judgmental and self-righteous smugness. Although it has come to have these meanings, it deserves rescuing because it sums up nicely the main features of the Christian's relation to God. John Calvin wrote forcefully on this point: piety is "that reverence joined with love of God which the knowledge of his benefits induces."[1] It defines religion: "Pure and real religion . . . [is] faith so joined with an earnest fear of God that this fear also embraces willing reverence, and carries with it such legitimate worship as is prescribed in the law."[2] Accordingly, it is a necessary condition of authentic knowledge of God, which "is that by which we not only conceive that there is a God, but also grasp what befits us and is proper to his glory. . . . Indeed we shall not say that, properly speaking, God is known where there is no religion or piety."[3] So, because everything embraced in the Christian life—love of neighbor, self-discipline, spiritual exercises, public worship, and so on—is done because of and in service to God, the traditional meaning of *piety* describes Christian spirituality well. It characterizes the beliefs and practices that are authentically Christian. Without piety, they lack a vital connection to God and become ends in themselves for our own edification or humanitarian gestures toward those around us. Piety—our reverence and love of God—sanctifies these practices and lifts them into a distinctively Christian sphere.

Spirituality and Theology

This book is a theological account of Christian spirituality. But isn't such a book superfluous? After all, the main thing in Christian spirituality lies in practicing it, not in knowing *about* it. There are at least two reasons why it is important to raise the issue of theology's relation to spirituality. First, there is a lingering perception among Christians that whereas theology is academic (in both the good and the bad sense of that term), abstruse, and unconnected to daily life, spirituality is practical, vital, and supremely connected to everyday life. Second, although Americans accept the need of experts in authorities in many areas of life, from auto mechanics to sports to politics, religion is an area in which Americans are reticent to abjure their own expertise.

A distinction may be of service. One sort of theology is academic theology. It veers in the direction of philosophy of religion and its concern is with the epistemological validity of religious ideas. This discipline is an important and legitimate intellectual endeavor. However, it is not directly concerned with the conduct of either the Christian life or any life and has little to contribute to Christian spirituality. There is a second mode of theology, a mode that exists for the church and its work and has an expressly confessional and ecclesial character. It has an essential connection to the Christian church and the lives of its members, even when dealing with fairly abstruse subjects. Its concern is pastoral, even when discussing matters that are not overtly pastoral. This sort of theology, insofar as it illuminates the nature of Christian spiritual practices, is the subject of this book. It is this mode of theology that pastors and church leaders must be competent in and that underlies Christian spirituality.

Unfortunately, the distinction between academic theology and confessional, ecclesial theology is sometimes not understood, and the latter is avoided because it is thought to be as remote from the Christian life as the former. Of course, we have to admit that sometimes even ecclesial theology assumes an abstruse form whose connection to the Christian life is uncertain and perhaps tenuous. This may be because such a form is needed in order for the theologian to do some hard but necessary conceptual work that does not lend itself to immediate practical application. Or it may be because the theologian has forgotten that Christian theology does have an essential connection to the Christian life and has allowed an academic or philosophical form to assume priority over the living substance of theology. This is a temptation that theologians must constantly resist. The problem in this case is not that theology as such is unconnected to the Christian life, but that the theologian has imprudently chosen an unsuitable mode of exposition. This choice contributes to the perception of theology's separation from life.

Finally, it must be acknowledged that one can be a fine Christian without an overt cognitive knowledge of theological subjects. Professional theologians lament this fact, but it is true. But ignorance, if not a vice, is no virtue. It is natural for fine Christians who are ignorant of theology to assume that, because they are fine Christians, theology has no importance for them. The problem here is that such people have not seen the extent to which their Christian faith depends on the theological work of others. They are analogous to mechanics who, through trial and error, might learn to correlate noises with malfunctions and thus acquire the skills of repairing. They might be ignorant of and therefore fail to see the value of engineering, but in fact their work presupposes the engineering that they disdain.

So, what is the connection between theology and spirituality? The answer is best obtained by attending to the several dimensions of the Christian faith. There are at least three such aspects or dimensions.[4] One is the regulative. This is what was called, in the patristic period, the rule of faith. The regulative dimension is that function of doctrine by which the Christian faith is distinguished from other systems of belief and by which boundaries are established for determining what are and what are not authentic expressions of the Christian faith. The regulative dimension of the doctrine of the Trinity, for example, stipulates the beliefs (such as tritheism) that are unacceptable for the church. The regulative dimension is typically expressed in creeds and other authoritative documents. However, we should not think of it as something narrowly cognitive, for it is also the rule of practice. One of the perennial problems of Christianity is the tendency to think of doctrine in almost completely cognitive terms. Doctrine has come to be a set of ideas toward which one has a cognitive attitude such as belief or disbelief or curiosity. But this view is unsatisfactory because it unduly separates belief from practice.[5] The fact that the regulative dimension of doctrine pertains to both belief and practice brings it into close connection with Christian spirituality. Its main contribution is to maintain the *Christian* character of spirituality. The rule of faith is that tool that the church has used over the centuries to preserve and inculcate authentic Christian belief and practice. Any belief or practice that the church may consider adopting must conform to or at least not contradict the rule of faith. In a world that is increasingly pluralistic, the regulative dimension assumes ever greater importance by reminding us of the distinctive aspects of the Christian faith. Adherence to the regulative dimension contributes to Christian spirituality by keeping us faithful to the normative aspects of the church's tradition.

A second dimension of doctrine arises from the fact that we are always located in definite intellectual situations and that we necessarily think in terms drawn from our intellectual situation. The easiest way to grasp this point is to examine the doctrine of creation. In the transition from the Old Testament to the New Testament to the patristic and medieval eras to the modern era, we observe Christians understanding the doctrine of creation in a variety of ways. It has been understood in terms of ancient Near Eastern cosmologies, Hellenistic philosophies, and modern science. Because this second dimension is concerned with understanding, I refer to it as the hermeneutical dimension. Throughout the ages, God's people have, we trust, striven to be faithful to the regulative dimension of the doctrine, even as they have understood the doctrine in ways drawn from their intellectual contexts. So, whereas the regulative dimension is comparatively constant and unchanging, the hermeneutical is relative to the leading ideas of a given era. Today, we have little alternative to understanding the doctrine of creation in terms of the natural sciences; Hellenistic philosophy and ancient Near Eastern cosmology are no longer options for us. The only true alternative is to abandon the attempt to understand, but this is, practically speaking, impossible. We find ourselves inevitably thinking in a scientific way because this is the prevailing mode of intellectual inquiry in our culture. This is not to say that Christians necessarily adopt the ideas of their culture uncritically. But even in our criticism of those ideas, we are apt to use those intellectual tools that are dominant in our culture. The hermeneutical dimension represents the act of understanding the Christian faith according to the ideas and intellectual methods that are available to us. It pertains to spirituality principally in two ways. First, it is an act of spiritual devotion to God to exercise our intellect in the attempt to understand the Christian faith. Although the results of such exercise are always (as history shows) more modest than hoped, those who offer their intellect to God in the work of the church are engaged in a worthy endeavor. The understanding of faith means, in effect, the sanctification of the intellect— its devotion to God's service. Second, reviewing the history of the hermeneutical dimension promotes our humility, for we observe in that history a variety of ways of understanding the content of faith. Prolonged meditation on this history compels us to acknowledge the human and therefore finite character of Christian attempts at understanding the faith. It brings home to us the fact that in human history there is no absolute perspective on the truth, that there is no level of understanding that is beyond critique and improvement. The power of this insight to promote our humility should not be underestimated.

The third dimension of faith is the one that connects theology most overtly to spirituality. This is the ethical dimension. The Christian faith has an ethical dimension because the character of our knowledge of God is determined by the character of God. With worldly things it is possible to have a knowledge that strives for objectivity and is distanced and dispassionate. But with God, distanced and dispassionate knowing is both inconceivable and undesirable. On the contrary, knowing God must take the form of becoming conformed to God. Since God is love, knowing God consists in or, at the very least, is closely associated with love. In the words of 1 John, "Everyone who loves is born of God and knows God. Whoever does not love does not know God, for God is love" (4:7-8). This is the ground of the ethical dimension of the Christian faith.

How are we to understand the relation of faith to ethics? We might suppose that the relation is one of cause (that is, believing causes us to act ethically in love) or obligation (that is, since we believe, we ought to act ethically in love). But it is better to represent the relation in much closer terms by saying that belief and ethical action are two aspects, distinguishable but not separable, of the Christian faith. Therefore, Christian belief is an ethical and not merely a cognitive act and Christian ethical action is not simply principled behavior but is also an act and actualization of faith. In other words, belief and action are two sides of the same coin of faith. In the Christian life, each is vital and presupposes the other. Neither can be authentic without the other. This conviction is stated succinctly when the Letter of James states that faith without works is dead. We can add that works without belief are not properly Christian, even if they are laudable. The Christian faith, then, does not merely imply ethical action, but in fact essentially includes such action. This insight reveals the close connection between theology and spirituality. The spiritual life of Christians, whether in the form of devotional exercises or expressly ethical activity in the world, is the Christian faith in one of its forms, the form of lived-out activity, just as belief is the Christian faith in another form, the form of cognitive affirmation.

A Few Assumptions and Remarks on Method

Considering the relation of theology to spirituality reminds us that theological thinking is thinking in an orderly way about theological subjects. To think in an orderly way is consistently to employ relevant and valid ideas in order to illuminate the subject. It is also to think within prescribed yet justifiable limitations.

For purposes of simplicity and convenience, this book is written from the perspective of the Christian tradition and entirely from within the circle of faith. I have ignored a host of difficult and deserving questions arising from extratheological disciplines. Chief among these questions are those regarding the status and validity of religious traditions beside those of Christianity. Adequate consideration of these questions would be possible only in a much larger and more technical work. As a result, this book is an exercise in confessional theology.

The basis of this exposition in the Christian tradition means that it relies heavily on the Bible and the tradition of Christian thought. Stated differently, it makes little use of the social sciences and other disciplines that can make a valuable contribution to our understanding of Christian spirituality. A book exploring this subject using these ancillary disciplines is something to be desired, but there is also great value in expounding spirituality from a strictly theological perspective. The loss due to narrowness of focus is balanced by a depth of insight, even if that insight is partial and requires supplementation. The confessional quality also means that I have, with respect to the Bible, ignored all critical issues of date, authorship, priority, influence, and so on. I will refer, for the sake of convenience, to the authors of biblical books using the names that tradition has given them. For example, I will refer to Paul as the author of Ephesians even though modern scholarship has cast doubt on his authorship. Although such critical issues are not without importance in other contexts, they are not vital for an understanding of the present subject.

Methodologically, this book is an exercise in systematic theology. The heyday of system-building in theology lies in the past. Nonetheless, the practice of systematic thinking in theology is indispensable. This practice consists in using, thoroughly and persistently, basic concepts to analyze a subject. Each such concept functions as does a diamond's facet. Each opens up to us the subject in a distinctive way and helps us think about the subject more completely. Of course, to think systematically is not the same as achieving comprehensive knowledge. This is because no single concept is the only means of grasping a subject, just as no diamond has only one facet, and because no systematic treatment could possibly employ every available concept. In theology, there will always be other possible facets, each yielding different insights. The only requirement is that concepts used in systematic thinking successively give us insight.

The four concepts that I have chosen are, first, the role and importance of embodied practices in Christian spirituality; second, the role and importance of the Christian community in the development of spirituality; third, the development and conduct of spirituality in a fallen world; and fourth, our relation to the triune God. The choice of embodied practices follows directly from the practical dimension of doctrine. The choice of the others follows from the fundamental realities of the Christian life: sin, grace, and the church. Although, as I have noted, these are not the only concepts that might be used to elucidate Christian spirituality, they are among the most central concepts.

Thinking systematically requires that we think dialectically. Thinking dialectically consists in thinking things together that are more easily thought apart. It is much easier to think of belief and action as two distinct things than to see their essential connection and to see that, in the Christian life, the one cannot be without the other. Dialectical thinking occurs when we refuse to allow these related concepts to be separated. Although, for analytical purposes, we may consider one in isolation from the other, in fact we recognize their inseparable unity. Dialectics, therefore, is not a method employed only in philosophy. On the contrary, it is the only way we have of construing such central Christian beliefs as the incarnation and the Trinity.

There are several sets of concepts relevant to corporate spirituality that must be approached dialectically. One is body and soul. It has been one of the accomplishments of modern biblical study to recover the Bible's sense of the wholeness of human existence and to help us see that, as the Bible represents it, humans are not souls lodged in bodies, but instead bodily creatures capable of self-transcendence. This recovery helps us resist a life-denying pessimism about the body that has characterized some philosophies and recognize the embodied character of all human phenomena. At the same time, we do not want to fall into the opposite error of crass materialism, as if words such as *soul* and *spirit* were mere delusions and empty concepts. Although there are plenty of good reasons for not wanting to revive the Platonic conception of the soul, a materialistic conception of the human self when put into the service of a reductionistic philosophy is no more congenial to the Christian faith. Instead we must think of terms such as *body* and *soul* together in their unity. *How* we are to conceptualize this union today, in a scientific era, remains an open and difficult question. It is enough for our present purposes to grant the importance of thinking of soul and body together, neither denying the

11

soul nor denigrating the body, and to regard ourselves as embodied persons in every aspect of our lives.

One consequence of the unity of our embodied condition is that the Christian faith has a twofold relation to the world. On one hand, the gospel calls us to conquer, resist, and overcome the world by means of Christian practices. This call presents the world as a spiritual problem that we must surmount through a Christian life lived well. In this book I call this the world-transcending impulse of the Christian faith. This phrase signifies that we are to go beyond this world through ethical and spiritual practices. On the other hand, this call is not a summons literally to abandon the world but is instead a call to overcome the world insofar as it has fallen into sin. Insofar as the world remains the good creation of God and the site of God's grace, we are called to affirm our created and embodied status. I call this the impulse toward participating in the world. It is what explains the fact that Christians over the centuries have thrown themselves into a great variety of activities aimed at cooperating with God's work of redeeming the world. These two impulses stand in a dialectical relation toward each other. Both together drive the Christian ethical life. But history shows that it is easier to practice spiritual world-transcendence exclusively or world-participation exclusively. It is more difficult to see them as two impulses of the ethical dimension of Christian faith. To think and live dialectically is to see them as distinct yet, ideally, inseparable in the unity of the Christian life. Schism and heresy are the results of failing to maintain this ideal unity.

Another set of concepts that we should approach dialectically is individuality and community. Observers of the American scene have long noted our tendency toward excessive individualism and, recently, the diminution of community. We have for too long considered the rights and importance of the individual in isolation from the role of the community in enabling individuals to live the good life. Meanwhile, the twentieth century witnessed numerous totalitarian regimes whose aim was the complete domination of human life. Here the supreme value was the community (or, at least, its despotic representatives), with individualism dramatically subordinated to that supreme value. What is called for in a Christian theology of spirituality is a dialectical understanding of community and individuality. In this understanding, neither term is thought without the other and, ethically, neither is exalted above the other. As a result, we will see that the embodied practices of the Christian life are inseparable from their setting in the Christian community—there is no community without these embodied practices and there can be no authentic practices without a sound and supporting community. The attempt to have one or the other alone invariably leads to error and excess.

Another leading concept that demands a dialectical approach is sin. The reality of sin means that the Christian life is conducted in the tension between the kingdom of God and the enduring reality of sin. The gospel proclaims that in the ministry of Jesus Christ the kingdom of God has appeared. But the New Testament knows as well that, although Christ is seated at the right hand of God, he is still putting his enemies under his feet. We are not yet at the time when God is all in all. For us, the kingdom of God coexists with the fallen world of sin. For the Christian, sin lies in the past but endures into the present. The kingdom exists in the present, but its complete victory lies in the future. This tensed present, then, is the epoch in which the Christian life is conducted. We live by the power of the Spirit but continue to be susceptible to the power of sin. We look forward hopefully to the future but all too often look back wistfully to sin's past. To understand the Christian life requires that we hold these two realities together—the power of God's kingdom and also the power of sin. It is this dialectical reality that causes the Christian life to be an eschatological existence, that is, the appearance of the eschaton (the triumph of the kingdom of God) in the midst of sinful human time.

Finally, our relation to God requires a dialectical treatment. The Christian says two things about this relation. First, we are not God. We are in no sense divine. The Christian tradition has always drawn the firmest of distinctions between God and us and forbidden any blurring of that line. Second, God is not a being that exists in isolation. God is not a thing that is remote and without relations. On the contrary, we have been drawn into God's trinitarian life. We exist in Christ. We live in the Spirit. We participate in the divine nature. These and other New Testament phrases point to the reality of our participation in God's life. So, in thinking about God, we must simultaneously uphold the utter transcendence of God and also our participation in God. To affirm the latter alone would be to assert our divinity. To affirm the former alone would mean falling into Deism.

There is only one way in which we can perceive the coherence of the Christian faith. That way is dialectical thinking. Without it and the practice that follows from it, we inevitably fall into serious error. Even in a subject such as Christian spirituality, we must constantly and carefully regard the way in which the Christian faith asks us to hold together realities that are more easily allowed to separate, but whose separation is a disaster for that faith.

A Preview of Subsequent Chapters

The remainder of this book falls into two divisions, chapters 2–3 and chapters 4–10. Chapter 2 is a brief examination of spirituality, generally considered, in America today. This will describe the cultural context in which the quest for Christian spirituality is conducted today. With an awareness of what is going on around us, we will be in a better position to note the distinctive features of Christian spirituality and also to observe the temptations to which American Christians are susceptible today. Chapter 3 is a summary of the theological foundation of Christian spirituality. In this book I am primarily concerned with describing the practices and communal setting of Christian spirituality; however, it is good at the outset to remember that the spiritual pursuit rests on God's grace toward us and presupposes such central realities as justification, reconciliation, and sanctification. Chapters 4–10 successively discuss some central features of Christian spirituality: baptism, faith, worship, discipline, virtues, the quest for justice, and our relation to the rest of creation. Of course, this list is far from comprehensive. There are other worthy aspects of the Christian life, such as peacemaking and evangelism, that deserve attention in other venues. But the selected topics illustrate well the theses enumerated above and illuminate the nature of Christian spirituality.

Notes

1. John Calvin, *Institutes of the Christian Religion*, trans. Ford Lewis Battles, ed. John T. McNeill. Vol. 20, Library of Christian Classics. 2 vols. (Philadelphia: Westminster Press, 1960), 1.2.1.

2. Ibid., 1.2.2.

3. Ibid., 1.2.1.

4. See Samuel M. Powell, *Participating in God: Creation and Trinity, Theology and the Sciences* (Minneapolis: Fortress Press, 2003), for a fuller discussion of this analysis.

5. At the same time, it is necessary to resist the temptation, to which our era is equally drawn, to put all the emphasis on practice and to diminish the cognitive dimension of faith.

CHAPTER TWO

SPIRITUALITY IN AMERICA TODAY

I received in the mail an eight-page bulletin from a major health care provider.[1] The bulletin was a set of articles on staying healthy. Topics included exercise, asthma, and vitamin D. There was also a short article, "Seeking Spirituality on Your Own Terms." The first line stated, "spirituality means different things to different people. It can be defined as the ways that one seeks and finds meaning and purpose in life events and relationships." The article went on to assert that spirituality can come to us in a variety of ways, including in religious experiences, nature, meditation, and the arts. Readers were encouraged to ask themselves questions such as whether they had ever had a moment when life seemed filled with meaning and whether they had ever felt comfortable in the knowledge that all is right with the world. They were advised that their answers to these questions "may provide clues to enhance your own spiritual well-being." In conclusion, readers were urged to "consider making spirituality a priority in [their] life" because "studies show that spiritual well-being is associated with better physical and mental health, better quality of life, and enhanced coping with adversity and illness."

This article, which, like the rest of the bulletin, is filled with good sense and sound advice, tells something of great importance about spirituality in America today. For one thing, it tells us that spirituality is no longer a matter about which the Christian church is the only or even a leading authority. Spirituality has become a matter about which the health care community is a source of information and guidance. Second, it tells us that spirituality and spiritual needs are matters of great particularity: "Spirituality means different things to different people." In this view, there can be no generic, one-size-fits-all approach to spirituality. On the contrary, spirituality is a reflection of our individuality and uniqueness. Third, it tells us that spirituality is a matter of finding meaning and purpose in life. It is not, it appears, a matter of becoming reconciled to a wrathful God and obeying the commandments of that God in hope of an eschatological salvation. It is instead concerned with becoming reconciled to the dynamics of human life and relationships. Fourth, it tells us that our spiritual well-being is in our own hands. We can do things that will enhance our spiritual condition. Fifth, it tells us that spirituality is an integral part of a larger phenomenon of human well-being. Spirituality is important because it usefully serves to improve every aspect of our human life.

Each of these points reveals why the Christian church today faces a daunting task not only in fulfilling its mission, but also in defining itself. In the past, the church enjoyed, if not a monopoly, then at least a dominant place in America's understanding of spirituality. Today, however, the church is just one of many sources of spiritual guidance. We are not accustomed to being one voice among many and are not sure how best to proclaim our message in this plurality of voices. We are also not sure how to frame our message in a context in which people think of spirituality as a reflection of their uniqueness. Christians have traditionally thought that everyone has the same spiritual problem—sin—and that there is one remedy that works for everyone—redemption in Jesus and reception of the church's ministry. We are in a better position in relation to the thesis that spirituality is about finding meaning in life, except that Americans today seem reluctant to affirm that there is *one* meaning of life, with its exclusive connotations. They are more comfortable with a plurality of meanings, individually sought for and achieved. The church likewise sees the value in having people take responsibility for their spiritual condition but isn't sure how the doctrine of grace fits with the American spirit of self-reliance and effort. Finally, the church acknowledges that true spirituality is associated with the good life in all its dimensions but should be worried that the connection between spirituality and our overall well-being will mean that modes of spirituality—including the Christian faith—will be evaluated pragmatically on the basis of their contribution to our overall well-being. The church has always resisted the message that authentic spirituality is a means of solving every human problem. In short, the church in America today is facing religious competition that is comparable only to the church's first centuries of existence in the Roman Empire. Whether we will flourish in this atmosphere of plurality and diversity remains to be seen.

The bulletin tells us one more thing, namely that religion, packaged with the new and improved name of spirituality, is alive and well in America. The persistence and indeed thriving of religion is a matter of some surprise to those who have followed scholarly thinking about religion over the last few decades. In the 1960s, there was some fear that religion in America would disappear, replaced by secularism. The death of God movement in theology and the beginnings of decline in church membership seemed to many to prophesy this decline. Moreover, the disappearance of religion had long been predicted by sociologists, convinced that, with the rise and spread of modern forms of social organization, the institutional forms of religion would be replaced by secular forms of life and religious beliefs and practices would evaporate under the pressure of increasing secularization. However, quite the opposite has occurred. Opinion polls regularly show that a high percentage of Americans hold religious beliefs. A clear majority believes in God and the afterlife. The growing power of fundamentalist movements and associated institutions such as Christian schools and home schooling networks likewise testifies to the prevalence of religion. Surveys show that even the scientific community is not uniformly atheistic or agnostic. Although the incidence of religious beliefs in the scientific community is lower than it is for the American population as a whole, the number of scientists reporting some sort of religious convictions is still remarkably high. This is especially significant since it was expected that scientific rationalism would lead the way in creating a secular America. So, if secularism is defined as a decline in religious interests and beliefs, then America is no more secular than it was one hundred or even two hundred years ago.

However, the refutation of the thesis of inexorably increasing secularization has little comfort for those concerned with the well-being of the Christian churches. For although religious belief is as or more pervasive than in the past, there has been a sizable shift of religious interest from Christianity to alternatives outside the church. Even if some of the membership losses in the mainline churches from the 1960s to the present have resulted in increases in evangelical churches, the fact remains that the Christian churches no longer have a monopoly on American religious life as they once did. Of course, we know that in every era of American history the church faced an uphill battle in its evangelistic task. But not until recently have Americans had so many alternatives to choose from. In the eighteenth century, the main options were few: Christianity, Judaism, and some form of Deism. The options expanded modestly in the nineteenth century with the rise of various forms of Spiritualism. But the last thirty or so years have witnessed an unprecedented increase in the number and types of religion available to the American public. In this situation, although the majority of Americans continues to identify itself as Christian, the Christian churches are no longer the main providers of religion.

It is appropriate in this context to use economic metaphors. In particular, the American religious scene today resembles a marketplace. Once upon a time each small town might have had a single general store that was an all-purpose, one-stop shopping venue. Today, multipurpose department stores have had a difficult time sustaining themselves through the rise of more specialized stores that focus either on particular types of goods (such as clothing or sports equipment) or on demographic niches (such as teenagers). The shopping mall provides an apt metaphor for religion today. The idea of the mall is that no single store can satisfy all of one's consumer needs. By analogy, Americans by and large have decided that no single church or religion can be expected to satisfy all of our spiritual needs. So, just as there has been a dramatic proliferation of shopping options, so there has been a proliferation of religious options. Americans come into the great religious mall and find there some large churches seeking to be full-service spiritual venues and also many smaller boutique religions that appeal only to a segment of the population, which seeks them out for very specific reasons. This means that for Americans, religion is a consumer-oriented commodity and they participate in religion more as consumers than as devotees. This is not to say that Americans think of religions as something to be bought and sold. It is to say that we tend to see religion as something that satisfies a need. But as our spiritual needs have become more refined and we have come to expect more out of life, there has been a tendency to engage in a "shopping around" attitude in one's approach to religion. The evidence of this tendency today suggests that people do not remain in the tradition in which they were raised, but instead seek out a church or tradition that best suits them and shows greatest promise of meeting their needs. Church-hopping and

18

tradition-shopping is not so much because people have changed their minds about doctrines, but more often because a certain church has a program (for children or teens, for instance) that corresponds to a need arising at a certain point in their life.

Because of our consumer approach to religion and the proliferation of religious alternatives, Americans have come to evaluate churches and religions pragmatically. Americans have always had a pragmatic bent, but we in the church like to think that in the past Americans were members of a given church because of theological convictions and loyalty to tradition. Today's situation, however, encourages us to look at a church in terms of its promise to help us in some way. Along with this goes the assumption that the full satisfaction of one's spiritual needs will require the use of several religions or churches, just as the full satisfaction of one's household needs requires shopping at several types of stores. So, a family's teens may be involved in one church because of its outstanding youth program, while the adults may belong to another church because of its inspiring worship services. Meanwhile, the family may make use of a city-sponsored yoga class for meditation and relaxation and a twelve-step program for addictions. Like a shopper in a mall, the contemporary American comes into the marketplace of religions with certain needs and problems and goes looking for activities and programs that promise to satisfy the needs and solve the problems. Those that fail to deliver on their promises may be abandoned as quickly as we return broken tools or ill-fitting clothing. The pragmatic approach means that Americans today have an eclectic attitude toward religion. This contrasts with traditional Christianity, which made exclusive claims and demanded total and undivided allegiance. Whether it always received that total and undivided allegiance is another question, but at least in American history there was a tendency toward institutional monogamy, if only because of a lack of alternatives.

If we ask why America has seen such a proliferation of religious options, one answer is that it is part of a long reaction to scientific rationalism, a reaction extending back to the early nineteenth century. The leaders of the Romantic movement, especially in Britain, were sharply critical of an exclusive devotion to the scientific approach to reality. It was, they felt, too analytical and too quick to deny the reality of fundamental values such as beauty. The Romantics emphasized two points of interest to us. First, they argued for seeing nature, not as so many disconnected things, but instead as a living whole of which humankind is an integral part. Second, they looked back beyond modern society to premodern societies and found in them wisdom that had escaped modern people. Although Romanticism as a literary movement died long ago, there are significant ways in which our contemporary religious situation has embodied these Romantic notions. First, the drive toward alternative forms of religion has been fueled by a distrust of the methods of the sciences and resulting technology. Reading the literature of new religious movements, one is often struck by the extent to which they are premised on a desire to recover a more holistic relationship to the natural world. Whether it is Kabbalah or neo-paganism or goddess worship, there is a conviction that there is more to the natural world than is discoverable by the sciences and that the truth that lies beyond the reach of the sciences is a wisdom of the greatest importance to our well-being. Second, the proliferation of religious alternatives has grown through a weariness and impatience with the Western European tradition. Neither the sciences nor Christianity (at least in its institutional form) are regarded as able to solve pervasive human problems. Indeed, they are not infrequently regarded as contributing to those problems. In response, there is a tendency to look to other non-Western, nonmodern traditions for wisdom. So, we see growing interest in the religions of other cultures, including in Native American cultures and Asian religions; in ancient and esoteric traditions, including Kabbalah and Celtic religion; in phenomena whose reality is denied by the sciences, including angels and astrology; and in alternative and holistic forms of medicine. When the sciences are valued, it is on the same pragmatic grounds. So certain forms of psychology (such as that of Carl Jung) are valued because they are thought to provide an alternative and rigorous path to the desired wisdom.

When churches and religions are evaluated pragmatically by consumers, then the idea of spiritual authority undergoes profound changes. Traditionally, the Christian church understood itself to be an authoritative institution. Its authority rested on the fact that it had been founded by Jesus, had received his authority and teaching, and had been supplied with his Spirit for its task. So it regarded its ministries as ministries of God's grace and its teaching as the communication of Christ's teaching. Theories of ministerial ordination varied across denominations, but there was a common understanding that ordained clergy had special authority with respect to preaching, teaching, sacraments, and other rites. In a consumer-oriented approach to religion, however, authority is shifted from the institution and its ordained representatives to the consumer and to those spiritual advisers with whom the consumer chooses to invest authority. In other words, we come to the religious marketplace today with the attitude of *caveat emptor* ("let the buyer beware"), an attitude in which we have been schooled through our participation in the national economy. In an unregulated economy, consumers have the responsibility of being informed about their purchases. From automobiles to electronic equipment, it is the consumer who must become an expert and choose the product that best accords with his or her needs—hence the ostensible purpose of advertising, which is to inform us. It is no different with religion. Faced with a vast and bewildering array of religious options, it is the consumer who must seek and experiment until those options are found that satisfy spiritual needs. The idea of an authoritative institution, with sole possession of the means of salvation and the only authentic representatives of God, is quite out of tune with today's pluralistic situation. Instead of authoritative representatives of God—with the power of dispensing necessary sacraments—clergy are apt to be valued as spiritual guides. But this pragmatic basis for being valued shows us that their authority rests not on their institutional status, but instead on their competency and their ability to address the spiritual needs of seekers.

The marketplace character of religion and the altered conception of authority mean a change in the conception of the church. In the past, with limited geographical mobility, even rootless Americans tended to show some loyalty to their church. The nineteenth-century debates between Presbyterians and Methodists over issues of free will and predestination testify to the extent to which denominations stood for particular constellations of belief. If one was a Methodist by conviction, then joining a Presbyterian church was unthinkable. Along with doctrinal conviction went the fact that one's ties to a church might be familial. One's parents and grandparents might have been members of a church, especially if they were immigrants and the church bound them not only to a religious tradition, but to a national culture as well. But a consumer orientation (in combination with increased geographical mobility) reinforces the individualistic tendencies of Americans and tends to overcome the corporate dimension of church life. It does this by convincing us that each person is unique and that this uniqueness is essential for defining one's identity. If each person is regarded as unique, then there will be a tendency to be suspicious of institutions, which tend to offer one-size-fits-all spiritual remedies. In a consumer-oriented society like ours, what is most important is the well-being of the individual, and that well-being is generally defined as the satisfaction of needs and the supplying of wants. More important, consumer goods come to be seen not merely for their utilitarian value, but also as means of expressing our individuality— hence the multitudinous variety of automobiles, grooming products, and so on. All this carries over into religion. In today's climate, general remedies to human problems are unfashionable; tailor-made approaches based on a wide range of options are more in touch with sensibilities today. As a result, megachurches with a diverse range of ministries flourish while small congregations languish. In a megachurch, nearly everyone can find some sort of ministry that will address needs. In a small church, the possibility of finding a specific ministry is much reduced. All this means that churches are not likely to be communities founded on shared beliefs, customs, practices, and values. They are more likely to be loose assemblies of people who happen to find at least part of what they need at a given church but who may well belong to an array of other equally loose and short-term spiritual communities that address other needs.

The individualism inherent in today's spirituality manifests itself in the fact that spirituality today is often cast in terms of self-fulfillment. Of course, the Christian tradition has from the beginning taught that faith in God, love toward God and neighbor, and eschatological blessings are indeed the fulfillment of our created nature. But in doing so, that tradition spoke from the assumption that all human beings have the same spiritual need and that the gospel and the ministries of the church are the one authentic answer to that need. It is distinctive of recent writings about spirituality to assume that self-fulfillment is not the fulfillment of our generic created nature, but instead something that can be discerned only through a process of self-discovery. In other words, spirituality has been assimilated to the sort of psychology associated with Carl Rogers. One of the fundamental aspects of Rogers's approach to therapy was the premise that each person must discover for and by himself or herself the sorts of things that are truly good and fulfilling. Great psychological harm, Rogers believed, resulted from attempts by one person to determine for another the sort of life to be lived. Naturally Rogers understood that there were constraints to the process of self-discovery. He did not mean that whatever the individual decided was good truly was good. He understood that individuals make mistakes in judgment. Nonetheless, the thrust of his approach was to grant individuals the time, emotional space, and personal support required for the process of discovery and to avoid dictating to others the precise nature of the good they were seeking.

Although it is doubtful that many writers about spirituality have read Rogers, it is obvious that ideas like his passed over into the general stock of socially accepted ideas and thus have had an effect on spirituality. The result is that, in America today, there is a pervasive sense that spirituality is a quest to discover what is good for the individual. This quest requires that we come to know ourselves in our uniqueness and then find spiritual paths that are appropriate to who we are. In the Christian world, this attitude appears in the notion (which I have heard laypeople express) that the large number of American denominations is justified by the fact that each appeals to a different sort of person, some finding more meaning in structured liturgy, others in charismatic spontaneity.

The emphasis on spirituality as a means of self-fulfillment, with its attendant individualism, fits well the modern partiality toward pluralism and diversity and the suspicion of universal solutions and master narratives of truth. It breeds dogmatic relativism, which is the phenomenon of individuals exhibiting absolute certainty about their own self-discovered truths while granting complete validity to the self-discovered truths of others, even if the two truths are not in agreement. This phenomenon is possible because spiritual truth today is not generally regarded as accurate statements about a transcendent reality, but instead as practical insights, won through experience, into the appropriate paths of one's unique spirituality. One can be dogmatically absolute about one's truth because one has found it to be pragmatically useful in becoming spiritual, while happily acknowledging that one's truth may not be pragmatically true for another person. This is one reason why religious institutions like churches do not enjoy widespread and automatic authority. Because the spiritual quest is a process of discovering pragmatic truths, the individual on the quest must be the ultimate arbiter of what works. No amount of testimony by the church that millions or billions of Christians have found satisfaction in the church's way is necessarily convincing, for the individual on the quest may find himself or herself to be different. Experience is a more trustworthy guide than are authoritative institutions, no matter how ancient.

This emphasis on pragmatic truth and experience means that spirituality has become a subject of self-help instruction. Just as bookstores abound in books of self-help psychology, so they abound with volumes of self-help spirituality for, in the contemporary conception, all spirituality is ultimately the result of a process of self-help with close ties to popular psychology. A leading instance of the union between self-help psychology and spirituality is M. Scott Peck's *The Road Less Traveled*. Peck's book is loaded with helpful and sound advice for life. But there is no mistaking the fact that his book is a work not only of psychology, but also of psychologically oriented theology. Apart from its musings about God, inspired by Carl Jung, it is notable for two things: its individualism with respect to attaining the goal of spirituality and its emphasis on individual responsibility. Each of these implies the other. True spirituality is something achieved by effort and experience. No one can obtain it for others. Consequently, responsibility for becoming a spiritually mature person rests solely on the individual. The purpose of Peck's book is to indicate helpful tips for navigating the path toward spirituality. Nowhere in the book does Peck counsel the reader to seek out authorities such as pastors. Authoritative doctrine, church sacraments and rites, and other institutional artifacts do not even come into consideration as possible aids in becoming spiritual. Becoming spiritual is largely a matter of exercising certain practical disciplines and expanding one's mental horizon. For this purpose the vast self-help literature serves as the new scriptures.

These are some of the features of spirituality in America today. They pose for the church and its leaders the great challenge of defining the Christian life in such a way that it is distinguished from the rather vague religious background that forms the marketplace of spirituality.

Note

1. *Mayo Clinic HealthQuest* (Rochester, MN: Mayo Foundation for Medical Education and Research, May 2004).

Sources Consulted and Recommended

Bellah, Robert, Richard Madsen, William M. Sullivan, Ann Swidler, and Steven M. Tipton. *Habits of the Heart: Individualism and Commitment in American Life*. Berkeley: University of California Press, 1985.

Besecke, Kelly. "Speaking of Meaning in Modernity: Reflexive Spirituality as a Cultural Resource." *Sociology of Religion* 62, no. 3 (2001): 365-81.

Cady, Linell E. "Categorical Imperatives: Religion, Spirituality, and the Secular in American Life." *American Journal of Theology & Philosophy* 25, no. 2 (2004): 140-56.

Collins, Kenneth J. "What Is Spirituality? Historical and Methodological Considerations." *Wesleyan Theological Journal* 31, no. 1 (1996): 76-94.

Dawson, Lorne L. "Anti-Modernism, Modernism, and Postmodernism: Struggling with the Cultural Significance of New Religious Movements." *Sociology of Religion* 59, no. 2 (1998): 131-56.

Dean, William. *The American Spiritual Culture and the Invention of Jazz, Football and the Movies.* New York: Continuum, 2002.

Dinges, William D. "American Catholics and the Joseph Campbell Phenomenon." *America* 168, no. 6 (1993): 12-19.

Isherwood, Lisa, and Elizabeth Stuart. *Introducing Body Theology.* Introductions in Feminist Theology. Cleveland: The Pilgrim Press, 1998.

Lee, Richard Wayne. "Strained Bedfellows: Pagans, New Agers, and 'Starchy Humanists' in Unitarian Universalism." *Sociology of Religion* 56, no. 4 (1995): 379-96.

McGuire, Meredith B. "Why Bodies Matter: A Sociological Reflection on Spirituality and Materiality." *Spiritus* 3, no. 1 (2003): 1-18.

Peck, M. Scott. *The Road Less Traveled: A New Psychology of Love, Traditional Values and Spiritual Growth.* New York: Simon & Schuster, 1978.

Schneiders, Sandra M. "Religion vs. Spirituality: A Contemporary Conundrum." *Spiritus* 3, no. 2 (2003): 163-85.

Stark, Rodney. "Secularization: The Myth of Religious Decline." *Fides et Historia* 30, no. 2 (1998): 1-19.

Sylvan, Robin. *Traces of the Spirit: The Religious Dimension of Popular Music.* New York: New York University Press, 2002.

Wuthnow, Robert. *After Heaven: Spirituality in America Since the 1950s.* Berkeley: University of California Press, 1998.

———. *Christianity in the Twenty-first Century: Reflections on the Challenges Ahead.* New York: Oxford University Press, 1993.

CHAPTER THREE

THE THEOLOGICAL FOUNDATIONS OF CHRISTIAN SPIRITUALITY

T he purpose of this chapter is to set forth the biblical basis of Christian spirituality—not spirituality itself, but its prelude. In particular, I will show how the four theses enumerated in chapter 1 (pertaining to embodied practices, community, spirituality in a fallen world, and participation in God) are expounded in the Bible. I will not discuss here particular spiritual and ecclesial practices. They will be the subjects of subsequent chapters. Instead, my goal in this chapter is to state the theological presuppositions of Christian spirituality.

The Practice of Christian Spirituality

The Christian life bears upon our inwardness as subjective beings as well as upon our behavior. It is about our thoughts and feelings as well as our conduct. This point must always be remembered, for, as the Gospels plainly show, outward observance of God's law may fall short of pleasing God if we fail to act with the right motives. Mark 7:20-22 is a testimony to this point. Here Jesus warns against an understanding of purity that has to do only with physical and behavioral matters and teaches instead that purity and impurity have to do with the things that come from the heart.

At the same time, it is possible (as history shows) to overvalue the inward life of subjectivity at the expense of the more public and embodied dimension of the Christian life—the domain of actions and speech. It is, sadly, too easy to regard the Christian life as one of good intention and right relation to God and to forget that right intention and right relation become empty abstractions if they are not joined to faithful practice and speech. There are several reasons why the importance of embodied practices needs emphasizing today. For one thing, American Protestantism has been deeply affected by the heritage of revivalism, which tended to present the Christian life in terms of peak religious experiences and commitments. Of course, the revivalistic traditions often joined to this understanding some rather strict behavioral standards and hence acknowledged a practical dimension to the Christian life. Nonetheless, this tradition may have inadvertently encouraged people to think of the Christian life as essentially composed of dramatic conversion experiences and to downplay the importance of distinctively Christian practices. Second, there has been a long-standing Protestant suspicion of Roman Catholic piety and devotional practices. This may have inclined Protestants to overemphasize faith (often transformed into cognitive belief) as the essence of the Christian life to the neglect of specific practices. Third, to the extent that Protestants did emphasize the practical aspect of Christianity, some (especially in the revivalist tradition) tended to represent it negatively, that is, as worldly activities that should be avoided. Fourth, the dominance of Christianity in the cultural life of America has meant that, until recently, there was considerable continuity between being a Christian and being an American. Christian virtues were American virtues and vice versa. This fact made it easier for distinctively Christian practices to be overlooked—it's difficult to think of the church as distinctive when it seems to have no boundaries in the national community. Fifth, and most important for the contemporary situation, the growth of religious pluralism has resulted in a proliferation of religious practices, drawn from various traditions, with a resulting relativizing of all practices. In today's context, prayer, meditation, fasting, and other religious activities do not seem to have anything distinctive about them. In a culture in which people eclectically engage in Buddhist, Native American, Celtic, and other practices, the distinctiveness of Christian practices is easily lost. Because of these many factors, it is vital to remember that the Christian life is something conducted publicly and that we are not beings of pure inward subjectivity, that we are social beings and not just individuals, and that we are beings of deed and speech and not just beings of thoughts and feeling. In short, we must think dialectically about human life, training ourselves to recognize the unity of thought and deed, of feeling and speech, and learning to prevent the separation of the unities, to which our culture so readily inclines.

The theological basis of embodied practices is the embodiment of God in Jesus Christ. The significance of the incarnation for our subject is twofold. First, it tells us that the corporeal is a fit vehicle for God. It is neither intrinsically evil nor resistant to God's will. It is instead capable of being used by God and of revealing God and of being united with God. Second, the incarnated God is the exemplar of the life that Christians are to live. The Christian life is based on and follows not philosophical ideas, but instead a historically particular life, a life we are to embody.

These insights into the corporeal and the incarnation lead us to consider what we may call the sacramental principle, expounded (in the New Testament) mostly consistently in John's Gospel. In this Gospel, physical miracles of Jesus are, at several important points in the narrative, employed to signify some spiritual truth. The physical loaves and fish in chapter 6 point to Jesus, who is the bread of life (6:48-58). The healing of a blind man (chapter 9) is the physical correlate of Jesus, who is the light of the world (9:5) and whose work is to bring spiritual sight (9:39). In each case, some common physical thing or event possesses great symbolic value. In Johannine terms, these events are signs that point to Jesus' glory (2:11). This is the insight that underlies the sacraments. Although the various streams of the Christian tradition understand the efficacy of the sacraments in different ways, all sacramental practice rests on the conviction that in the giving and receiving of physical substance, God's grace and presence are given to us in a distinctive way. This is the sacramental principle. But this principle does not apply only to the sacraments. It applies also, for instance, to preaching, in which very human words mediate to the hearer the word of God. In this event, physical acts—the spoken words and hearing those words—are essential to our receiving God's word and God's grace (Romans 10:17). This is not to say that God cannot communicate the divine word without preaching and hearing. But it is to say that deeply rooted in the Bible is the conviction that God's grace and presence to us is always mediated by finite realities. And since we are corporeal beings, those mediating realities are themselves corporeal. This point about the sacramental principle and preaching is also the basis of Christian iconography. John of Damascus, who wrote in the midst of the iconoclastic controversy (eighth and ninth centuries), argued that, through the incarnation, matter as such has been filled with grace and power, enabling it to be an instrument of salvation. Moreover, we, being corporeal, require some type of image (he was particularly concerned with visual images) if we are to receive God's communication to us. Both visual and auditory images are means by which we gain understanding of divine matters.

These considerations bring us back to Jesus Christ, who is himself the sacramental principle. This is expressed in the New Testament's portrait of Jesus Christ as the true image of God (2 Corinthians 4:4 and Colossians 1:15) and the word of God (John 1:1 and Revelation 19:13). The witness of the New Testament is that the life of this man is the revelation of God and, even more, that this man is God among us. In Jesus Christ, corporeality and divinity are inseparably joined, and matter stands utterly and obediently in the service of God. This means that Jesus Christ is analogous to the sacraments, preaching, and icons. In these, too, we find the union of the corporeal and the spiritual. In them material substance is the bearer of God's grace and presence.

The complement of the New Testament's teaching about corporeality and its fitness for divine service is the doctrine of holiness. Perhaps, however, it is better to speak of *sanctification*, for this Latin-based term has reference not just to the state of holiness, but also to things being made holy (*sanctus* = holy, *facere* = to make). The point is that corporeal realities are not, at least from our perspective, automatically holy and fitted for God. For this they must be consecrated.[1] This is true above all for us. Like all other corporeal things, we must become fitted for God through consecration and a process of sanctification.

Discussion of sanctification brings us to a consideration of human existence from a theological perspective. A way to think of the unity of our inwardness and our outward conduct is to think of the human person as embodied and to regard the complete range of human activities, including thinking and feeling, as acts of an embodied person. As has been noted by modern biblical scholarship, the Bible account of creation encourages us to think in this direction. The account of God's creating humans found in Genesis 2 goes out of its way to emphasize that humans are made from dirt (2:7). Even though we are animated by the breath of life, which is the Spirit of God, this does not distinguish us from other living beings, for they, too, live as God gives this breath; and both we and they die when it returns to God (Psalm 104:29-30). The Old Testament, then, begins with an affirmation of humankind's embodied existence. It shows no tendency to denigrate the body or to suggest that the body is foreign to the true human self.

The situation in the New Testament is a bit more complicated because by the first century Judaism had developed a concept of human spirit that entailed the possibility of spirit existing apart from the body. Revelation 6:9-11 gives witness to this belief. Here John sees the souls of the martyrs, resting under the heavenly altar, crying out for vengeance. This passage points to the conviction that the righteous, upon death, exist with God in heaven, awaiting the resurrection of their bodies. There is also in the New Testament, it must be admitted, an anxiety about the status of the body that we do not find in the Old Testament. This appears most notably in Paul's letters, which speak of the body being sown (that is, dying) in dishonor and weakness (1 Corinthians 15:42), and of the law of sin that is at work in our body (Romans 7:23). These related passages suggest that Paul regarded the body in its current condition as problematic. In spite of this anxiety, even the New Testament betrays no tendency to devalue the body. Although Paul wished to be delivered from "this body of death" (Romans 7:24) and longed "to be clothed with our heavenly dwelling" (2 Corinthians 5:2), he nevertheless envisioned our ultimate state as an embodied one—the spiritual body mentioned in 1 Corinthians 15:44. The problem for Paul is not the body itself, but sin, which has infected the body just as it has misused God's law (Romans 7:7-12). What is needed is not an escape from the body, but the transformation of our bodies so that they are freed from the power of sin and death (1 Corinthians 15:51-57).

What is the significance for spirituality of our embodied condition? First, it means that we are not beings of pure spirit. We have a range of experiences that no spirit being would have. This includes bodily desires, memory, physical sensations, feelings, and emotions. Even our rational thought has its basis in our sensuous life and has an essential connection to our emotions. All of these come into consideration in a discussion of spirituality, which is not about our spirits abstractly considered, but is instead about our existence as concrete, bodily beings.

Second, our embodied condition means that we live in the world and necessarily have an ethical and spiritual orientation to the world. Because of this orientation to the world, the Christian faith has an inescapably ethical dimension. As we survey the history of Christianity, we observe that the ethical dimension of faith manifests itself in two impulses, which are of the greatest importance for spirituality. One impulse is expressed by Jesus' statement in John's Gospel that "in the world you face persecution. But take courage; I have conquered the world!" (16:33). This is supplemented by 1 John's rhetorical question, "Who is it that conquers the world but the one who believes that Jesus is the Son of God?" (5:5). These verses indicate the premise on which the impulse toward transcending the world rests, the conviction that this world has become the place of sin—not that the physical universe itself is sinful, but that it is the arena in which sin flourishes. In this conception, *world* no longer has reference to the physical cosmos in its materiality, which is the good creation of God. Instead, as in John's Gospel, it refers to humankind and demonic powers as they are arrayed against God and God's followers. It is this world and its sinful effects that disciples are called to flee. World-transcendence, then, does *not* mean denying or hating the good cosmos that God created, even if it has become the place where sin occurs. It also does not mean physical flight from the world, for, by virtue of our participation in the world, we are worldly beings through and through. There is no escaping our created nature as inhabitants of this world. Besides this, any attempted escape from the sinful world would be futile, for we would bring the fallenness of the world with us. What are the ethical implications of world-transcendence? Any general sort of answer would be exceedingly abstract, for world-transcendence is always pursued in particular ethical and spiritual contexts. For this reason, it is best to point to examples.[2] Perhaps the most lucid example in Christian history is monasticism. Although Christian monasticism began literally as an attempt to physically flee the world by finding refuge in the desert, it quickly developed into the pursuit of perfection through the practice of ascetic and spiritual disciplines. Other examples in Christian history abound, including Martin Luther's concept of the believer's spiritual lordship; John Calvin's teaching about self-denial; and the devotional exercises, ascetic practices, mystical contemplation, and acts of political resistance engaged in by Christians over the centuries.

At the same time, this impulse toward ethically transcending the world coexists with another impulse that induces us to participate ethically in the world. This impulse is, in part, grounded in the confidence that the world remains God's good creation and that Christians, as creatures, remain a part of that world. We have, whether we recognize it or not, an essential solidarity with the rest of the created world. It also rests on the conviction that God has not abandoned the world. As a result, we see in history Christians participating in the world both in routine ways (such as in family life and labor) and also in attempts at reform (such as in the American Social Gospel movement and contemporary liberation theologies). Psalm 104 is instructive in both these regards. This psalm places humankind squarely in the midst of that created world, side by side with other animals. Like other animals, humans have to work (v. 23), are dependent on God's goodness in providing food (vv. 14-15), and, as noted above, live and die by the breath of God (vv. 29-30). Participation in the world is not sheer existence in the world in the way in which plants or animals participate in the world. By "participation" I mean the sort of participation that is distinctive to humankind. This means a spiritual and ethical participation that involves the totality of our being. Although we do participate in the world through the physical and biological dimensions of our being, our participation involves as well our spiritual and ethical dimensions. Affirming that human beings participate in the world in every dimension of our being means, first, that every aspect of human being is a part of the created world. There is no part of us that is foreign to the created world and that has its home in an unworldly reality. Human beings are thoroughly a part of the world. This affirmation means, second, that the created world is and remains God's world in spite of the presence of sin in it. It is for this reason that Christians are called upon, in the interests of spirituality, not to forsake this world, but instead to cooperate with God in its redemption. At the same time, we must acknowledge that a spiritual and ethical participation that is God-pleasing is not something automatic but instead is a task set before us. Human beings, by virtue of our humanity, participate in the world. However, we participate under the condition of sin. This implies that we must exercise critical judgment when considering our participation. Experience shows that our affirmation of the world and of its created goodness easily passes over into sinful indulgence in worldly pleasures and into a sinful identification with the world that hinders our devotion to God. Our created participation in the world, then, must be set over against the other focus of our spirituality, world-transcendence.

We are not surprised that Christians have found it difficult to do justice to both impulses simultaneously and evenly. Inevitably, we tend toward one or the other. But it is important to keep in mind that neither world-participation nor world-transcendence alone constitutes the ethical dimension of life in the Spirit. In fact, each taken alone represents a grave risk to the Christian life. History abounds with examples of believers who participated fully in the world without the transcending impulse. One result has been that Christians have identified with the world so thoroughly that we have often identified some worldly phenomenon, idea, or institution with the kingdom of God. We lose all capacity to hear the prophetic word that calls for a critical distance between us and the world. Another result has been our immersion in the mundane pleasures of life that make it exceedingly difficult to engage in the training in righteousness that 2 Timothy speaks of. A one-sided emphasis on world-transcendence brings another set of problems. For instance, extreme apocalyptic movements that regard the created world as evil and that envision salvation as deliverance from this world suffer from an abundance of the transcending impulse and an undervaluing of our participation in the world. The same is true for movements advocating extreme practices of asceticism. Life in the Spirit, then, is the ideal balance between these two impulses, participation and transcendence. Such a balance is, under the conditions of sin in which we labor, impossible. We, individually and the communities of which we are a part, will inevitably veer toward the one or the other. In pessimistic eras and times of persecution, Christians will lean toward world-transcendence. In optimistic times, we incline toward world-participation. It is the task of the church in general and its leaders in particular to help disciples discern the appropriate forms that spiritual transcendence and participation should take and avoid an unhealthy imbalance between the two impulses. By striving for balance, we can attempt to be faithful to God's call to overcome the world even as we remain in the world and affirm God's good creation.

Third, embodiment signifies our essential finitude. Because we are bodily creatures and finite, we are subject to limitations that no perfection of spirituality can overcome. There is no spiritual state in which our memory is flawless, in which our thinking is without error, in which our feelings and emotions are always appropriate. Even those most advanced on the path of Christian spirituality remain limited in the functions that make us human, quite apart from the effects of sin. Spirituality does not elevate us above our essential finitude. Indeed, it is the mark of a truly spiritual person to acknowledge that finitude, both as an act of self-knowledge and as a way of honoring the creator, who alone is infinite.

Our finitude is both an empirical fact and a theological conviction. The empirical character of this judgment does not require extensive citation. Every one of us feels our limitations: limitations of knowledge, of physical strength, of memory, of courage and character. There is also the fact that one's life has a definite beginning and a definite and inevitable ending. Theologically considered, finitude is expressed in the doctrine of our creation in the image of God. On one hand, this doctrine expresses the belief that humans are made for God and that our highest good lies in the knowledge and love of God. On the other hand, the fact that we are the image of God discloses our essentially derivative character. We are not the original, the prototype, but instead are formed in the image of something that is original and primary. As an image, we cannot be other than finite, for to be an image is to be limited, in one's being, by that of which one is an image. So, even though the Bible places humankind at the apex of creation, it always leaves us in the finite world. Nothing, not even eschatological salvation and our participation in God's trinitarian life, annuls our essential finitude.

A necessary part of Christian spirituality is acknowledging our finitude. It might seem unnecessary to insist on this point. After all, since our finitude is a matter of empirical observation, denying it is pointless and emphasizing it seems otiose. But the Bible takes a different view because our finitude creates the possibility of sin. This is not to say that our finite condition is itself sinful or that it causes us to sin. It is only to say that knowledge of our finitude is an ontological condition in which sin can take place. This is because, in recognizing our limitations, we spontaneously desire to transcend them. Ezekiel's oracle against Tyre illustrates this point as it poetically portrays the king of Tyre as opposing God to such an extent as to aspire to divinity:

> Because your heart is proud
> and you have said, "I am a god;
> I sit in the seat of the gods,
> in the heart of the seas,"
> yet you are but a mortal, and no god....
> You were the signet of perfection,
> full of wisdom and perfect in beauty....
> You were blameless in your ways
> from the day that you were created,
> until iniquity was found in you....
> Your heart was proud because of your beauty;
> you corrupted your wisdom for the sake of your
> splendor. (28:2, 12, 15, and 17)

This passage points to an important aspect of human existence, namely, our capacity for transcendence. Because we are not only finite but also aware of our finitude, there is within us a drive to transcend our limitations. This can take salutary forms, as in works of creativity and imagination, in developing our innate capacities, in friendship and sexual union, and in ameliorating undesirable social conditions. In each of these we escape from blind repetition of the past and orient ourselves toward something greater than us and toward the future. But this drive can also take malignant forms. Few of us would overtly and consciously think ourselves equal to God, but we are prone to overcome our finitude at the expense of others. Violence, intimidation, humiliation, and other forms of dominance are testimonies to the direction that our drive for transcendence can take when we are unmindful of God. For this reason, Paul had to warn his readers "not to think of [yourselves] more highly than you ought to think" (Romans 12:3) and "in humility [to] regard others as better than yourselves" (Philippians 2:3). Humility, which is an essential aspect of Christian spirituality, is rooted in acknowledging our finitude and accepting our place among creatures. It is a way of honoring the creator by accepting the limitations inherent in human nature. Of course, it must also be noted that the drive for transcendence can be crushed and destroyed. This is one of the enduring contributions of feminist theology. Such destruction happens when, for instance, violence and intimidation compel people without power to curtail their hopes and when their development as human beings is stunted. In these cases, the natural and good desires of transcendence, self-assertion, and self-actualization are not allowed to express themselves. On the contrary, those oppressed by violence and intimidation progressively withdraw from self-assertion and instead become passive recipients of that violence and intimidation. In these cases, spiritual health is not curbing our overweening drive for transcendence, but instead regaining an appropriate desire for transcendence and a capacity for self-assertion.

Another effect of the idea of finitude on spirituality is that we are reminded that, regardless of the extent of our spiritual maturity, there are some aspects of human nature that even the most mature Christian character does not aid. It is important to draw a distinction between the results of sin and the limitations of our nature due to our finitude. The former contradict our created nature and are overcome—slowly—through God's grace. The latter, however, do not contradict our nature—they *are* our nature. The finest disciple who ever lived suffered from defects of knowledge, memory, strength, courage, and so on. Even Jesus Christ, the eternal Word existing under the condition of human existence, lived with the limitations of knowledge and energy that we all experience. As John's Gospel states it, when Jesus sat down by Jacob's well, he did so because he was "tired out by his journey" (4:6). Sadly, developing a well-formed Christian character does not make us more intelligent or physically more capable. Additionally, we must be realistic about our capacity for appreciable change in our fundamental personality traits. Paul was irascible before his conversion and he was irascible after. Peter was no model of courage before Pentecost and continued to lack moral fortitude after, if Paul's account of the events in Antioch is taken at face value (Galatians 2:1-14). It is fervently to be hoped that the inexorable effect of God's grace upon us will over time soften the hard edges of our personality and ameliorate our weaknesses; however, Christian spirituality is pursued under the condition of our essential finitude. We cannot escape the fundamental limitations of our nature, even if we can spiritually transcend the world and its sin. This fact is no justification for laziness, as the New Testament's frequent exhortations demonstrate. But it is a call to acknowledge that our transformation and renewal through grace leaves us human. It is not within the scope of salvation to alter this fact. At the same time, we must acknowledge that we do not know the full potential of grace to transform us, prone as we are to settle for a life that is no worse than the lives of those around us. We may assume that history has never yet seen the person whose cooperation with God's grace brought to full effect the power mentioned in the prayer of Ephesians that we might know "the immeasurable greatness of [God's] power for us who believe" (1:19).

The Practice of Christian Spirituality in Community

The Bible assumes the importance of community for spiritual well-being to such an extent that it does not bother to argue for it. In the ancient setting, with a collectivist form of social organization, the over-riding significance of the community was taken for granted. In our cultural context, however, we cannot take it for granted. In fact, it is something that we must recover in some measure if we are to understand and practice Christian spirituality. Fortunately, although the Bible does not argue formally about the importance of community, it expresses this point indirectly and yet so forcefully that we can hardly miss the point. Yet it is important to reinforce the connection between community and spirituality because of the forces in American society that tend to fragment communities.

Both in philosophical discourse and in our cultural ethos, American culture has witnessed a widespread and dramatic interest in and emphasis on individuality. There were and are good reasons for this emphasis. Politically, it has been important to assert individual rights against the potentially overweening power of the state. Philosophically, it has been important to recognize the role that individual subjectivity plays in human knowledge. Culturally, there is value in encouraging individual expression of talents and desires as an antidote to bland uniformity. However, there can be too much of a good thing. It is no exaggeration to assert that in our day individual subjectivity has become a high and virtually unquestioned principle. Unfortunately, the baneful effects of rampant subjectivity and inwardness are all around us, from the legal obsession with individual rights to the privatization of religion to the increasing social isolation of the individual and loss of community. So, it may be that in our cultural situation the church will find it necessary to emphasize the important connection between community and spirituality more vigorously than would be necessary in other cultural situations.

One way to appreciate the central importance of community is to take account of the Bible's teaching regarding election. This doctrine has been one of the most contentious doctrines in Christian history. I will not attempt an adequate exposition here. The point I do wish to make is that, within the Bible, the object of election is normally the community—first Israel, then the church—and not individuals as such. Although this observation does not solve every problem associated with the doctrine of election, it does indicate the great importance that the community has for the salvation of its members. A classical statement of Israel's faith in this matter is Deuteronomy 7:6: "You are a people holy to the LORD your God; the LORD your God has chosen you out of all the peoples on earth to be his people, his treasured possession." Here God is represented as surveying the nations and selecting Israel to stand in a special relation to God. Moreover, Deuteronomy expressly states that this selecting was not done on the basis of Israel's size (7:7) and its righteousness (9:4), but instead because of God's faithfulness to the covenant made with the patriarchs (7:8). This shows us that the object of God's choosing is a corporate entity—those descended from Abraham—and not individuals.

The salvation of individuals is made possible by their participation in the elect community that God has set apart.

This perspective on community and election helps us make sense of some of the New Testament's teachings. Two representative passages are Ephesians 1:4-5 (God the Father "chose us in Christ before the foundation of the world to be holy and blameless before him in love. He destined us for adoption.") and Colossians 3:12 ("As God's chosen ones, holy and beloved ..."). Contrary to our tendency to interpret these passages as teaching God's election of individuals in their individuality, in light of the Old Testament background it is most sensible to interpret them as describing the election of a corporate entity, the church considered as the body of Christ. If we press the analogy between the church and Israel and interpret passages like these with the help of Deuteronomy 7:6, they reinforce our sense of the central place that the community has in the Bible's understanding of salvation and spiritual well-being. Putting it briefly, the possibility of a spiritual life at all is largely tied to membership in the community.[3] Not surprising, the New Testament speaks in the harshest of tones of those who have left the community or have been expelled from it because of sin: they have been handed over to Satan for discipline (1 Corinthians 5:5 and 1 Timothy 1:20) and are antichrists (1 John 2:18-19). Although this sort of rhetoric is unfashionable for today's pastor, the point it makes is clear—salvation and spiritual well-being are found only within the church, so that leaving the church has calamitous results for one's spirit.

Election is an important concept not only because it shows us the importance of community for understanding spirituality, but also because it defines that community as holy, which is a fundamental presupposition of Christian spirituality. Election creates a *holy* community. This is seen clearly in Deuteronomy 7:6, in which the juxtaposition of holiness and election suggests a close conceptual connection. Israel and then the church are holy because God has singled them out for special divine service. Because of this selection, Israel and the church stand in a special relation to God, one that distinguishes them from the nations and that lays distinctive obligations on them. The Bible's teaching about holiness may be summarized under three points: separation, purity, and righteousness.

The theological motif of separation is central to the creation story of Genesis, in which God is portrayed as performing various sorts of separation: dry land from water, light from darkness, and so on. Prominent among these is the separation of the seventh day from the first six and

God's endowing the seventh day with a special purpose. The seventh day is holy precisely because God has separated it from the other days and thereby brought it into special relationship to God. Thus we see, even in the story of creation, the connection between separation and holiness. This connection is further illustrated by the laws regulating Israel's priests. They were distinguished from the rest of the people because of their service in the temple. As a result, some regulations applied to priests and not to other Israelites. These additional regulations express their holiness and their separation from the rest of Israel. Obedience to the regulations maintained their distinctive holiness and allowed them to minister before the holy God. But it is not only the priests who were holy, although it is true that they were in a special state of holiness. The Old Testament represents Israel as a whole as a distinguished, priestly people, with special regulations applying to them and not to other nations, regulations that expressed and maintained their holiness. This conviction is expressed clearly in Leviticus: "I have separated you from the peoples. You shall therefore make a distinction between the clean animal and the unclean.... You shall be holy to me; for I the LORD am holy, and I have separated you from the other peoples to be mine" (Leviticus 20:24-26). In the New Testament, this same idea is expressed in 1 Peter 2:9: "You are a chosen race, a royal priesthood, a holy nation, God's own people, in order that you may proclaim the mighty acts of him who called you out of darkness into his marvelous light." In this passage, the church is expressly likened to priests and is called holy. It is especially important to note that holiness is an attribute of the church as a corporate entity. In this way, the church occupies the same status of being a separated people that Israel occupied. The individuals can be holy only as they participate in the holy community. In the biblical traditions, then, separation combined with election implies holiness.

Purity is a second aspect of the community's holiness. It appears in Leviticus 20, in which Israel is called upon to distinguish the clean from the unclean. Although the rationale for this sort of distinction is generally lost on modern audiences, it signifies an important point in the Old Testament, namely, that some things that are forbidden to the holy people are allowed to the rest of humankind. Because Israel was a priestly nation (Exodus 19:6), it must live by stringent laws of purity from which other nations were exempt. The temple priests, of course, lived by even more stringent laws. What was true of Israel is true of the church as well, although New Testament writings have mostly dropped the ancient obsession with ritual purity and food laws from the concept of purity. Instead, by the New Testament period, purity had come to mean honorable sexual behavior (as in 1 Thessalonians 4:3-7 and 1 Corinthians 5:7). Moreover, it is something that can be compromised by evil thoughts and motives and by things such as avarice, envy, and pride (Mark 7:20-22), and not by eating unclean food or coming in contact with corpses.

Mention of evil thoughts and motives brings us to the third feature of holiness, righteousness. For the Old Testament, righteousness is an obligation laid on those who are holy: "You shall be holy, for I the LORD your God am holy. You shall each revere your mother and father, and you shall keep my sabbaths.... Do not turn to idols or make cast images" (Leviticus 19:2-4). It might have been thought (and judging from the prophetic literature, ancient Israelites customarily did think) that the holiness of Israel bore no special ethical consequences. After all, the reasoning went, if Israel was elect and holy, then it stood, by virtue of that election and holiness, in a unique relation to God, nothing else being necessary to maintain that relation except for ritual purity. The Old Testament writers, however, were eager to correct this impression. As Leviticus 19:2-4 admonishes, Israel must be righteous precisely because it was called to be holy. Holiness, then, could not simply be a matter of purity and temple service. Holiness also had to issue forth in ethical comportment of the highest degree. That is why in the biblical tradition holiness begins to shade into righteous behavior. Not surprising, in the New Testament, in which temple service and ritual purity are not part of the Christian life, holiness is virtually equivalent to righteousness. Accordingly, the New Testament makes express the connection between holiness and righteous conduct that is still somewhat latent in Leviticus: "Do not be conformed to the desires that you formerly had in ignorance. Instead, as he who called you is holy, be holy yourselves in all your conduct" (1 Peter 1:14-15). The expression of holiness in conduct is righteousness.

In summary, the church, like Israel, is elect and therefore both holy and called to be holy. Its holiness consists in being separated from other communities, in being pure, and in acting righteously. Individuals can be elect, holy, and righteous only as they are incorporated into this holy community. The quantity of metaphors found in the New Testament to signify this incorporation and to convey the significance of community signal the importance of this point. Some have already been mentioned: holy priesthood, chosen race, holy nation. There are many others such as the body of Christ (Ephesians 1:23 and 4:15-16), the household of God

(Ephesians 2:19, also in 1 Peter 4:17 and 1 Timothy 3:15), the holy temple (Ephesians 2:21-22) and the spouse of Christ (Ephesians 5:25-30). To be a Christian is to be a member of this new reality, to be incorporated into this corporate existence.

This emphasis on community raises an issue. Surely we do not wish to state that the Holy Spirit is found only within the church. Was there no life in the Spirit before the appearance of the church? Is there none today outside the church? These questions arise for at least two reasons. First, there is a persistent conviction in our society that access to God requires no institutional or communal membership. Second, we are aware of people outside the Christian community who exhibit virtues, and from this we rightly conclude that Christians do not have a monopoly on virtue.

To these points the Christian church must tirelessly insist on the importance of the Christian community for authentic spirituality. We must insist on this point above all because of its biblical warrant. As 1 Corinthians and Galatians indicate, the notion of being a Christian apart from being in the body of Christ is absurd. But there are other pertinent considerations. For one, true spirituality will be in agreement with our created nature, one result of which is human society. Belief that humans are social beings is not a uniquely Christian conviction. As far back as Aristotle, philosophers had noted that our well-being depends on the character of our relationships. If this is true, then authentic spirituality cannot occur apart from some sort of human community, and its essence will be essentially connected with the character of that community. For another, there are intensely practical and pastoral reasons, exhibited in history, for connecting spirituality with community. John Wesley's experience in the revival of the eighteenth century is instructive. Having attained great success in gaining converts, Wesley found that they were soon lost. In response, he developed the class meeting, the forerunner of modern accountability groups, in order both to provide nurture and to create accountability for converts. This illustrates the point that discipleship cannot be successfully practiced outside community. Further back in Christian history, the experiences of early monasticism point to the same insight. Initially, those interested in pursuing the monastic life simply went out into the desert to seek perfection through a solitary life. But, over the course of time, those in the monastic movement noted that the solitary life encouraged eccentricity and, sometimes, loss of good judgment. In response, Christian monasticism developed in a more communal direction, for example, in the Benedictine movement.

Benedictine life was intensely communal with, once again, provision made for spiritual nurture and also regular accountability.

But perhaps all that these arguments establish is that *some* sort of community is necessary for authentic spirituality. Perhaps it is important only that we pursue spirituality in and through *some* community. The question remains, Why is incorporation into the Christian community necessary for authentic spirituality? To this question two answers are appropriate.

First, it is not necessary to believe that the church is the only place where the Spirit of God can be found working. It is theologically legitimate to draw a distinction between life in the Spirit, which is a function of being incorporated into the body of Christ, and the work of God in the world. It is entirely appropriate to acknowledge that the Lord of the universe is free to act anywhere and at any time. Experience shows that throughout history and in many cultures there have been people who, like Cornelius (Acts 10), have been devout and fearers of God. It would be theologically disastrous to avow that such people have achieved this devotion strictly through their own native abilities and without the leading of God's Spirit. At the same time, it is important for the church to affirm that it is through the ministries of the body of Christ that God's grace is administered, the gifts of the Spirit are distributed, and the fruit of the Spirit is cultivated. The church, in this affirmation, is like the sacraments in this respect: Like them, the church is the ordained means by which God ordinarily and graciously comes to us. But the reality of these ordained means does not at all exclude extraordinary means through which God in God's freedom may act within the church or outside the church. At the same time, the possibility of these extraordinary means at God's disposal does not reduce the church's obligation to be faithful to its calling as the ordained means of God's grace.

Second, it is a matter of Christian conviction that there is the closest possible relation between membership in this community and Christian spirituality because this community is the eschatological community. This community is eschatological because the promised age of the Spirit has arrived in the life, death, and resurrection of Jesus Christ and is present in the church's continuation of his ministry. This means that this community represents the appearance of the eschatological kingdom of God. Of course, it would be a mistake to claim that this community *is* the kingdom of God. On the contrary, it is an anticipation of the fullness of God's kingdom in the midst of history. The historical anticipation of the kingdom takes the form of a community because, as Jesus portrayed it, the kingdom is like a banquet to which many will gather from the east and the west (Luke 13:29; 14:15). The church is the community that anticipates, proclaims, and celebrates this kingdom. Although the church does not perfectly embody the kingdom of God, it is the community whose task it is to bear witness to the coming kingdom by anticipating it both in hope and practice.

The Practice of Christian Spirituality in a Fallen World

The incarnation and resurrection of Jesus Christ introduce the transition from God's original creation to God's new creation. In so doing, they bring about a new mode of being—eschatological existence.

Christian eschatology is based on the premise that the kingdom of God has arrived in the person and ministry of Jesus Christ and that the age of the Spirit has come. It includes the observation that the kingdom of God coexists with the fallen, sinful world, so that, although the kingdom is present, its full manifestation lies in the future. To say that the Christian life is an eschatological existence is to say that it partakes of the age of the Spirit in the context of the present evil age. Because God's kingdom has not yet overcome the power of sin, the Christian life includes the reality of temptation and the possibility of falling back into the life of sin. As noted above, our participation in the trinitarian life of God means our spiritual transcendence over the world. However, this transcendence is neither automatic nor necessarily permanent. On the contrary, it requires our decision and resolve. Although the establishing of a Christian character can make this resolve more spontaneous and continuous, there always remains to us the possibility of falling back into the life of sin that constitutes our past. The Christian life, then, is poised between the past, which is our life under the power of sin, and the future, which is our life in God's kingdom. The purpose of pastoral exhortation in the New Testament is to strengthen the disciples' resolve to press onward toward God's future and to leave behind the past. The problem of the Christian life and the reason that pastoral exhortation is required is that the past (the life of sin) is not simply in the chronological past (as, for example, the year 1901 is in the past). The chronological past is one that is irretrievably gone and has reality only as it resides in the memory. Ideally, the past that is our life under sin would be of this sort—it would be something that we merely remember and that would have no continuing effect on us. We have a sense of this ideal possibility insofar as we have turned our backs on sin, have a measure of freedom from sin, and live in the hope and expectation of God's future. However, our past creeps into the present whenever we lose sight of God's future and allow that past once again to be our future. We are, then, constantly being summoned: by God into the future of freedom and salvation and by the past into a life of sin and death. These two times are the framework of the Christian life.

The New Testament describes the past of sin in various ways. In the Johannine literature, it is the world that, although it is passing away, remains a possible object of love for the disciple (1 John 2:15-17). In Paul's letters, it is the flesh, which opposes life in the Spirit and which the Christian must crucify (Galatians 5:17, 24), and it is the former self that must be put off (Ephesians 4:22). Regardless of the metaphor used to describe it, what is being discussed in these passages is the subtle power of sin and its residual effects in us. We experience this power and these effects because of our proximity to the world and because of its allure for us. That is why, in John's Gospel, Jesus prays that disciples may be protected from the evil one, for although they do not belong to the world, they must remain in the world (17:11-18). As Paul's exhortations in 1 Corinthians and John's in Revelation 2–3 remind us, it is all too easy for disciples to fall back into the world of sin. Although Paul spoke of those who are mature (or perfect [*teleioi*]) and spiritual (1 Corinthians 2:6), he judged members of the Corinthian congregation to be "fleshly" (1 Corinthians 3:1). Here, it seems, we discover an entire congregation that, poised between God's future of salvation and their own past of sin, were definitely tilted toward the past and were experiencing its effects in their corporate life.

For this reason, we must recognize the essentially ambiguous character of holiness and righteousness in eschatological existence.[4] The Bible knows of a day when all of God's enemies, even death, will have been subdued (1 Corinthians 15:24-26). However, we have not yet arrived at that day. In the language of Paul, we are still in that time when Jesus Christ is reigning and subduing those enemies. They remain at large. But the problem is not simply that they remain. It is also that they are subtle and attractive. They are not only public and visible enemies such as that which John described, a great political and manifest entity persecuting God's people and blaspheming God (Revelation 13). They are also the pervasive, tempting desires to which we may all succumb and which, in our darker moments, we often secretly wish to enjoy—greed, malice, envy, and the like. To live eschatologically, then, is to live with face toward God's future and with back to sin's past, but also with the constant awareness that the past, although dead and buried, can be instantly resurrected by our wavering from the future into which God is calling us. It is to live mindful of the fact that we exist tensed with the coexistence of the present evil age and the power of the age to come.

It is for this reason that the New Testament describes our holiness and righteousness both as an accomplished fact and as something that will not be accomplished until the eschatological day of God's triumph. First Corinthians 6:11 describes the completed aspect of holiness well: "You were washed, you were sanctified, you were justified." The use of the simple past tense in this passage portrays these acts of God as events available for simple narration, accomplished (presumably) at baptism.[5] At the same time, our sanctification is sometimes an object of prayer, sometimes an object of exhortation. In 1 Thessalonians, Paul placed sanctification expressly in an eschatological context when he prayed, "May the God of peace himself sanctify you entirely; and may your spirit and soul and body be kept sound and blameless at the coming of our Lord Jesus Christ" (5:23). Second Corinthians 7:1 ("Let us cleanse ourselves from every defilement of body and of spirit, making holiness perfect in the fear of God") shows holiness to be something about which believers must be exhorted. The fact that holiness is placed in an eschatological context and the fact that it is a matter of exhortation shows us that (passages such as 1 Corinthians 6:11 notwithstanding) holiness is not simply a once and for all event in the disciple's life. On the contrary, we are holy in a fallen world, which means that it is not a permanent possession but instead both a gift and something that must be persistently pursued and sought.

Christian Spirituality and Participation in God

The discussion of sanctification brings us to the fourth presupposition of Christian spirituality, our participation in the trinitarian life of God. Sanctification means being like God: we are to be holy because God is holy (Leviticus 19:2 and Matthew 5:48). Of course, we must quickly add that we are not holy in just the same way in which God is holy, for our holiness is finite, derivative, and contingent. For this reason, Ephesians speaks of our imitating God (5:1) and not of our becoming divine. Nonetheless, the Bible insists that we are to be like God. But it is also insistent that this is not a natural quality of human beings. We are not born being like God; the processes of socialization in family and society do not make us like God. Our becoming like God—our becoming holy— is the result of God's grace. It occurs only as we are drawn into and participate in the trinitarian life of the God who is love.[6] In turn, being drawn into this life means becoming conformed to Jesus Christ—the image of God (Romans 8:29)—and participating in the fellowship between the Father and the Son (1 John 1:3). Only in this way can we begin to escape the effects of sin and become new creatures, "created according to the likeness of God in true righteousness and holiness" (Ephesians 4:24).

There are several points to be made about the Trinity in relation to Christian spirituality. The first is the observation that every feature of the ideal Christian character is grounded in God. Love, justice, faithfulness, and every other quality finds its archetype and perfection in God. We can be loving, faithful, and so on only as we live in and through God. Even then our possession of these qualities is subject to the distortions of sin and the limitations due to our finitude. Nonetheless, to the extent that we have these qualities we have them because and to the extent that we participate in God. As Paul notes, in our prayers it is not so much we who pray as the Spirit of God that prays through us (Romans 8:26-27). In our striving it is not our effort alone but also God's working within us that leads us into a Christian character (Philippians 2:13). In short, a Christian character is not simply the result of our hard work, but also the effect of God's grace. But grace is not an impersonal power that comes upon us. It is instead God's life as we are drawn into that life.

However, this first observation is not sufficient, for it lacks the concrete sense of participation that we find in the New Testament. The notion that the virtues of the Christian life are archetypically in God and the exhortation to imitate God could lead to a Platonic conception of our relation to God, in which we would think of God as the original and perfect reality of which we would be defective copies. Although such a notion is not without an element of truth, it is not the whole of what the Christian tradition wishes to affirm. This leads to the second observation, that the life of Christian spirituality has a trinitarian structure. First of all, we are baptized into the name of the Father and of the Son and of the Holy Spirit. Then, we are said to dwell in Christ (Galatians 3:26) and to exist according to the Spirit (Romans 8:4-5). We are called on to pray and give thanks to God the Father (Romans 16:27 and Ephesians 5:20).

The trinitarian structure of the Christian life is summarized in Ephesians 2:18: "Through [Christ] both of us have access in one Spirit to the Father." These prepositions are to be taken seriously and not consigned to the sphere of mere metaphor.[7] As we live *in* the Spirit, our existence is directed *to* the Father *through* our participation in Jesus Christ and his body. The notion of participation in God's trinitarian life is hinted at in 2 Peter, which teaches that we are to become partakers of the divine nature (1:4), and in the metaphor of the vine and the branches (John 15:1-6). Elsewhere, John's Gospel speaks more directly of disciples being in the Father and the Son in just the way in which the Son is in the Father and the Father is in the Son (17:21). In other words, Christians are taken up into the trinitarian life of God and share in the love and fellowship that exists between the Father and the Son. As a result, we must affirm not only that the virtues of the Christian life are found archetypically in God, but also that we have these virtues only as we live in and through God. We participate in God not only as a copy participates in its original, but also in a more fundamental, even organic (to use the John's metaphor of the vine and branches) way.

The importance of this participation for Christian spirituality is that it gives us a language for describing the basis of both our holiness and our spiritual transcendence over the world. I previously discussed holiness in terms of separation, purity, and righteousness. Separation means that Christians are in some sense distinct from those outside the church. Besides all observable differences, the fundamental distinction is that the Christian life is a participation in God's trinitarian life in a way in which other forms of life are not.[8] The church and its members are set apart by their having come, through the resurrection of Jesus Christ, to dwell in God in a new and distinctive way. Purity and righteousness, in addition to describing our conduct in the world, also describe our fitness to stand in the presence of the holy God free from defilement and guilt. As the New Testament asserts, it is God who makes us fit to stand in the holy presence, and this occurs through our being drawn into God's trinitarian life of love. It is not as though God first examines us, finds us acceptable, and then admits us into the trinitarian fellowship. On the contrary, it is only as we are found in Christ and walk by the Spirit—as we live in God—that we are made acceptable to God. Our participation in the Trinity, then, is the basis of the life of sanctification as it is lived in the world. The same is true of our spiritual transcendence of the world. Although there is an important sense in which this is a matter of human striving and the subject of pastoral exhortation, there is also an important sense in which such striving and exhortation presuppose our life in God and the grace that is ours in that life. We can overcome the world in practice only because we are in Christ who overcame the world and because we have received the Spirit. Our transcending the world, then, is the actualization in practice of our relation to God, a relation of participation.

Notes

1. Perhaps from God's perspective, all corporeal things are already holy. If so, then what is lacking is not their own fitness for God, but instead our capacity to see their fitness. In this case, then it is our perspective that must be transformed and not corporeal things themselves.

2. See Samuel M. Powell, *Participating in God: Creation and Trinity, Theology and the Sciences* (Minneapolis: Fortress Press, 2003), for a fuller exposition and historical examples of world-transcendence.

3. I say "largely" and not "completely" because the Bible does know of occasional individuals (such as Cornelius in Acts 10) outside the elect community who exhibit spiritual qualities similar to those found in the community.

4. What is true of holiness and righteousness is true of salvation generally. It is both something that has been accomplished in the past and also something that will be fulfilled in the eschatological day.

5. First Peter 1:22 similarly speaks of disciples having purified their souls, and Hebrews 10:10 notes our having been sanctified by the offering of Christ's body.

6. It is important to note that, like all creatures, we participate in God in certain ways by virtue of our physical, biological, and social nature. However, these modes of participation do not bear on the question of holiness. Our participation in this way does not distinguish us from atoms, cells, and animal societies. Christian spirituality concerns our participation in God in a way that is distinctively human as that humanity is transformed in the new creation, the result of which is our being like the God who is love.

7. That the New Testament's language is metaphorical is obvious. Paul can say that we are in Christ but also that Christ is in us (Galatians 2:20). What is needed is to see the point that the New Testament is making through its metaphorical language.

8. In making this affirmation, it is important to remind the reader that, in this book, I am speaking from within the circle of faith and representing the affirmations of the Christian tradition without raising difficult philosophical issues. I am also purposely ignoring the vexing and deserving questions associated with religious pluralism.

BAPTISM

The Practice of Baptism

We are incorporated into the Christian community through baptism. This is an instance of the sacramental principle, which states that God comes to us not immediately in a purely spiritual way, but in a mediated way in and through earthly realities. Mediation is grounded in the incarnation, the supreme instance of God coming to us in the form of something utterly earthly. The church and its preaching, sacraments, and other ministries are likewise earthly forms in and through which God comes to us. Just as in the early centuries of the church, the incarnation was a scandal (that the *logos* had become human was a ludicrous proposition in the ancient world), so the Christian emphasis on mediation strikes some contemporary people as odd. People in our culture typically see no sin standing between us and God and, consequently, see no need of anything to mediate our relation to God. They also regard our knowledge of God as one of spiritual feeling or perception with no need of physical things and acts to mediate that knowledge to us. Today, the dominant feeling is that everyone stands in an immediate relation to God. The soul is in immediate contact with God.

To this the Christian church answers, as above, that the path of spirituality corresponds to our created nature. This created nature is not only social (so that life in the Spirit takes form in the community that anticipates the kingdom of God), but also corporeal. As a result, the path to spirituality lies along earthly ways. One way to help us feel the force of Christian belief about mediation is to concentrate on the physicality or sacramental character of the materials of baptism. In the ancient church, baptism sometimes involved not only water, but also oil, milk, honey, laying on hands, and speaking. Candidates were anointed with oil and received the laying on of hands in connection with their receiving the Holy Spirit. Milk and honey were given to signify the candidates' entrance into the promised land of salvation. Additionally, the candidate spoke words of confession. Above all was the water, which signified cleansing and also allowed the candidate to imitate Jesus, who was likewise baptized. Baptism, then, illustrates the point that God's grace comes to us in and through earthly realities. In the language of John's Gospel, realities such as water are signs. However, they do not signify arbitrarily, the way in which a street sign signifies. A street sign signifies because, in a given culture, there is agreement to use a geometrically shaped sign in a certain way. With a change in agreement, a sign with a completely different geometric shape could signify in the same way. Baptism, however, is different. It is no accident that the entrance into life in the Spirit is an act of cleansing. Hebrews preserves the connection between the purification of the body and that of the heart (10:22), reminding us of the Old Testament's concern with ritual purity as the prerequisite for approaching the holy God. It may be objected that 1 Peter goes out of its way to assert that the cleansing of baptism is not a matter of removing dirt from the body (3:21), indicating that the beginning of the Christian life is purely a matter of the heart, not of the body. But this objection misses the point of 1 Peter, which is that it is baptism that saves us. It does so because it is the appeal of a good conscience to God. Here we see the confluence of the heart (or conscience) and body that we found in Hebrews. It is in and through this physical act, joined with a willing heart and good conscience, that we are delivered into life in the Spirit. It was this confluence of the bodily and the spiritual that led John Calvin to comment on the appropriateness of using bread and wine in communion. As food, earthly bread and wine nourish the body and in this way are fit vehicles for communion, in which we feed spiritually on Christ and our souls are nourished.[1] This is why Calvin rejected a purely intellectual view of faith, according to which we receive Christ only in our understanding, and a purely spiritual view, according to which communion with Christ is simply equivalent to partaking of the Holy Spirit. On the contrary, there is, he taught, a real participation in Christ that is signified by our eating the bread and drinking the wine.[2] By analogy, the physical washing of baptism signifies the cleansing of the heart. But it is appropriate that this cleansing of the heart be exhibited by an act of physical washing so that we can be led to contemplate the truth that salvation is not only of the soul, but also the salvation of the entire self.

There is another type of immediacy that characterizes the contemporary spiritual pursuit, namely, the widespread view that there is nothing that we need to do in order to have a relationship with God. This is the view that we all enjoy, without any special effort on our part—a relationship with God, so that all that is necessary is for us to realize this fact. In this way, spirituality comes to be separated from spiritual disciplines, religious practices, and ethical comportment. This view is peculiar because our culture acknowledges the ncomessity of discipline and practice in areas such as sports and music. It likewise knows that human relationships cannot be sustained in the absence of performing specific acts. But religion is for us an exception. It is commonly supposed to be something effortless, instant, and immediate; for God is thought to make no extraordinary demands of us, and on the path to God we discover nothing more challenging than coming to know and accept that God loves us. In this sense, religion is like dieting. Whereas most people acknowledge that skills such as athletics and music require years of training and discipline, we have come to think of losing weight as something as effortless as religion, by virtue of dieting plans that claim (or are popularly believed to claim) that weight loss can be achieved by following a plan that, making minimal demands on us, makes dieting easy. The quick and painless fix of dieting is thus the counterpart to religion without cost.

The Christian church, however, has always recognized that the Christian life is a demanding one. Second Timothy, for instance, states that we have received the spirit of self-discipline (*sōphronismos*; 1:7); calls on us to suffer for the gospel (1:8); urges us to be strong in Christ's grace (2:1); likens us to soldiers, athletes, and farmers (2:3-6); exhorts us to flee from youthful passions (2:22); and reminds us that Scripture is useful for training (*paideia*) in righteousness so that we may be equipped for good works (3:16-17). The picture we receive from this and similar passages is that the Christian life is an active and costly life. This picture does not diminish the role and primacy of God's grace. Paul's words in Philippians remind us "it is God who is at work in you, enabling you both to will and to work for his good pleasure" (2:13). The Christian life is one of activity not because we are in it alone, without God's help, but because of the eschatological nature of that life. I will address this feature later in the chapter. At this point we may note that the assertion that the Christian life is an active life is simply the acknowledgment that God's grace demands from us a faithful and grateful response that takes the form of conforming our lives to that of Jesus Christ. In contrast to our culture, in which religion is regarded as something automatic, effortless, and immediate, the Christian tradition has argued that Christian religion is heavily invested in doing. This doing begins with baptism and the catechetical steps associated with baptism. As a result, the character of baptism as an act should never be overlooked or de-emphasized. Indeed, the church confesses that it is in and through this bodily act of baptism that we are inducted into the body of Christ. Our relation with God does not happen without our active response that involves the totality of our being. The activity of God ordinarily does not happen without human activity. It is not *equivalent* to that activity (otherwise the transcendence of God is lost), but it ordinarily takes place alongside that activity. In other words, God's actions *coincide* with ordained human actions. This coincidence of the divine and the human excludes three spiritual aberrations. First, it excludes the presumptuous view that human deeds anticipate God—that God acts only in response to our acting. Second, it excludes the temptation toward quietism, the view that we are to wait passively until God acts. Third, it excludes our culture's temptation to overlook the active and bodily dimension of spirituality in favor of a purely spiritual and immediate relation to God. To this third temptation the Christian tradition responds that God saves us, but not without our active cooperation not only in having faith, but also in bodily deeds such as baptism.

There is another respect in which the bodily aspect of baptism is vital for Christian spirituality. I refer here to the temporal or narrative structure of baptismal events. If our relation to God were something immediate (that is, utterly unmediated by earthly realities) and purely spiritual, then it would have no temporal structure; we would always, without interruption, stand in relation to God. The only development would consist in our gradual awakening to that fact. But because we are saved as whole beings who are deeply immersed in temporality, there is a temporal aspect to the process of salvation. At the broadest level, salvation encompasses the sum total of God's acts from creation to eschatological consummation. More immediate, the deeds associated with baptism mark and indeed effect the temporal structure of salvation: repentance, catechism, initiation, confession. They do so not because these deeds magically work salvation through their sheer performance, but because, through God's covenant of grace, God's saving act coincides with these ordained human acts.

What are these human acts in and through which God gives grace in baptism? Generalization is difficult because of the variety of baptismal customs among Christian churches, but the following seem universal: repentance and amendment of life (in the case of adult baptism); learning the faith (either prior to baptism or, in the case of infant baptism, later through confirmation); public confession of faith (again, either before baptism or, through confirmation, after baptism), and baptism itself. These acts are stations on the road to salvation and provide some of the temporal structure to the path of spirituality. Of course, this list should not be taken to indicate a strictly chronological order. Repentance is certainly not limited to the time before baptism, and baptism is not the last time believers are expected to confess the faith publicly. But these events do show us that the way of spirituality has a narrative or temporal character. It has a beginning, a time of development, and a consummation. Baptism pertains especially to the beginning, which has its own narrative structure because repenting, learning, confessing, and being baptized are distinct acts that occupy time and take place in a sequence.

In this section I have been urging consideration of the character of baptism as deed. Although baptism does not (or should not) occur without the devotion of the heart and the willingness of the mind, merely subjective feelings, thoughts, and wishes cannot validly substitute for it (except under specified conditions). Least of all can the church tolerate the view, which one hears occasionally, that the baptism required by the New Testament is a spiritual baptism in the Holy Spirit and not water baptism. A merely subjective approach does not involve the totality of our being, just as a merely physical baptism—without heart and mind—would not be valid. There is an analogy here to the christological debates of the fourth and fifth centuries, in which the importance of Christ's having a full and complete human nature was argued. Just as a Christ who was only divine and not human could not be the savior, so a relation to God that is only spiritual and overlooks the body falls far short of salvation. At the same time, it is important to remember that, as a sacrament, baptism signifies a reality without being that reality itself. Although baptism is the ordained means by which we are inducted into life in the Spirit, the church has always recognized that baptism is not absolutely indispensable and that extraordinary circumstances that prevent baptism do not disqualify us from salvation. In the third century, for example, Cyprian addressed the question of whether catechumens were to be considered saved if they had been martyred before being baptized. He responded that such catechumens were by no means considered unsaved, for their martyrdom represented a baptism in their own blood and they had been sanctified by their suffering.[3] In the same spirit, the contemporary catechism of the Roman Catholic Church affirms that, in the case of catechumens who die before baptism, their desire for baptism together with their repentance and love, ensures their salvation.[4] The lesson to draw is that baptism is an *ordinary* means of grace. It is the appointed way of entrance into life in the Spirit, but not an indispensable way in extraordinary cases. Consequently, the church is right to insist on the centrality of baptism without being legalistic about it in uncommon cases.

World-Transcendence and World-Participation

THE IMPULSE TOWARD TRANSCENDING THE WORLD

Another aspect of the corporeal character of baptism pertains to the impulses toward world-transcendence and world-participation. The New Testament is especially insistent on the importance of baptism in the pursuit of world-transcendence. For example, we find connected to baptism the language of rebirth (Titus 3:5), the image of being clothed with Christ (Galatians 3:27), and the image of being buried and raised with Christ (Colossians 2:12). These passages, and others less directly connected with baptism, point toward the believer's transcendence of the world. We are reborn, an affirmation that implies an advance beyond our natural birth. We have been clothed with Christ, which (according to Romans 13:14) implies the necessity of leaving behind the desires of the flesh. Then, we have been buried and raised with Christ. This points to the fact that life in the Spirit is in an important sense discontinuous with our former life in the world. We are, in a word, a new creation (2 Corinthians 5:17). Although we do not through baptism physically leave the world (in spite of the realized eschatology of Colossians, with its teaching that we have already been raised up with Christ), we have begun spiritually transcending the world, by being rescued "from the power of darkness" and transferred "into the kingdom" of the Son (Colossians 1:13).

There are definite, world-transcending ethical consequences of baptism. For one thing, it means that disciples have transcended and must no longer be regulated by social constructs that are not in harmony with the kingdom of God. These include gender, economic, and ethnic categories (Galatians 3:27). Here transcending the world means not the destruction of these categories, but their transformation. The church did not abolish the distinction between, for example, male and female. However, it did seek to modify the relation of husband and wife by summoning husbands to love their wives. Likewise, the church did not, even in its own communities, eliminate slavery, but it did try to ameliorate the conditions of slavery by impressing on masters their own status as slaves of Jesus Christ. Transcending the world, in these cases, involved trying to remake these social categories according to the law of love but also within the limitations imposed by the surrounding society.

A more dramatic instance of world-transcendence associated with baptism is freedom from sin in the form of vice. First Corinthians 6 speaks to this issue. According to 6:11, we have been washed, justified, and sanctified, a status that is clearly contrasted with the lives of the Corinthians prior to baptism. Their previous lives were characterized by vices of all sorts—fornication, adultery, drunkenness, and so on (6:9-10). The world-transcending character of baptism is evident in the affirmation that no one who practices these vices will inherit the kingdom of God (6:10). This point is made more fully in Romans 6. Here the argument is that, because in baptism we have been buried with Christ, we should no longer live in sin (6:2-4). Having died, we are free from sin (6:7). Moreover, the resurrection of Christ, as a pledge of our future resurrection, implies that our life must be characterized by newness (6:4). As a result, we should think of ourselves as dead to sin and, in Jesus Christ, alive to God (6:11). World-transcendence in this passage has a double edge. On one hand, it means freedom from sin. On the other, it means a new life in Christ, an anticipation of the resurrected life.

The transformation implied in baptism affects not only our practice, for example, leaving sinful vices behind, but also our state of mind. Because we have been raised up with Christ, we are to set our minds on heavenly things, for Christ is in the heavens, and not on earthly things (Colossians 3:2). Indeed, we are to kill off whatever is earthly—fornication, impurity, passion, and so on (3:5). For what is required is a transformation of the mind (*nous*), so that we can discern God's will (Romans 12:2). Then we will be of one mind and will think in ourselves that which was in Jesus Christ (Philippians 2:2-5).

Baptism, then, launches us into the pursuit of world-transcendence. The goal is to conquer the world as Jesus conquered the world (John 16:33) while at the same time, like God, loving the world (3:16). Consequently, this conquering does not mean the destruction of the world. Our transcending the world does not mean that we fight the world on its own terms and with its own weapons (2 Corinthians 10:3-5). On the contrary, the disciple's fighting is done with the armor of God—truth, righteousness, faith, the helmet of salvation, and the sword of the Spirit (Ephesians 6:10-12). That is why 1 John professes that faith *is* our victory over the world (5:4). Faith does not *bring* victory. It is our victory, for faith (understood as our faithful response to God's work in Christ) is a short-hand term for what I have been describing as transcendence. Faith is the state in which we turn our back on sin and live toward God in newness of life.

THE IMPULSE TOWARD PARTICIPATING IN THE WORLD

Because of its apocalyptic setting, the New Testament tends to place the emphasis on the world-transcending focus of the Christian life. However, it does not neglect our participation in the world. Through baptism's initiation into the Christian life we are, ideally, freed to participate in the world without danger of identifying with the world. Without world-transcendence, this freedom is impossible. Without world-transcendence, the things of this world become for us occasions for sin and objects of idolatry. However, by spiritually transcending the world we gain a cautious freedom that enables us to have a wholly different attitude toward the world and the things in the world. For this reason, 1 Timothy argues for the propriety of marriage and eating on the basis of thanksgiving and the sanctification of these things through prayer and the word (4:3-5). Some (in the ancient context) were urging ascetic practices in the form of abstinence as a means of greater spirituality. Their ethic was exclusively one of world-transcendence. In 1 Timothy, however, authentic spirituality lies in the direction of self-control (3:2, 11)[5] and devotional piety in the form of thanksgiving and prayer. Paul likewise allowed for the eating of meat insofar as it was eaten in faith (Romans 14:1-6), warned against a false religiosity that means unnecessary denial of the body (Colossians 2:16-23), and regarded marriage favorably as an image of Christ's relation to the church (Ephesians 5:25-33). In each of these passages, the goodness of some created reality is affirmed and to a certain extent celebrated, with the provisos that these created realities may be enjoyed only insofar as doing so is compatible with Christian piety and as the enjoyment of these things is regulated by the need to live soberly.

Apart from these express passages, we can make some general remarks on the world-participatory focus of baptism. First, the materiality of baptism testifies to world-participation. The fact that we are initiated into salvation through earthly medium implies that this salvation is not an escape from the earthly. As John of Damascus argued regarding icons, material reality is indeed a fit vehicle for God's grace and accordingly is to be honored by us. Second, baptism is our entry into the new creation. The new creation is not a contradiction of the first creation, but is instead its renewal. The new creation does not bring the first creation to an end, but rather brings it to completion. It is notable, in this regard, that Revelation, with its stark apocalypticism and its teaching about the new heavens and new earth, presents the new heavens and earth as continuous with and in fact as the perfection of this sinful world. For one thing, the new earth is built around the new Jerusalem, which, although fabulous, is quite material. For another, there is the tree of life. Its presence in the new earth is a clear signal that Revelation understands the future to be a return to the beginning narrated in Genesis. As a result, we conclude that the new creation into which baptism introduces us is this created world in its restored goodness. All the essential elements of the first creation reappear in the new creation without the results of sin. Here we find our renewal in the image of God (Colossians 3:10), a renewed wisdom in the person of Jesus Christ (1 Corinthians 1:24), and a new law—the law of love (James 2:8; for Paul the law of the Spirit of life [Romans 8:2]). In the new creation, then, the elements of the first creation are renewed and not canceled out. Baptism, then, draws us into a new world that is the first world in a new form. It is for this reason that baptism is also the ground of our participation in the world.

The Practice of Baptism in Community

Community

We do not know precisely the historical conditions under which baptism came to be the event by which people were inducted into the Christian community. Presumably the practice of baptism and its significance were adopted from Jewish practices. However, we can observe in Paul's letters the theological reason for linking baptism to community membership. In 1 Corinthians, in which Paul was contending with the Corinthian inclination to value one gift above another, he argued that Christ, like a body, is a unity that embraces many members (12:12). It is into this unity that we have been baptized (12:13). So that we do not think that this talk about the body is merely a metaphor, Paul affirmed that disciples *are* the body of Christ (12:27). This point is reinforced in Galatians 3:27-28, in which Paul states that, regardless of ethnicity, gender, or social status, disciples are one in Christ as a result of having been baptized into Christ. In these passages we find several affirmations. First, there is the closest possible connection between the Christian community and the risen Lord. We are Christ's body. That is why, upon hearing of the divisions among the Corinthians, Paul could exclaim that Christ himself was being divided (1 Corinthians 1:13). Second, this body is a unity, in spite of earthly distinctions. Third, it is the act of baptism that incorporates us into this body.

This notion of Christ's body and its unity supports a conclusion that later Christian writers drew about the importance of the community: there is no salvation outside this body. In 1 Corinthians, this view appears in the argument that, within a physical body, every organ performs a vital function and that, by analogy, in the body of Christ every spiritual gift is vital (12:14-26). It does not take much imagination to extend this argument by affirming that, just as in a physical body, no organ can survive without connection to the body's unity, so in the church, no one can be a disciple without a living connection to the unity of Christ's body. The soundness of this conclusion is shown by the fact that John's Gospel argues the same point with a different metaphor: Jesus is the vine and we are the branches. This means that we cannot bear fruit unless we abide in Jesus. Apart from our connection to Jesus we can do nothing. Without this connection and its resulting fruit, we are thrown away and wither (John 15:1-6). Later Christian writers such as Cyprian formalized this conviction with the slogan that one cannot have God as a Father without having the church as a mother. This slogan states compendiously the conviction of the early church that membership in the church—the body of Christ—is necessary for salvation. Baptism, as the point of entry into this community, has an unsurpassed importance in Christian spirituality.

Authority

A second aspect of baptism as a communal event is the role of clergy. From the beginning, baptism has been administered by ordained clergy. This reflects the church's interest in the function and exercise of discipline and authority. As the entrance into salvation and into the church, baptism was the one point in the early church at which clergy could easily regulate membership in the church and enforce behavioral and doctrinal standards. As long as baptism was preceded by a lengthy period of instruction, during which the church expected baptismal candidates to amend their moral lives, baptism had a disciplinary function. Through its practice, the church could assume at least a minimal degree of doctrinal knowledge and ethical comportment among its members. The fact that baptism took place under the direction of the bishop and that the ceremony involved the bishop laying hands on the candidates symbolized this regulatory and disciplinary function. The bishop embodied the authority and ethos of the community. The insistence (by the early writer Ignatius) that nothing should be done without the bishop was given concrete expression in the early baptismal ceremonies. Naturally, the church came to acknowledge that baptism was not absolutely required for salvation. Candidates who were undergoing catechesis but died before baptism were understood to have received the benefit of baptism because of their earnest desire for baptism. Nonetheless, the point remains that baptism was always regarded not only.as a communal event, but also as an authoritative event. That is why it was always (except in emergencies) carried out by ordained clergy. Only they had the authority to decide who were fit to be members of the church. This reminds us that we should not separate the issue of community and communal practices from the issue of authority. The church's existence as a community has always gone hand in hand with the exercise of spiritual and institutional authority. The early practice of baptism makes this point with great clarity.

The Practice of Baptism in a Fallen World

In post-Christian America, spirituality has little connection with eschatology, except for the widespread assumption that everyone except the most evil will be with God in heaven after death. This is all the more reason that the eschatological nature of Christian existence must be articulated. *Eschatology* in this context refers not to an apocalyptic world-view, but instead to the relation between what has often been called the already and the not yet in the Christian life. Christian spirituality is a life in which the power of God's future kingdom is present now and coexists with the power of the present evil age. The kingdom of God is present in power, but not in the fullness to come in the consummation of all things. The kingdom is present but also hidden. Like the wheat amid the weeds, it subsists alongside the fallen powers of this age. Christian spirituality is the life of this kingdom and its power, but it is also a life that feels the residual effects of the present age. Although, in the words of 1 John, "the world and its desire are passing away" (2:17), its passing is not yet complete. Hence disciples must still be admonished not to love the world (2:15). As believers, we have been crucified with Christ yet must be exhorted to die to sin. We stand, as it were, in two worlds—the new world of God's kingdom and the old world of sin. Although freed from sin, we continue to feel its effects and are liable at any time to return to the love of the world. To say that Christian existence has an eschatological character is to affirm, in the words of Hebrews, that we "have . . . been enlightened, and have tasted the heavenly gift, and have shared in the Holy Spirit, and have tasted the goodness of the word of God and the powers of the age to come" (6:4-5). But it is also to acknowledge that God's kingdom has not yet proved victorious. Jesus Christ has not yet "destroyed every ruler and every authority and power" (1 Corinthians 15:24).

All this implies that sin remains an issue for those who have been baptized. Baptism signifies the forgiveness of sin and, as our introduction to life in the Spirit, the beginning of freedom from sin. It is important to see why this is so. Sin is, first, the refusal to acknowledge and honor the creator and, second, the effects of that refusal. This is Paul's argument in Romans 1: in spite of the knowledge of God available to humankind (1:19-20), we have obstinately refused to honor and thank God (1:21), have worshiped creatures instead of the creator (1:25), and have failed to acknowledge God (1:28). As a result, we have fallen into every sort of degradation, examples of which are enumerated in 1:29-31. Baptism signifies the forgiveness of sin and the beginning of freedom from sin because baptism is an act of obedience. In this act we acknowledge not only the existence, but also the righteousness of the creator who is also the judge, and we submit to God's righteousness. It is this understanding of sin and baptism that underlies Paul's conviction that his calling was to bring about, among Gentiles, the "obedience of faith" (Romans 1:5,

16:26). Faith, for Paul, is an act of obedience, for in it we respond thankfully to the gospel and submit to the God who, through Jesus Christ, has brought about our redemption. Baptism, then, as the public and bodily exhibition of faith, shows forth both the admission of our sin and also our submission to God. It signals our peace with God and the end of our condemnation. It also marks our rebirth and our renewal in the Holy Spirit (Titus 3:5).

However, as already noted, life in the Spirit is an existence that transpires between the power of God's future and the power of sin's past. That is why Paul could, on one hand, teach that we *have been* sanctified in baptism (1 Corinthians 6:11) and, on the other hand, pray that we might be sanctified (1 Thessalonians 5:23). Our renewal in the Holy Spirit is both an accomplished fact and also an eschatological reality that will be completed only in the fullness of the kingdom of God. To use the language of world transcendence and participation, we may say that our spiritual transcending of the world remains incomplete and that our participation in the world often amounts to our identification with the fallen world. We have tasted the freedom that transcendence brings but have not allowed it to rule in our lives. The power of sin's past clings to us and prevents our participation in the world from being a cooperation with God and instead makes it an idolatrous loving of the world.

Our failure to transcend the world appears in the New Testament frequently. Take for example the Corinthians, who are carnal (*sarkikos*) and not perfect (*teleios*). Although Paul did not hesitate to affirm their justification and sanctification, they were also deeply immersed in the world and its desires. Several of the churches of Revelation afford us more examples of Christians who were indeed living in the Spirit but in whom the present evil age clung tenaciously. These examples point to one of the central features of eschatological existence—the persistence of sin in believers. This vexing pastoral problem has elicited a host of responses from the church, all in the attempt to come to terms theologically with this sin. In 1 John, for example, we find the root of what will later develop into the distinction between mortal and venial sins in the contrast between sin that does not lead to death, which is a proper object of prayer, and sin that leads to death, which is *not* a proper object of prayer (5:16). Although the demarcation between the two types is unclear, the fact that the Johannine community made a distinction is significant. It signals the community's awareness of spiritual shortcomings and its pastoral strategy for dealing with them redemptively. This issue was revisited in the third-century controversy over repentance. By about A.D. 200, the church had developed a protocol for dealing with weighty, public, and deadly sins such as fornication and apostasy. It involved, as Tertullian described it, a public process, supervised by clergy, in which those who had sinned grievously were readmitted to the church by grueling self-abasement. This involved prayer, fasting, weeping and groaning, and dress and demeanor appropriate to those seeking forgiveness. The controversy was whether, for those who had sinned grievously, repentance was possible at all and, if it were, how many times in a life forgiveness could be obtained. The debate raged through the first half of the third century, with rigorists such as Novatian denying the possibility of readmitting apostates and moderates such as Tertullian allowing the possibility of one act of post-baptismal repentance in a lifetime. The church eventually settled on the policy not restricting the number of acts of repentance. It also incorporated a general confession of sin into its various liturgies as a sort of minimal preparation for communion. Through all this we can see the church wrestling with the legacy of sin in believers.

It should be noted that it is not only the practice of sin after baptism that is theologically problematic. It is also the fact that we *can* return to sin—that is, that life in the Spirit transpires under the condition of sin. Numerous New Testament passages address themselves to this possibility: Hebrews speaks of the possibility of our failing, like the ancient Israelites, to enter into God's rest (4:1, 11); Romans raises the possibility of our failing to remain in God's kindness and consequently being cut off from the new Israel (11:22); John's Gospel is concerned that we will fail to abide in Christ and, like unfruitful branches, will be thrown away (15:6); and Galatians presses Paul's fear that his churches will return to the authority of the law, thus unleashing once again the power of sin. Eschatological existence means that "sin will have no dominion over" us (Romans 6:14) but also that we may allow it to have dominion over us. It is the possibility of a return to the former life, which remains with us unshakably, no matter how advanced in the way we are.

As a result, the New Testament is filled with exhortations. It is important to note that exhortation would not exist if life in the Spirit were not eschatological existence. If the kingdom of God were here in its fullness and the power of sin were utterly dead, then exhortation and admonition would be needless. If eschatology were realized (as some Corinthians believed), then there would be no exhortation—we would all be walking spontaneously and continuously according to the Spirit. We would be in the condition described by Jeremiah 31:34, quoted in Hebrews 8:11: "They shall not teach one another or say to each other, 'Know the Lord.'" But experience shows that exhortation and warning are necessary as means of calling us to faithful obedience. The eschatological nature of life in the Spirit also means that striving and discipline are needed. Authentic Christian spirituality is not without cost and effort. If the kingdom were present in its fullness, then there would be nothing in this world to make the Christian life difficult. We would all willingly and gladly and unfailingly obey the command of God. As it is, life in the Spirit is work—sometimes hard work—for which training, discipline, and striving are required. At the same time, this striving is not a merely human deed. Living in the Spirit means that our exertions are also the work of God. Although there is no progress in the Christian life without our exertions, that progress is in fact the result of God's working in us. As Paul expresses it in Philippians, "The one who began a good work among you will bring it to completion by the day of Jesus Christ" (1:6). Life in the Spirit, then, is ultimately a life of hope, a hope that the author of the new creation will bring that new creation to its appointed end.

Baptism and Participation in God

If we ask about the character of the God that is represented in spirituality today, then we must admit that this God is essentially a creator but not a redeemer. Whether the spirituality is of the pagan/wiccan sort or is more overtly theistic, the God that appears in today's spirituality is regarded in some sense as a creator. However, because today's spirituality does not regard the spiritual life in eschatological terms and consequently does not accept the Christian conception of sin, it sees no need to conceive of God as the redeemer. Not surprising, this spirituality lacks a trinitarian conception of God. For if God is seen as creator only and not also as redeemer, then (to use the categories of H. Richard Niebuhr), the result will be monotheism either of the first person (a transcendent source of all) or of the third person (an immanent source of all). But there will be no need for the second person and no need for a conception that encompasses all three persons in their relations. The eschatological character of Christian spirituality compels Christian theology to think of God in trinitarian terms. It is impossible for us to conceive of God as simply the transcendent creator or as the inspiring Spirit within. On the contrary, we must think of God first and last as Jesus Christ, the Father of Jesus Christ, and the Spirit of Jesus Christ.

But it is possible to have a trinitarian conception of God without understanding fully its implications for our understanding of life in the Spirit. It is possible to think of baptism into the name of the Father, Son, and Spirit as merely bringing us into relation with the Trinity. The Christian tradition, however, has understood life in the Spirit, and baptism as its beginning, in more profound terms. The place to begin is with Paul's view of the believer's relation to Jesus Christ.

As noted previously, Paul taught that in baptism we are dead and buried with Christ (Romans 6:4). More important, in baptism we come to share in Christ's new life. Paul's letters have two ways of representing this. Colossians presents a realized eschatology in which, in baptism, we have already been "raised" with Christ, our resurrected selves being for now "hidden with Christ in God" (3:1-3). Romans and other letters of Paul represent a less realized eschatology, in which we share eschatologically in Christ's resurrected life. As Paul argued in Romans, Christ's resurrection means that now, in the midst of this world, we can walk in newness of life (6:4). But our own resurrection (in the perspective of Romans) lies in the future and is a matter of faith and hope (6:5, 8). Nonetheless, the point common to both presentations is that, in baptism, we have begun the resurrected life.

However, Paul was quick to point out that this resurrection life is had in Christ. It is not something that is given to the individual person as a possession. Instead, in Paul's conception, to receive the resurrection life is identical to being in Christ. We are, then, resurrected into Christ's own resurrected being. This is how we are to make sense of Paul's words in 1 Corinthians 12 that we have been baptized into one body (v. 13). It is true that this body into which we have been baptized is the church, but the church is the body of Christ (v. 27). Baptism, then, marks not only our membership in this community, but also our eschatological participation in the resurrected life of Christ. That is why Paul could affirm that "it is no longer I who live, but it is Christ who lives in me" (Galatians 2:20). We—our former selves—have been crucified (Romans 6:6). Our new self *is* the life of Jesus Christ within us. However, this new self is still an eschatological reality. We have not yet been actually raised. For that reason, we have this new life only by faith: "The life I now live in the flesh I live by faith in the Son of God" (Galatians 2:20). However, there is more to be said about baptism. It is not only our incorporation into the body of Christ and our participation in Christ's resurrected life. It is our participation in the trinitarian life of God. It is, accordingly, important that the early form of baptismal liturgy by which believers were baptized in the name of Jesus (Acts 2:38) was replaced by the longer form referring to Father, Son, and Spirit (Matthew 28:19). Christianity is not a religion about Jesus Christ. It is instead the religion that worships Jesus Christ, the God and Father of Jesus Christ, and the Spirit of the Father and of Jesus.

We get some indication of the trinitarian dimension of baptism in those New Testament passages that link baptism to the Holy Spirit. Among these are the narratives about John the Baptist, according to which he prophesied about the coming one who would baptize with (or in) the Holy Spirit (for example, Mark 1:8), the various places in Acts in which reception of the Holy Spirit is associated with baptism (e.g., 2:38), and Titus 3:5, which connects the washing of rebirth and our renewal by the Holy Spirit. These passages go beyond the assertion of Ephesians 2:13-14 that we have been sealed with the Holy Spirit and that the Spirit is the eschatological pledge of our eventual redemption. They suggest that, in baptism,[6] we receive the Spirit as promised in Joel. Having the Spirit not only holds us over until the eschatological consummation, but also now in the midst of this age enables us to live the life of the resurrection. Although the New Testament's teaching about baptism and the Spirit does not show the same degree of development as does its teaching about the relation of baptism of Christ, there is enough to justify the assertion that, for the New Testament, baptism is to be thought of not just christologically, but along trinitarian lines.

The way toward a systematic understanding is indicated by Paul's teaching about life in the Spirit in Romans 8. In the first part of this chapter, Paul's language suggests an external relation between the believer and the Spirit, using phrases such as "walk according to the Spirit," "live according to the Spirit" and "set our minds on the things of the Spirit" (8:4-5). This language could be taken to imply that the Spirit represents for Paul a moral ideal that believers are to use as a pattern. However, the remainder of the chapter shows us that Paul had something quite different in mind. According to 8:9, the Spirit of God and of Christ dwells in us, and, consequently, we belong to God and have become God's children (8:14-15). The Spirit, as the Spirit of adoption, is here represented as that by which we are drawn into a relation to God the Father. Moreover, we find in Romans 8 express affirmations of the coincidence of divine activity and human activity, a coincidence that is due to the Spirit. First, Paul asserted, when we cry out "Abba! Father! it is that very Spirit bearing witness with our spirit that we are children of God" (8:16). Second, when we pray without knowing what to pray for: "That very Spirit intercedes with sighs too deep for words . . . according to the will of God" (8:26-27). Our relation to the Spirit, then, is not an external relation but a much more intimate one. In our communion with God the Father, it is the Spirit that is speaking through us, so that our words are also the Spirit's words.

For a fuller view of the trinitarian dimension of Christian spirituality, we must supplement Paul's theology with that of John. Unexpectedly, the Johannine literature says little expressly about life in the Spirit. However, it does enlarge our understanding of our relation to God. It does this by representing disciples as being drawn into the unity of the Father and the Son. Initially, John's Gospel presents the Christian life as one of abiding in Christ: "Abide in me as I abide in you. Just as the branch cannot bear fruit by itself unless it abides in the vine, neither can you unless you abide in me" (15:4). However, later the perspective broadens when Jesus prays "that they may all be one. As you, Father, are in me and I am in you, may they also be in us. . . . The glory that you have given me I have given them, so that they may be one, as we are one, I in them and you in me, that they may become completely one" (17:21-23). In this passage two things are asserted. First, disciples are to exhibit the same unity among themselves that the Father and Son enjoy with each other. Second, disciples are incorporated into the relationship of mutual indwelling that exists between the Father and the Son.[7]

In conclusion, we may say that the Christian life is lived in and through God. The New Testament has many ways of stating this point, but the various passages all converge on this affirmation. Baptism, then, is all that has been previously noted: entrance into the community, a bodily act, an ethical act, and the beginning of eschatological existence. But we would miss the most profound aspect of the New Testament's teaching if we neglected baptism's role in inducting us into the trinitarian life of God. It is in baptism that we are drawn, by the power of the Spirit, into the eternal fellowship between the Father and the Son and participate in their shared life. This is an important point because there will always be a temptation to think of the Christian life simply as a life of moral reformation, just as there is an opposite temptation to ignore the moral dimension of this life. Nonetheless, life in the Spirit is not equivalent to a life of moral development. It is not simply equivalent to a life of self-discipline and spiritual exertion, although self-discipline and exertion are required. It is, in addition to these things, a life in God, not a life that springs spontaneously out of human nature. In other words, it is a life of grace. But God's grace is not a power that God implants in us to enable us to live a certain way. Grace is instead God's trinitarian life itself insofar as it draws us into itself and transforms us into the image of God. This drawing and transforming does not happen without the mediation of earthly things and the coincidence of human activity. But it is not reducible to the effects of those earthly things and those human activities. Grace, in short, is a shorthand expression for the conviction that we are partakers of the divine nature (2 Peter 1:4) and consequently are enabled to be imitators of God (Ephesians 5:1). Baptism is our entrance into this life of grace.

Concluding Meditative Prayer

We praise you, our God, who in the beginning caused creation's dry land to appear from the primordial water touched by a mighty wind. We ask, Lord, that today your new creation may come forth from the baptismal water, sanctified by the touch of your Spirit. We praise you, our God, who in the time of Noah destroyed the sinful world with water and gave the dove as a sign of deliverance. We ask, Lord, that you would destroy our sin by the water of baptism and send the divine dove upon us as a sign of salvation. We praise you, our God, who sent to us Jesus Christ to be the savior. Grant to us, Lord, that, like him, we may fulfill all righteousness by submitting to baptism. Grant that the heavens be opened up to us and that your Spirit come upon us as a dove. We praise you, our God, who has made us the spouse of Christ and has cleansed us with the washing of water with the word. Grant to us, Lord, that we may remember the baptismal vows with true repentance and thus find forgiveness of sin in your mercy. May we live worthy of the divine name into which we have been baptized. Blessed are those who have washed their robes and made them white in the blood of the lamb. Blessed are those who have been saved through the water of rebirth and renewal by the Holy Spirit. We confess, our Lord, that we have not lived lives worthy of our baptism. We have been faithless to the covenant of grace and have not repented as we ought. Preserve us, Lord, from sin and its effects. Deliver us from the evil one and the devices of evil. Lead us always in the spirit of repentance. We pray for those who have faith and those who do not yet have faith.

We pray for those who have not yet been enlightened, have not yet tasted the heavenly gift, not yet shared in the Holy Spirit, have not yet tasted the goodness of the word of God and the powers of the age to come.

You, our God, who once created by separating the waters and now creates anew with water, we praise.
We praise
   the Father, whose children we are in the new creation,
   through the Son, with whom we die in baptism and with whom we are
      raised to new life,
   in the Spirit, who is given to us in baptism as a pledge of redemption
      and with whom we have been sealed.
We praise the holy Trinity, the beginning and end of the new creation in baptism.

Notes

1. John Calvin, *Institutes*, 1.17.3.
2. Ibid., 1.17.7 and 11.
3. Cyprian, *Letter* 72, ¶22.
4. *Catechism*, ¶1259.
5. See also 2 Timothy 4:5; Titus 2:2.
6. Or, it must be said, somehow in connection with baptism, for Acts shows great variety in representing the connection between baptism and receiving the Holy Spirit. In chapter 8 of Acts, the Samaritan Christians are baptized by Philip but cannot receive the Spirit until the apostles from Jerusalem lay hands on them. In chapter 10, the Spirit falls on Cornelius before he is baptized.
7. Curiously, there is no mention of the Spirit. Yet it is natural to think of the Spirit in this context, for the Holy Spirit is "the Spirit of Truth" who "will guide you into all the truth" (John 16:13). In the Johannine view, it is the Spirit that brings about the disciples' relation to Christ. The Christian tradition was not wrong in connecting the Johannine dots when it attributed to the Spirit the role of incorporating us into God's Trinitarian life.

Sources Consulted and Recommended

Ambrose. "On Repentance." In *Ambrose: Select Works and Letters*. Vol. 10, *Nicene and Post-Nicene Fathers of the Christian Church*, 2nd ser. Peabody, MA: Hendrickson Publishers, 1995.

Augustine. *The First Catechetical Instruction*. Translated by Joseph P. Christopher. Vol. 2, *Ancient Christian Writers*. New York: Newman Press, 1978.

Bradshaw, Paul F. "The Gospel and the Catechumenate in the Third Century." *Journal of Theological Studies* 50, no. 1 (1999): 143-52.

Calvin, John. *Institutes of the Christian Religion*. Translated by Ford Lewis Battles. Edited by John T. McNeill. Vol. 20, *Library of Christian Classics*. Philadelphia: The Westminster Press, 1960.

Catechism of the Catholic Church. Liguori, MO: Liguori Publications, 1994.

Cyprian. "Letter 72." In *Letters (1-81)*. Translated by Sister Rose Bernard Donna. Vol. 51, *The Fathers of the Church: A New Translation (Patristic Series)*. Washington, DC: The Catholic University of America Press, 1965.

———. "The Unity of the Church." In *Treatises*. Edited by Roy J. Deferrari. Vol. 36, *The Fathers of the Church: A New Translation (Patristic Series)*. Washington, DC: The Catholic University of America Press, 1958.

Cyril of Jerusalem. "Lenten Lectures." *The Works of Saint Cyril of Jerusalem*. 2 vols. Translated by Leo P. McCauley and Anthony A. Stephenson. Vols. 61 and 64, *Fathers of the Church*. Washington, DC: The Catholic University of America Press, 1969–1970.

Hippolytus. *The Apostolic Tradition of Hippolytus*. Translated by Burton Scott Easton. Cambridge: University of Cambridge Press, 1934.

John Chrysostom. *St. John Chrysostom: Baptismal Instructions*. Translated by Paul W. Harkins. Vol. 31, *Ancient Christian Writers: The Works of the Fathers in Translation*. New York: Newman Press, n.d.

Tertullian. "On Baptism." *Latin Christianity*. Vol. 3, *Ante-Nicene Fathers: The Writings of the Fathers down to A.D. 325*. Edited by Alexander Roberts and James Donaldson. Peabody, MA: Hendrickson Publishers, 1995.

———. *Treatises on Penance: On Penitence and on Purity*. Translated by William P. Le Saint. Vol. 28, *Ancient Christian Writers*. New York: Newman Press, 1959.

CHAPTER FIVE

FAITH

The Practice of Faith

World-Transcendence and World-Participation

The practical dimension of the Christian faith is faith when it is embodied in living subjects who act in the world. Because faith is an aspect of our embodied existence, and therefore includes an orientation to the world, it exhibits the twofold structure of world-transcendence and world-participation.

THE IMPULSE TOWARD TRANSCENDING THE WORLD

The point of departure for understanding the world-transcending character of faith is 1 John 5:4: "This is the victory that conquers the world, our faith." But the attempt to grasp the significance of this verse must begin with an analysis of faith. To this end, the distinction between *fides quae creditur* ("the faith that is believed") and *fides qua creditur* ("the [act of] faith by which something is believed") is an aid. Broadly considered, *fides quae creditur* is the *content* or *object* of the Christian faith; *fides qua creditur* is the subjective act of faith.

This content of faith—the *fides quae creditur*—is designated in the New Testament in various ways, including in symbols such as the kingdom of God and the new creation. Later, the church gave formal and more technical expression to the object of faith through its creeds. But a bit of reflection reminds us that the object of faith is not merely something that we should believe in the narrow sense of belief. We may entertain beliefs about the weather or the fate of our local sports team, but the Christian church means something quite different by *fides quae creditur*. This is because the gospel summons to us to experience the object of faith in a more than cognitive way. We are called on not only to believe something about the kingdom of God and the new creation, but also to enter into this new creation and to become members of this kingdom. So, *fides quae creditur* is more than simply the object of cognitive belief. To think otherwise is to overlook the ethical dimension of faith. When we take into account the ethical dimension of faith, then we see that its object is in fact a new reality, a new way of existing both individually and corporately. Of course, this reality is not narrowly practical—it also encompasses intellectual or dogmatic content. It is both a matter of thought and also the subject of practical activities. *Fides quae creditur*, then, engages the totality of our embodied being.

The transcending character of *fides quae creditur* becomes clear if we attend to its description as, for instance, the new creation or the kingdom of God. These denote that act of God by which judgment is rendered on the sinful world and by which that world is redeemed from the effects of its sin. They symbolize the new reality that God is creating in contrast to this fallen world. This reality is the subject of the Christian faith, which has given verbal articulation of this reality in scripture, creed, preaching, teaching, hymns, and other forms. This faith is about a reality that is transcendent, first, in the metaphysical sense of not being a mundane reality and, second, in the ethical sense of constituting a contradiction to this world. This new creation is the *no* of God's judgment on human sinfulness, even if it is also God's *yes* of redemption from that sin. This *no* constitutes one part of its transcendent charcter. (It is important, however, to keep in mind that contradiction is not negation. The new creation is God's judgment on the world, but it does not imply the canceling out of the world. Even the sinful world is the world that God loves.) But the *yes* constitutes another part, for the *yes* of redemption has a transcendent source. To affirm this faith—to confess the *fides quae creditur*—is to affirm the reality of a world of God's making that goes beyond this fallen world.

Besides the content or object of faith, Christian faith is also an act, *fides qua creditur*, the act of affirming and living that content. The question before us is, How can the act of faith be a transcending act? How does it constitute our transcending the world? The answer becomes evident if we consider a typical New Testament affirmation, the confession that Jesus is "the ruler of the kings of the earth" (Revelation 1:5). In the first century, the act of affirming this statement was a transcending act insofar as it required believers to go beyond what they could see and beyond what generally counted as common sense. After all, Caesar professed to be the supreme power, and empirical evidence of that claim was everywhere for believers to see. To affirm the lordship of Jesus meant discounting the evidence of the senses and believing in a new and different reality. The transcending character of the act of faith lies in its going beyond the evident facts of common sense toward the eschatological truth of God's kingdom and the new creation. It is for this reason that Paul portrayed faith as an act of obedience in response to the proclaimed gospel (Romans 1:5). If faith were merely a species of belief, resting on an inference from evidence, then it could not reasonably be commanded, for no one thinks of ordering someone to make certain inferences or form certain opinions. Inferences and opinions are, at least ideally, governed by the rules of logic and evidence. They are not matters of conscious choice. As it is, however, the act of faith is an ethical act, that is, it is about our orientation to and life in the world and in God's kingdom. Logic and evidence are not irrelevant to this faith, but faith also has an essential element of decision about it. It is, in part, our decision as to whether we will continue the life of sin unmindful of God or whether we will leave sin behind and embrace the kingdom of God and the new creation. As noted previously, the content or object of faith is the world of God's new creation. The act of faith is the act of turning from the world proposed by sin (and its effects in human society and culture) and living in the new creation. Hence, faith is related to conversion in a way that belief and opinion are not. John's Gospel has a pointed way of making this point. It grounds faith in a prior disposition and in God's election. It teaches, for example, that our wanting to do God's will is a condition of knowing Jesus' truth (7:17) and that in order to hear God one must first belong to God (8:47). That is why, according to this Gospel, the Jews fail to believe: they are not among Jesus' sheep (10:26). If faith were an ordinary sort of belief, then we would say that they do not belong to Jesus' sheep because they do not believe. In fact, however, believing is not, for John's Gospel, a result of logical inference. It instead rests on belonging to God, a status that, the Gospel implies, is an act of God. In Paul's theology, there is a similar emphasis on divine activity as the ground of faith: "The one who began a good work among you will bring it to completion"

(Philippians 1:6). "It is God who is at work in you, enabling you both to will and to work for his good pleasure" (Philippians 2:13). Not surprisingly, faith is said to be a fruit of the Spirit (Galatians 5:22). So, according to the New Testament, the act of faith has not only a transcendent object (that is, the kingdom of God and the new creation), but also a transcendent source—God. Hence it should not be regarded merely as a human act or as an inference from evidence. It is instead grounded in our participation in God's trinitarian life. As a result, we must conclude that the act of faith is no merely worldly phenomenon. It is rather an act by which we transcend this sinful world and become oriented to the world of God's new creation.

Paul's first letter to the Thessalonians gives us a concrete example of this act of faith as a new orientation. Paul described the Thessalonians thus: They received the gospel "in power and in the Holy Spirit and with full conviction" (1 Thessalonians 1:5). They became imitators of Paul and of Jesus (1:6), and it had become widely known that they had "turned to God from idols, to serve a living and true God, and to wait for his Son from heaven" (1:9-10). For the Thessalonians, faith meant hearing this message as the very word of God and responding to it by abandoning the worship of other gods and embracing the worship of the God proclaimed in the gospel. Their faith and reorientation to the living God had resulted in their love for one another (4:9-10) and underlay Paul's exhortation to keep awake and be sober (5:6), that is, to behave properly (5:8). Faith here is described not only as a belief about something, but additionally as a rather complete change in understanding. Their view and worship of the divine and their ethical comportment were both significantly altered with their new faith. To speak of their faith is to affirm that they had left behind the conceptions and behaviors of their former life and had embraced new conceptions and new behaviors. This is what it means to say that the act of faith is an act of spiritual transcendence.

THE IMPULSE TOWARD PARTICIPATING IN THE WORLD

Although faith in the form of *fides quae creditur* has a transcending aspect, as discussed above, it is important to remember that the kingdom of God is (eschatologically) an earthly reality and not something other-worldly. Put differently, faith bears upon our participation in the world. This point becomes evident through a consideration of biblical eschatology. In the words of Revelation, in the eschatological kingdom of God "the home of God is among mortals" (Revelation 21:3). In contrast to the popular view that Christian eschatology is about our going to heaven, where God is, biblical eschatology is about God's coming to us. Moreover, God's new creation is continuous with and not a negation of the first creation. It is true that 2 Peter indicates the destruction of the first creation (3:10-13) and that Revelation speaks of the first creation passing away (21:1). But Revelation also, by mentioning the presence of the tree of life in the New Jerusalem (22:2), depicts the new creation as a return to the original state of creation. Further, the new earth is said to be without a sea (21:1)—a clear indication that we are in the realm of the symbolic and that we are not to think of the new heaven and earth as materially different realities from the first heaven and earth. Additionally, theological anthropology shows the continuity of the first and new creations. The new *anthropos* (Ephesians 4:24) is not brand new and materially distinct from the former self, but is instead the former *anthropos* purified of sin and redirected to God, being renewed in righteousness and true holiness. The New Testament, then, wants us to regard the content of faith as being oriented to this world—not this world in its present sinful state, but insofar as it is the object of God's new, creative, and redeeming activity—the new heaven and the new earth. Consequently, the content of faith, although it is world-transcending, is not something otherworldly, unless we take the word *world* in its sense of fallen humanity. On the contrary, faith denotes our participation in the world of God's creation.

Faith in the form of *fides qua creditur* is likewise a mode of our participation in the world. This can be seen from the historically relative character of faith in the form of *fides qua creditur*. It is not only the content or object of faith that is historically relative, but also the subjective act of affirming that faith. Faith in this sense is our obedient response to the gospel. But this faith is always situated or embodied, that is, it is always an act that arises out of and can be understood only in the total context in which we live. That is why there is no such thing as faith in general. As an act, the decision of faith (as well as the decision against faith) cannot be understood as the act of a context-free intellect dispassionately considering alternatives. Instead, the act of faith is the act of a person occupying a particular historical place and time. It is the response of our entire being to God's call to us in the gospel. To say that it is the act of our entire being means that it cannot be separated from the sum total of our desires, our hopes and fears, our beliefs, and the other aspects of our lives, all of which are particular and perhaps unique, being the product of our life histories. We hear the gospel in ways shaped by our tradition and also by the concrete circumstances of our lives. What did it mean to have faith in the first century? For Jewish Christians it meant accepting the messianic claims about Jesus and then coming to terms with their Jewish heritage—interpreting their identity as Jews in the light of the gospel. For Martin Luther and John Calvin, faith meant receiving assurance of salvation in contrast to the perceived uncertainties of the medieval system. Even these examples describe faith at an excessively general level, for it overlooks the ways in which particular contexts would have conditioned the act of faith. To understand someone's faith, we would have to see his or her life history and know what brought him or her to this act.

All this points to the fact that faith is an act that involves the totality of our being. As a result, although (as described above) faith has a transcending aspect, it also has a world-participating aspect. It remains always that act of a creature whose being is woven into the fabric of the world.

FAITH UNDER THE CONDITION OF FINITUDE

The world-participating nature of faith leads us to an understanding of the essentially finite character of faith. I have reference to the fact that, although the content of faith (*fides quae creditur*), the new creation, is a matter of revelation, our understanding of that reality and the verbal forms in which we know it do not enjoy the status of revelation. Our understanding of the faith—our concepts, our images, and our language—is not, like the new creation itself, transcendent and divine, but is instead thoroughly historical. I have elsewhere referred to this aspect of faith as the hermeneutical dimension.[1] But this means that the Christian faith is always received and affirmed by human minds that occupy very particular intellectual contexts and that are formed not only by the Christian tradition, but by many other intellectual factors as well. Hence, we must acknowledge the perpetual corrigibility of doctrinal formulations, which Paul Tillich referred to as the Protestant principle. According to the Protestant principle, all doctrines and creeds are human productions and consequently do not have ultimate authority and are subject to correction. Although the church is understandably conservative with respect to the rule of faith and rightly regards it as practically unchangeable, the *understanding* of the rule of faith has a high degree of historical relativity, as the history of Christian thought shows. This helps us understand the error of the various forms of Christian fundamentalism, whose representatives do regard certain understandings or verbal forms (whether the Bible or creeds) as being matters of revelation and as being incorrigible. Fundamentalists do not realize that the Christian faith, although expressing God's revelation, is always believed and understood by people in diverse intellectual settings with historically relative ways of thinking.

The church acknowledges the finite character of faith whenever it admits that the language of theology is highly metaphorical, symbolic, and analogical. One of the classical formulations of this conviction is found in the thought of Thomas Aquinas, according to whom literal statements about God are impossible because of our creaturely status. Our knowledge of God is, accordingly, proportionate to our finite cognitive powers. In the twentieth century, Paul Tillich made a similar point in his dictum that all statements about God are symbolic, except for the statement that God is being itself. Thomas's and Tillich's presentations of the finite character of faith are not beyond improvement, but virtually all Christian theologians have acknowledged the main point that our understanding of God is not infallible and that the language we use to depict God is not literal.

These considerations help us understand the difference between doubt and unbelief. Although in popular use they are often used interchangeably, it is valuable to draw a distinction between them. Unbelief is a manifestation of sin. It is the creature's refusal to acknowledge the creator and to submit to the creator's law. Doubt, however, is an intellectual condition characterized by puzzlement that results from the finite nature of human thought. Every Christian doctrine can be doubted because each makes intellectual claims that cannot be completely substantiated either through evidence or logic. That is why Christian faith contains an element of decision. No one can come to have Christian faith in a strictly intellectual way by contemplating intellectual arguments. Although the assertions of Christian doctrine are not contrary to logic and evidence, they are not completely entailed by logic and evidence. Belief in these teachings requires something more than ratiocination. For this reason, there will always be some, perhaps many, who entertain doubts about all or some of these teachings. They are, in fact, intellectually puzzling in certain respects. Even lifelong disciples, who affirm these doctrines with all their being, may find themselves puzzled and doubtful about them. It cannot be otherwise, given the fact that our intellects are finite.

There are two other perennial problems connected with the Christian faith. These problems arise because this faith contains an ethical dimension. One is the tendency to reduce faith to belief. The other problem is the difficulty of expressing, in a conceptually clear and spiritually healthy way, the relation of faith to good works. These tendencies result from the inclination to divorce faith from the practice of life and instead to consign it exclusively to the spiritual domain of life. If this spiritual domain is conceptualized as mind, then faith is represented as intellectual belief, and the first tendency arises. If the spiritual is conceptualized as soul, then faith is pictured as something inward and subjective, and then the second tendency arises.

The Tendency to Reduce Faith to Belief: The Excessive Intellectualizing of Faith

In spite of considerable effort over the centuries, theologians and church leaders have never been completely successful in conveying the notion that Christian faith is not simply a matter of belief. As early as the Letter of James we can see the church insisting that belief, narrowly conceived, falls far short of authentic Christian faith. To be sure, Christian faith involves the act of belief. There is a set of theses, intellectual affirmation of which is necessarily required if one is to be a Christian disciple. We would certainly consider someone confused if that person professed to be a Christian but consciously and in an informed way denied that Jesus was in any sense God incarnate. Nonetheless, energy must be continually expended to convince people that Christian faith is *more than* intellectual belief—that, in fact, it has everything to do with the practice of life.

Part of the problem is endemic to Christianity. What I mean is that Christianity, unlike some religions, is a religion of doctrine. It is not simply a mode of life characterized by customary ways of eating, speaking, worshiping, and so on. It is not simply a set of practices. It also has a dogmatic content that has been formally expressed in creeds and other documents. This is the Christian faith in the form of *fides quae creditur* discussed previously. As noted, the church expects that its members will intellectually and verbally affirm these doctrines, taking into consideration the fact that people vary with respect to cognitive development. The problem is that there is a tendency, reinforced in the past by church practices, to make Christian faith begin and end with the affirmation of these doctrines, hence the phenomenon of people who believe Christian doctrine (in some sense) but whose lives do not give any evidence that this doctrine has had any effect on the practice of life. The extreme of this phenomenon is the nominal or cultural Christian, who has undergone baptism and confirmation and whose next exposure to the church will be a Christian burial.

Against this tendency pastors and theologians must labor ceaselessly in the effort to convince church members that the Christian faith is operative not only cognitively but also practically. In fact, instead of using the rhetoric of faith and practice, it would be better to speak of the intellectual or cognitive aspects of Christian faith and the ethical or practical aspects of that faith. In this way, Christian practice might be seen as an essential aspect of Christian faith—practice is the Christian faith appearing in the form of deeds, just as creeds are that faith appearing in the form of verbalized statements of belief.

The Relation of Faith to Good Works: The Excessive Spiritualization of Faith

The New Testament is adamant on two points. First, we are saved by God's grace and not by or because of our works (Titus 3:4-5). Second, we are to abound in good works (Titus 2:14). How to come to an adequate understanding of these two affirmations, which the New Testament obviously does not regard as contradictory, has been a challenge in Christian history. Nonetheless, the general outlines of an adequate understanding are simple: God's grace is prior and primary in our salvation, yet this grace, so far from rendering good works otiose, is the source of good works. We have been newly created for the purpose of engaging in good works (Ephesians 2:10), and it is by the power of the Spirit that we are able to produce them (Galatians 5:22). Where does faith fit into this understanding? It is probable that faith would never have been regarded as a problem in connection with good works if it were not for a debate within the New Testament on this subject. As is well known, Paul's theology makes a rather sharp distinction between the righteousness that results from faith in Jesus and the righteousness that results from obedience to the law of Moses. It is also well known that this teaching was more than a bit controversial in Paul's day. There are signals in the New Testament that Paul's hearers and readers had a difficult time understanding exactly what Paul was stating. Some of the Corinthians, for instance, seem to have interpreted Paul's teaching as implying freedom not only from the law of Moses, but also from every sort of moral restraint. Second Peter 3:16 acknowledges that Paul's letter contains some ideas difficult to grasp and easy to distort. Moreover, we know from Galatians that Paul had to contend with a sizable and active group of rather conservative believers who regarded his teaching about faith and righteousness as a total repudiation of Christianity's Jewish heritage. It was in this context that the Letter of James stated the issue succinctly and gave it an enduring and polemical form: citing Abraham (as had Paul), this letter asserts that we are made righteous by our works and not only by our faith (2:24)—a clear rebuke to Paul's theology.

As a result of this first-century debate, faith became central to the Christian understanding of the necessity and nature of good works. This is not something to be lamented. On the contrary, if faith had not been drawn into relation to good works, then faith and practice would have been utterly separated—something that is intolerable for the church, even if it is pervasive. What, then, is the best way of understanding faith in relation to good works? Fortunately, we are not compelled to choose between Paul and James. The idea of the canon forbids us from opposing one source to another. Instead we must attend carefully to what each source is truly concerned about. For Paul, the primary insight is that the law of Moses, far from being a means of righteousness, has become (in a fallen world) the law of sin and death. Consequently, no amount of obedience to this law can render us righteous. Following this law actually accomplishes the opposite of righteousness—it unleashes the power of sin and brings about our condemnation. In Paul's view, Jews are ignorant of the righteousness that God gives and instead pursue their own righteousness (Romans 10:3). The only way truly to become righteous is to become obedient to the gospel, that is, to believe the message of what God has accomplished in Jesus Christ (10:4) just as Abraham believed and acted on God's promise (chap. 4). The issue to which the Letter of James addresses itself is quite different. Here the concern is with the neglect of good works. For this letter, faith that is not accompanied by good works is a dead faith (James 2:17) and, we may add, not properly Christian faith at all. It is instead mere belief (James 2:19).

This analysis does not completely reconcile the theology of Paul and the theology of the Letter of James. There remain important differences. But it does indicate that the issue of good works in Christianity is a subtle one and must be treated dialectically. On one hand, good works of any sort do not save us—only God's grace saves us. On the other hand, salvation without good works is inconceivable. It is faith that mediates between these two points. Faith is that attitude of receptivity by which

God's grace becomes effective within us and salvation becomes actual. At the same time, faith that is authentic and living is productive of good works, so that we are justified in saying that there is no valid Christian life where there are no good works.

For the purpose of appreciating this point, the Gospel and first letter of John are exemplary. John 15 contains Jesus' remarks on the vine and the branches. Of particular interest is his emphasis on bearing fruit. Not only is bearing fruit a consequence of abiding in Jesus, the vine (vv. 4-5), but also it is the purpose of Christ's calling the disciples (v. 16). But what is the fruit of which Jesus speaks? It has everything to do with love: disciples are to abide in his love (vv. 9-10), and this includes loving one another just as Jesus has loved the disciples (v. 12). To ensure that we not misunderstand what is entailed by this love, 1 John asserts that love must take concrete form: it must consist in action and not only in word (3:18) and, even more concrete, must be exemplified in meeting the material needs of a fellow disciple (3:17).[2] These verses state unmistakably that love is a matter of good works. Love that is not manifested as good works toward other disciples is not authentic love. It is not even possible to love God without good works (4:19-20). Finally, love in the shape of good works is given a christological rationale and form as disciples are commanded to lay down their lives for one another just as Jesus laid down his life for us (3:16; 4:9-11). However, the Johannine tradition wants us to see our love as something not only commanded, but also grounded in the nature of God. God is love; consequently, disciples are to love one another (4:7) and those who love abide in God (4:16). Love, then, is not only a response to God's command. It is also the way in which we participate in God's eternal life. Moreover, love is the highest form that our knowledge of God can take. First John flatly states that no one has ever seen God (4:12). We may take this to imply that God cannot be known in the ways that human beings normally know things. God is not an object of cognition as other things are. On the contrary, there is only one authentic form of knowing God—love: "Everyone who loves is born of God and knows God. Whoever does not love does not know God, for God is love.... If we love one another, God lives in us" (4:7-8, 12). In these compressed sentences is contained a profound picture of the Christian life, in which good works, considered as expressions of love, are not merely human deeds, but also the life of God within us or, alternatively stated, the manifestations of our participation in God's eternal life of love. In this perspective, good works—love—are not something added to the knowledge of God. They are in fact the only form of knowing God that 1 John recognizes as authentic, for the reason that God is love. If God were a thing, then God could be known by us sensuously or conceptually. But since God is love, our acts of loving and our abiding in love mean that we are conformed to the nature of God. Only thus is it possible for us to know God and only this love is the knowledge of God. For 1 John, any other supposed way of knowing God is bogus.

This brief meditation on the Gospel and first letter of John bring to light the importance of what we may call the ethical or practical dimension of faith. This is not the only dimension of Christian faith. It is, however, exceedingly important, for it prevents us from seeing the ethical conduct of life as merely an implication or result of faith, as though one could have faith and then possibly engage in an ethically upright life. On the contrary, attention to this dimension compels us to recognize that the ethical is not a consequence of faith but is instead a form of faith. We customarily think of faith as either verbalized in creeds (*fides quae creditur*) or as an act of affirmation (*fides qua creditur*). But these are only two forms of faith. The ethical is a third form. In other words, the practice of the Christian life is itself the exercise of faith. It is an affirmation of faith just as the recitation of a creed is an affirmation. This fact explains why Christian writers have always wanted to say that those who persistently do not practice life in a Christian way really do not have faith. If faith were merely cognitive belief, then it might be possible to believe in one way and practice in another way. As it is, belief and practice are two forms of faith. This point is made repeatedly in the Pastoral Epistles. As is well known, these letters emphasize sound doctrine. What is not so often noted is that this sound doctrine has a decidedly practical aspect. As 1 Timothy puts it, "The aim of such instruction is love that comes from a pure heart, a good conscience, and sincere faith" (1:5). Moreover, this letter declares that the object of our faith is not only the "sound words" of Jesus, but also "the teaching that is in accordance with godliness" (6:3). These passages makes it clear that sound doctrine not only is a matter of having right cognitive beliefs, but also pertains to right living as well. This point is reinforced in the famous statement of 2 Timothy about inspiration: the affirmation that "all scripture is inspired by God" is often quoted, but the following words are less frequently cited: "And is useful for teaching ... and for training in righteousness, so that everyone who belongs to God may be proficient, equipped for every good work" (3:16-17). The inspiration of scripture here is manifestly linked to its function of training us in righteousness and the production of good works. Titus 2:1-2 supplies the detail implied by 2 Timothy 3:16: "Teach what is consistent with sound doctrine. Tell the older men to be temperate, serious, prudent, and sound in faith, in love, and in endurance." This text makes it abundantly clear that "sound doctrine" has a most intimate connection with vital Christian characteristics such as temperance and prudence. In conclusion, then, the New Testament compels us to affirm that the Christian faith includes a practical or ethical dimension and that a persistent failure to practice the Christian life signals the absence of living faith.

This extended discussion of New Testament teaching is necessary because stating and living the proper relation of faith to works is a perennial struggle in Christianity. Although cognitively affirming the doctrines of Christianity in the face of doubt is challenging, doing so (history shows) is easier than living the doctrines of Christianity. This perennial struggle takes two main forms. The first has already been mentioned—the neglecting of good works. The second is perhaps more pervasive. It is the neglect not of good works, but of good works that are distinctively Christian.

The first problem may be specially (although not uniquely) associated with the revivalistic heritage of American Protestantism. On one hand, this heritage generated tremendous spiritual energy that sustained a significant degree of social activism and great attempts at social reform. On the other hand, it also, especially under the influence of fundamentalism and premillenial eschatology, exhibited tendencies toward otherworldliness. It has showed, at times, a highly individualistic devotional quality, in which the sum of religion consists in the individual's relation to Jesus, a relation sometimes portrayed in excessively sentimental terms. Praise songs have reproduced, with up-to-date rhythms, the sentimentality of the personal relationship with Jesus, a relationship often indistinguishable from the romantic relationships portrayed in modern ballads. At the same time, this heritage has had an overemphasis on a theology of glory. By this I mean that, alongside a personal relationship with Jesus, the height of religion has been regarded as an experience, with significant emotional overtones, of the presence of God in a way that anticipates the heavenly state. The goal of the Christian life is, in this case, described as a continual abiding in the presence of God, an abiding that is continuous with eternal life with God in heaven. In this way, one's earthly life not only anticipates the eschatological state, but also is the temporal beginning of that state. The effect has been to place a certain kind of emotional experience and individual focus at the center of the Christian life, an experience and a focus that do not, in themselves, encourage a profound involvement in the world. To the extent that this heritage produced an ethical posture, it was sometimes of the rather rigidly legalistic sort, in which the Christian ethical life was depicted mainly in terms of what Christians do *not* do. I do not wish to give the impression that the revivalistic heritage has been uniformly negative in consequence or that its effect has been to discourage good works. My point is only that this heritage and its theology, as they developed under pressure from fundamentalism and premillenial eschatology, do not exactly *encourage* good works. And since, as experience shows, getting Christians to perform good works is difficult enough, having a theology and a tradition that do not sufficiently encourage them constitutes a problem.

Today, in the early years of the twenty-first century, the effects of the revivalistic heritage have been amplified by our religiously and epistemologically pluralistic culture, which encourages us to think of religion in individualistic terms and in terms of subjective (and hence private) experiences. It is in this pluralistic setting that the second problem arises, namely, the neglect of good works that are distinctively Christian. The problem here is not that Christians are deliberately disregarding such works (although some are). The problem instead is that we are no longer clear about just what a distinctively Christian good work would be. The fact that America has a massively Christian heritage means that many things that Christians do (or should do) are performed today, not for consciously Christian reasons, but instead because Christian practices (for example, public charity) have found institutional and, in many cases, secular forms. At the same time, we are more aware than ever before that people of other faiths and even people who are not overtly religious can and do engage in practices that Christians do. Atheists can and do give a cup of water to strangers, Buddhists can and do practice peacemaking, and so on. Fortunately, the quest for practices that are *distinctively* Christian does not require limiting ourselves to practices that are *uniquely* Christian. As the parable of the good Samaritan shows, the kingdom of God is found wherever people do what is pleasing to God. In the words of Acts 10, "In every nation anyone who fears [God] and does what is right is acceptable to [God]" (v. 35). The church's task is not to guard a truth and a practice that is unique, but instead to be faithful to the call of God. Nonetheless, the task remains of identifying and strengthening those practices that are distinctively Christian.

The Practice of Faith in Community

Community

One of the pervasive features of religion in America today is the privatization of belief. Americans do not like to be told what to think, and this resistance applies to our religious beliefs. As a result, churches are faced today with the daunting task of upholding doctrines in an age with little use for doctrines and of speaking authoritatively in an age that either distrusts or simply ignores authorities.

How did we get here? The answer is found in the American character's long memory, stretching back to the struggle for religious liberty in the seventeenth century. It was in this century that separation of church and state, freedom of conscience, and the principle of toleration became matters of urgent concern. After the struggles in Europe to maintain the union of church and state and the resulting use of coercion by the state to enforce doctrinal uniformity, Protestants were ready for the state to take a hands-off approach. At the same time, philosophical currents were urging a more tolerant political attitude toward nonestablished churches and heterodox ideas. When Protestants emigrated to America, these two convictions, liberty and toleration, became deeply embedded in the national character.

Recent developments have made America less overtly Christian but have also reinforced the notions of liberty and toleration. Among these recent developments are the reality of cultural and religious pluralism, the resulting popular acceptance of relativistic modes of thought, and the declining importance of institutions of all sorts. At the beginning of the twenty-first century, there is little doubt that most Americans operate with a practical relativism. A great many people believe that their religious and moral views are the right ones; but, in a culture marked by a high degree of pluralism, it has become virtually impossible for ordinary people (to say nothing of intellectuals, who long ago assimilated the implications of pluralism into their thinking) to maintain their conviction about the rightness of their beliefs. They are pretty sure their views are correct; but, given the vast diversity of opinion surrounding them, they have no other response than to allow other people the right to hold their opinions and to enter into a tacit pact whereby everyone agrees not to discuss publicly matters of religion and morality. It is an odd combination of absolutism and relativism. Individual beliefs are held to be the right ones, but, with no generally accepted way to substantiate that conviction, people act as though the beliefs of everyone else are equally valid. Exacerbating this tendency is the declining importance of institutions. Once upon a time, one's church provided him or her with a bulwark against uncertainty and the acid of relativism. Now, however, with a consumerist approach to religion (whereby we choose churches on the basis of our needs), it is increasingly difficult to think of churches and our membership in churches as providing much certainty. The experience of the Roman Catholic Church in recent decades is instructive. Although American Roman Catholics support the church both financially and in attendance at worship, and although they have great respect for the Pope, they have collectively decided that in certain matters (such as the use of artificial means of birth control) they will follow their own counsel and not the dictates of the church. This example illumines the problem that faces any institution today that wishes to be an authoritative source of moral and intellectual guidance.

In this context, toleration means not only granting the political right to hold an opinion but also the implied promise not to have one's opinions challenged. Whereas the political struggles of the seventeenth and eighteenth centuries were about restricting the power of the state to regulate belief, toleration today is the guaranty that I will be allowed to hold my opinions without being challenged by anyone—hence the great irritation people feel when evangelical Christians want to press them for a decision about Jesus Christ. Such an insistence seems to be a breach of the rule of toleration that polite society has drawn up, rules that specify that religious beliefs should not be challenged. In this cultural situation, the Protestant emphasis on religious liberty and freedom of conscience has been popularly transformed into the absolute right of individuals to determine truth. But in a highly pluralistic society, this individual determination of truth takes the form of practical relativism as described above. As a result, Americans have become quite at ease with the notion of something being true "for me," with the assumption that it may not be true for all.

We should not assume that this emphasis on individual judgment is all bad. Nothing would be gained for the cause of Christ by forcing people— either through overt coercion or subtle manipulation—to affirm Christian doctrines, as was the custom in previous centuries. Such belief would not be the living faith that God wants. The world has had enough experience with despotic regimes of all sorts to be convinced of the value of the individual's autonomy and of political measures that ensure that autonomy. However, it is no exaggeration to say that the problem of the contemporary American church is not a lack of autonomy, but a surfeit. The task set for today's church is to find a way of being authoritative while avoiding the temptation to be authoritarian. In short, it is imperative that the church recovers the communal dimension of the Christian faith in response to and in judgment of the overly privatized belief that characterizes American spirituality today.

The communal dimension is an inescapable aspect of authentic Christian faith. This is shown most notably in the form of the ancient creeds: *We* believe in God, the Father almighty. The Apostles' Creed ("*I* believe ...") is not an exception, for its origin as a baptismal creed reminds us that the baptismal candidate was affirming not his or her idiosyncratic beliefs, but instead the faith of the community into which he or she was being incorporated. This communal dimension of faith is expressed in the notion of the rule of faith, first reported by Irenaeus and Tertullian. The rule of faith, as they presented it, is the apostles' teaching, which has been transmitted through the church. Its importance lies in the fact that it preserves the church's doctrinal integrity over time and keeps the church in living continuity with the apostles. It does this by drawing a circle that demarcates the boundaries of authentic Christian faith. The rule of faith, accordingly, has a vital function in the life of the church. As a test of acceptable belief, it is normative. It is not just a statement of what Christians believe, but constitutes the church by determining what Christians should believe and what the church should teach.

In discussing the rule of faith, I have shifted the focus from the subjective act of believing, the *fides qua creditur,* to the content of faith, the *fides quae creditur.* I have argued that the rule of faith is inescapably communal. But we should not overlook the communal dimension of *fides qua creditur.* This can be seen if we attend to the ways in which people come to believe. Unlike religions in which truth is obtained by intuition, the Christian church has insisted from the beginning that the truth about God comes to us through the influence of this community, whether in the form of missionary preaching or the nurture of religious education or the informal influence of godly example. As Paul stated, "How are they to believe in one of whom they have never heard? And how are they to hear without someone to proclaim him?" (Romans 10:14). There is a twofold reason for the communal dimension of *fides qua creditur.* First, the doctrine of sin reminds us that the human mind is not able to discern the truth about God, at least not sufficiently to effect salvation. Humans have, we are told, become "futile in their thinking," and our "senseless minds" have become "darkened" (Romans 1:21). As a result, the human mind is not able to know the truth about God without the help of God. This brings us to the second reason, which is the doctrine of the incarnation and which proclaims that the truth of God—God's word to us—appeared among us in the form of a human being. As a result, there is no way to know God adequately apart from the mediation of this being. As John's Gospel states, "No one has ever seen God. It is God the only Son . . . who has made him known" (1:18). Of course, it is not Jesus Christ alone who is the means of authentic knowledge of God. John's Gospel is emphatic that, once the visible presence of Jesus is taken away, the knowledge of God is given by the Spirit (16:13-15) and through the testimony of the disciples (15:27). But these qualifications do not alter the main point. We can come to the proper knowledge of God only through the historical mediation of Jesus Christ, the community that he founded, and the Spirit of that community.

Authority

These two doctrines, the incarnation and sin, point us to the final aspect of the communal dimension of faith—the issue of authority with respect to the Christian faith. This is a difficult issue for a couple of reasons. First, as already discussed, respect for and trust in institutions is at an all-time low in America. The days when an institution such as the church could count on people accepting its views on the basis of implicit trust are not likely to return soon. In a consumer-oriented society like ours, people reserve the right to make their own judgments on matters of importance. As a result, even when an institution is respected and trusted, its members feel free to pick and choose among its tenets as they construct their beliefs. The Roman Catholic Church in America has discovered this as it has maintained its stance against artificial means of birth control in the face of massive disregard of that stance. This fact makes it exceedingly difficult for a church to proclaim doctrines with dogmatic certainty. Second, our pluralistic culture has been accompanied by a relativistic view of truth. Claims to absolute truth are generally met either by amused rejection or by a more complex strategy whereby a belief is held to be absolutely true for some people but not for others.

In the light of these facts, how can the church today maintain some sense of doctrinal authority? The first step is to be clear that the church's teaching is authoritative only for those in the church. This is a statement of empirical fact, not of theological truth. Theologically considered, Christian doctrine is the truth about God whether or not people realize and accept it. It is the continuation of the preaching of Jesus and the apostles and it carries their authority. Empirically considered, the church's teaching is authoritative only for those who accept it. This point seems obvious today, but it is instructive to remember that, until recently in America, the beliefs of the church had, to some extent, a normative status for society at large. A majority of the population affirmed at least some of those beliefs at some level even if they cared little for the church. Today it must be recognized that to speak of authority with respect to the church's faith means to speak about those who have some allegiance to the church. The church's authority will probably never again be valid for those outside the church—except to the extent to which they find some aspect of the church's doctrine to be attractive and choose to incorporate it into their beliefs. Once this point is recognized, then it becomes clear that doctrinal authority is ultimately about the well-being of the church and its life and that it is not about the relation between the church and those outside the church. The church is concerned about the purity of its faith only because it is convinced that this purity is essential for the church's faithful obedience to God and its continued existence as the people of God. For this doctrinal purity some form of authority is required.

The Practice of Faith in a Fallen World

There is not much patience in American spirituality for the notion that sin is an important factor in our knowledge of God. Americans today seem comfortable with the concept of a God who is the creator; but, lacking much doctrine of sin, they seem to regard the knowledge of God as something unproblematic. The theology found in popular media (for instance, the television show *Touched by an Angel*) testifies to this, although Americans do acknowledge plenty of diversity with respect to specific beliefs—hence the practical epistemological relativism of American spirituality. More scientifically minded people may identify empirical or logical obstacles to the knowledge of God, but this still dif-

fers from the theological conviction that more is involved in our ignorance of God than just the inherent limitations of the human mind. The
more that is involved is sin. As a result, it is important to consider faith
in a fallen world, which is also a part of the context of our existence.

With respect to faith, sin takes the form of unbelief. The first thing is
to remind ourselves that unbelief differs from doubt. Doubt is an epistemological condition. It may appear in the form of skepticism (when
doubt is adopted as a philosophical method) or perplexity (when we lack
enough facts to arrive at a state of knowledge). But faith is not exclusively
or even principally an epistemological issue although it contains a cognitive dimension. Instead, as previously discussed, it is an act of obedient
response to the gospel. It is a way in which we honor and acknowledge
the creator. That is why Paul's argument in Romans 1 culminates in the
indictment that humankind is without excuse. We do, in fact, know
God's eternal power and divine nature. Yet we have not honored God or
given thanks to God (1:20). Our sin, according to Paul, is not the epistemological matter of being ignorant of God. It is instead our steadfast
refusal to acknowledge God. Similarly, the letter to the Hebrews exhorts
us not to have "an evil, unbelieving heart that turns away from the living
God" (3:12). Who exemplifies such a heart? Not those with intellectual
doubts but instead those who, like the ancient Israelites, harden their
hearts "as in the rebellion" against Moses (3:15). These are they who
heard the word of God but did not benefit from that hearing because they
lacked faith (4:2). But to lack faith in this situation was not to entertain
doubts. It was rather to fail to enter into the land because of disobedience
(4:6).

It is because unbelief is a matter of decision more than of epistemology
that Jesus refused to provide a sign to the Pharisees (Matthew 12:38-39).
If faith were primarily epistemological, then offering a sign—some sort of
evidence—would be expected as a means of securing intellectual certainty. However, the Gospels are adamant that what the Pharisees lacked
was not information or proof, but instead was the willingness to acknowledge Jesus as the Son of God. Their asking for a sign was a testimony to
their desperate spiritual condition, for they did not recognize their sinful
disobedience to the message of Jesus. On the contrary, they believed that
the appropriate stance toward Jesus could be obtained simply by acquiring the requisite information.

The New Testament document that most develops this theme is the
Gospel of John. John's Gospel presents the reader with two reasons to

accept Jesus Christ: the signs and the witnesses. For this Gospel, the signs that Jesus performed offer indisputable proof that he was from the Father. Accordingly, there are several episodes that culminate in someone accepting Jesus because of his signs. These include the disciples believing because of the miracle of wine (2:11) and the official believing because of a healing miracle (4:53). At the same time, this Gospel states expressly that these miraculous signs do not in themselves create faith. Jesus' brothers are not convinced of his divinity in spite of the signs (7:1-5), and the signs are acknowledged to have had no effect on the Jews in general (12:37-43). The same is true of the witnesses to Jesus. These include John the Baptist (5:32-33), Jesus' works (5:36), the Scriptures (5:39), and Moses (5:46). Yet, the Gospel concludes, none of these finally proved sufficient to create faith among the Jews. The reason for this is that confessing Jesus rests on much more than just having enough information. One must have a prior disposition toward God in order for these evidences to be convincing. In the words of the Gospel, we must want to do God's will before we can recognize the truth of Jesus' words (7:17), and we must first belong to God before we can hear the words of God that Jesus speaks (8:47). Unbelief, then, does not arise from a lack of information, but is instead failure to have this disposition toward God—not wanting to do the will of God. Conversely, faith is not the conclusion of a logical argument but is instead having this disposition and letting it become concrete in a faithful response to the gospel.

Unbelief is one form that sin takes with respect to faith. Another is heresy. Immediately it is necessary to observe that it is not completely clear what *heresy* means in a situation such as ours, in which there are numerous denominations, each with its doctrinal tradition and standards. Although denominations are, generally speaking, less pugnacious and more conciliatory toward one another than in previous generations, it is still far from clear how we should use the term *heresy*. It does not seem either appropriate or useful to declare traditions other than our own heretical simply because they do not share our doctrines. This tempts us to assume that heresy must deal with some inner core of Christian beliefs, which could only be what all Christian denominations have in common. But finding this common core of beliefs has proved to be difficult, particularly since what one tradition regards as vital is often not so regarded by other traditions.

Some help may be gained if we attend to the ethical dimension of faith. The Christian faith pertains to the "teaching that is in accord with godliness" (1 Timothy 6:3). This implies that heresy is more than holding beliefs that are, by Christian standards, false. The falsehood that characterizes heresy is not just believing a wrong idea, but believing and practicing an idea that is not in accord with godliness. But here a question arises: some Christian doctrines seem to have only a remote connection to godliness. How, then, can not affirming them or affirming contrary doctrines fail to be in accord with godliness? For example, the doctrine of the Trinity, as popularly represented, seems more than a bit speculative and unconnected to the Christian life. Nothing relevant to godliness seems jeopardized by rejecting this doctrine.

It is the fault of the church and its teachers and pastors that the ethical dimension of the doctrine of the Trinity has lain among us undeveloped and idle. Fortunately, there are signs that this state of affairs is changing. Although a complete rehabilitation of the ethical dimension of this doctrine is still in the future, we can nonetheless state that there is a difference between a verbal affirmation of this (or any other) doctrine and a practical affirmation. This distinction is possible because the Christian faith has, beginning with the proclamation of Jesus, come to be stated verbally. It has an intellectual content that is the subject of affirmation and understanding. It also has an ethical dimension, as previously discussed. In a fallen world, in which human existence loses the wholeness and undivided unity that God wills for us, it becomes possible for us to affirm that faith verbally and intellectually without affirming it practically. This is called hypocrisy. But it is also possible for people to affirm some aspect of the Christian faith practically and ethically even while denying it verbally and intellectually. Thus, some Christians in history have had serious reservations about the doctrine of the Trinity, especially in its creedal forms. Yet it is certainly possible for such doubters to be practicing trinitarian faith in the conduct of their lives. This is possible because God is love and love can be practiced even if one is not in full verbal agreement with the church on a doctrinal point.

None of this discussion is intended to minimize the importance to the church of doctrinal precision or agreement. Both are useful and desirable. The point is only that, because of the multidimensional character of Christian faith, one can be *practicing* the teaching that accords with godliness even while disputing the verbal forms in which those teachings are to be framed. A given teaching on this account is not to be judged heretical primarily because of its divergence from these verbal forms. It is to be judged instead in terms of its accordance with godliness—its propensity to help disciples live the Christian life. The fact that faith has a hermeneutical dimension means that Christians will have different understandings of the faith. History shows that sometimes these differences are severe. Yet it is to be hoped that a difference in understanding does not necessitate a difference in Christian character.

Sin affects Christian faith in a third way, a way related to the communal dimension of faith. As discussed previously, the church plays a vital and central role in nurturing Christian faith. Consequently, authority becomes an important issue in doctrinal integrity. However, in a fallen world, the church's authority is subject to distortion. It is not difficult to find examples in church history of the distorting effect of sin on the exercise of authority. The phenomenon of conversions either overtly coerced or at least encouraged by force or incentives is one example. Another is the history of overly zealous heresy-hunting, which even the early church did not escape. Even more extreme is the occasional offshoot of the church that becomes destructively manipulative of its members and seeks to control the details of their lives. In all these cases, churches' legitimate attempts to ensure orthodoxy and orthopraxis are corrupted by sin's propensity to substitute human structures and desires for the kingdom of God. Against this propensity the church must continually seek a path between institutional authoritarianism and excessive individual autonomy.

Faith and Participation in God

The Christian life is an eschatological existence. This means that faith is the form that the knowledge of God takes in our current state. In the words of Paul, "Now we see in a mirror, dimly" (1 Corinthians 13:12). Philosophically considered, it might be thought that faith is a deficient form of knowledge—the sort of knowledge one has if sufficient evidence is lacking, as when we say, "I *believe* it may rain tomorrow," because we do not *know* whether it will rain. In this case, we prefer knowledge to belief. But this is a poor understanding of Christian faith. Christian faith is not a poor cousin to logically or empirically certain knowledge. It is, on the contrary, the sort of knowledge appropriate to embodied beings, living eschatologically, whose object of knowledge is the God who is love.

We know things as we bring our minds into conformity with the nature of those things—as we allow them to shape our thinking. This is true both in scientific thinking and in the realm of personal relations. In scientific thinking, knowledge is increased as we allow new phenomena to alter our conceptions and as we make our theories pliable enough to fit the phenomena. Without this pliability, we can know things only as they conform to our customary modes of thinking. In this way we miss the distinctive characteristics of phenomena and lose the opportunity to enlarge the scope of our theories. It is no different in personal relations. Here true knowledge of the other person requires that, to some extent, we set aside our preconceptions and wishes and instead allow the nature of the perceived object to shape us. All of this applies to our knowledge of God. If God is love, then it follows that the authentic knowledge of God consists in love and results from allowing the God who is love to shape our thinking and indeed our entire being. Of course, there are limits to the extent to which, in a fallen world and in our eschatological existence, the nature of the God who is love can transform our natures. That is why the Christian life of faith and love is also a life of hope—the eschatological nature of our existence points us to the unambiguous future of God's kingdom, when our nature will be utterly transformed into a reflection of the God who is love. In the meantime, the life of love, although fragmentary and imperfect, is the form that the authentic knowledge of God takes.

But how does this relate to faith? If love is the form that the knowledge of God takes, then what can we say about faith? After all, Paul asserted that love is superior to and more enduring than faith (1 Corinthians 13:2, 13). It is true that faith is strictly an eschatological phenomenon. In the fullness of God's kingdom, there will be no need for faith, whereas love—the nature of God—endures everlastingly. However, this should not cause us to miss the important point that, as long as our existence is eschatological, there is an indissoluble unity between faith and love. My previous remarks on the ethical or practical dimension of faith were an attempt to state this point clearly. Authentic Christian faith is something active and practical. Its perfection is found in love for God and neighbor. Love, in fact, is the practice of faith. And, as noted, faith without works of love is a dead faith and is not really Christian faith at all. (The case of love without Christian faith is more difficult, since it involves the possibility of someone being conformed to the nature of God apart from authentic faith, something the New Testament does not countenance.) So, in view of the indissoluble bond between faith and love, we are justified in affirming that the ethical dimension of faith is the form that authentic knowledge of God takes in our eschatological condition.

It is not enough to say that faith is the form that the knowledge of God takes and that loves means our being conformed to the nature of the God who is love. To accurately portray things, we need stronger language. Such language is provided in 2 Peter 1:4: God "has given us . . . his precious and very great promises, so that through them you may . . . become participants of the divine nature." On the basis of these words, we may say that faith (in its union with love) is our participation in the God who is love. This means that our relation to God is not that of one thing imitating another. Our relation is instead that of one thing dwelling in another. John's Gospel provides a fuller account of this mutual indwelling. There we learn that, like a vine and its branches, there is a mutual indwelling between Jesus and disciples (15:4). Moreover, this mutual abiding is the ground of disciples' fruit-bearing—their works of love (15:5). It is not only or primarily Jesus and the disciples who enjoy this abiding. For this Gospel, one of the fundamental truths is that Jesus and the Father abide in each other (10:38). And, just as the indwelling of Jesus results in the disciples' good works, so that indwelling of the Father is the basis of Jesus' works, so that his words and works are really those of the Father (14:10).

For the New Testament, then, the Christian life is not only a life that imitates God, but also a life that lives in God and in which God lives. This means that this life must be thought of as graced, that is, lived by the power of God. That is why Paul wrote that "it is God who is at work in you, enabling you both to will and to work for his good pleasure" (Philippians 2:13) and why love and faith are among the fruits of the Spirit (Galatians 5:22). Although (as will be discussed in chapter 7) the Christian life is a demanding one that calls upon us to exert and discipline ourselves, it is at the same time a graced life that endures through the life of God within us. This life, in short, is our participation in God.

The New Testament wishes to be very specific about the character of divine love. It is the love that transpires between the Father and the Son and which is inspired in us by the Holy Spirit. For this reason, it is necessary to say that faith, in its unity with love, is our participation in the trinitarian life of God. The basis of this assertion is John 17:21-23: "As you, Father, are in me and I am in you, may they also be in us. . . . The glory that you have given me I have given them, so that they may be one, as we are one, I in them and you in me, that they may become completely one." This passage states that disciples are drawn into the unity and fellowship of the Father and the Son. We are in this way made part of God's trinitarian life of love. However, what about the Holy Spirit? Here we must admit that the doctrine of the Spirit is underdeveloped in this

Gospel in particular and in the New Testament in general. However, as noted above, a way forward is offered in Paul's theology. If faith and love along with the other gifts come to us as a life in the Spirit, then it is not difficult to conclude that our abiding, through love, in the unity and fellowship of the Father and Son is effected by the Spirit. It is in the power of the Spirit that we come to participate in God's trinitarian life. This occurs as, in the Spirit, we come to manifest the fruit of the Spirit. In short, it is faith, in its unity with love, that is our participation in the Trinity. That is, it is as our faithful response and obedience to God is elicited by the Spirit and is manifested in works of love that our participation in the Trinity is actualized.

So far I have been discussing participation in God in terms of the ethical dimension of faith, for this dimension has the most overt connection to love. It is not, however, only the ethical dimension of faith that is our participation in God—the hermeneutical dimension (that is, its function of understanding) is relevant as well. Ancient Christians allowed that all human beings participate in the Logos by virtue of their created rationality. But this level of participation, although theologically important, does not bear on Christian spirituality—there is nothing either distinctively Christian nor distinctively spiritual about it. We must look further for the way in which faith, in its hermeneutical aspect, is a participation in God. For help we turn to the ancient slogan "faith seeking understanding." This slogan depicts the fundamental structure of Christian thinking. As embodied beings, our thinking necessarily begins somewhere, namely in the situation in which we find ourselves—our tradition, our prejudices, our experiences. "Faith seeking understanding" states that there is a proper task for the intellect—understanding the faith. But it also states that Christian thinking begins with and remains faithful to the Christian faith (the *fides quae creditur*). This means that thinking—the application of the intellect—must be sanctified. The Christian intellect is not allowed to assume just any premise or to arrive at just any conclusion. It is bound by the rule of faith, by the "teaching that is in accordance with godliness" (1 Timothy 6:3). Thinking, for the Christian, is an activity that is faithful not only to the rules of logic and evidence, but also to the consensus of the Christian tradition as it bears on the rule of faith. Thinking that follows the paths of the rule of faith is thinking that is consecrated to God. It is a thinking that is holy because it has submitted to God's truth and faithfully follows the way of that truth. Such thinking is a participation in God because God is the holy God. In such sanctified thinking, our nature is conformed to the nature of the God who is holiness itself. Of course, this concept of the sanctification of the intellect should not be confused with a demand that has sometimes been placed on disciples, the demand to believe what some ecclesiastical authority decrees simply on the basis of its institutional authority. Acceding to this demand is not the sanctification of the intellect, but rather the unholy sacrifice of the intellect—not the spiritual worship that Paul urged in Romans 12:2, but the killing off of the intellect at the behest of human authorities for their own security and sense of control. As was noted previously, in a fallen world, the church sometimes confuses its own declarations with the word of God and thereby wrongly demands obedience to those declarations. In these situations, it is an act of the highest piety to call attention to this sin and to insist on the true holiness of faithful thinking.

Thinking according to the slogan "faith seeking understanding" is a participation in God because of its holiness. But there is an additional sense in which such thinking is a participation in God. This additional sense appears to us when we attend to what theologians and mystics have insisted on, namely that human thought, with its finite limitations, is not capable of comprehending God and that true knowledge of God passes beyond the concepts and categories that human thinking uses. In other words, in authentic knowledge of God, God is not the object of thinking in the customary sense, with its propensity toward categorization. God cannot rightly be located in any category of thought. On the contrary, God lies outside all such categories, and the thinking that approaches God must abandon categorical thinking. The thinking appropriate to God instead has a more participatory and unitive character. In other words, it has the character of love. If God is love, then the knowledge of God can have no higher form than our love for God. But what does this love consist in? We cannot do good works for God as we can and should for the neighbor. In the case of God, love is not so much active as a matter of abiding in, to use the words of John's Gospel. In abiding, we incorporate ourselves into God and God into ourselves to such an extent that our being and identity come to be utterly defined by that incorporation. This is the ultimate form that the understanding of faith may take. It is truly an act of understanding, for it is obtained by following a path of thinking. Yet, unlike typical thinking, it ends not with an object classified in some category, but rather in a state of wisdom, a state in which we live in God and God lives in us.

Concluding Meditative Prayer

We praise you, our God, whose word we believe, whose faithfulness we trust with a sure faith, and who has made us hearers and doers of the word. You, Lord, we praise, who are most free yet most faithful, most incomprehensible, yet most revealing. Lead us, our Lord, always to your word and strengthen our faith in it. We praise you, our God, who came to us in Jesus Christ, the pioneer and perfecter of our faith. May we, like him, endure the cross for the sake of the joy set before us. We praise you, our God, who in the Holy Spirit has given us the gift of faith. Give us that faith and its victory over the world. Help us ask, with the demoniac's father, Lord, we believe, help our unbelief. We praise you, also, Lord, for your saints, living and dead, who are our models in faith. Blessed are those who are members of your holy temple, built on the foundation of the apostles and prophets. We confess that our faith is misdirected and that we are often faithless. Turn our faith, so often awry, aright and Godward. Preserve us, Lord, safe from error, schism, and heresy. Deliver us from the spirit of forgetfulness and obstinacy. Make us always remember you and your grace to us. Give us a true heart in full assurance of faith. We pray, Lord, that our faith may always be joined to faithfulness, that you would cause our hearts to cling to the apostles' teaching, that you would make us walk in the truth and do the truth.

You, our God, who keep faith with your covenant people, we praise.
We praise
> the Father, whose faithful grace sent to us your eternal word, Jesus Christ,
> through the Son, the Logos, in whom we believe and trust and who is the pattern of our faith,
> in the Spirit of truth, who inspires and nourishes our faith.

We praise you, holy Trinity, the alpha and omega of our faith.

Notes

1. See Samuel M. Powell, *Participating in God: Creation and Trinity*, *Theology and the Sciences* (Minneapolis: Fortress Press, 2003).

2. It is well known that the Johannine literature has a strongly sectarian character, according to which love and good works seem to be restricted to the members of the community. Although God loves the world (John 3:16), disciples are

never commanded to love the world and, in fact, are expressly told not to love the world (1 John 2:15). Although it is important for us to honor the message of this tradition and feel its force and allow its judgment on us, it is just as important that we recognize that other streams within the New Testament, notably Luke and Acts, express a universal scope for the Christian's love.

Sources Consulted and Recommended

Athanasius. "On the Incarnation." In *St. Athanasius: Select Works and Letters*. Vol. 4, *Nicene and Post-Nicene Fathers of the Christian Church*, 2nd ser. Peabody, MA: Hendrickson Publishers, 1995. Discusses the universal participation of human beings in the *Logos*.

Dayton, Donald W. *Discovering an Evangelical Heritage*. Peabody, MA: Hendrickson Publishers, 1976. Illustrates the tradition of social reform in American revivalism.

Irenaeus. "Against Heresies." In *The Writings of Irenaeus*. 2 vols. Translated by Alexander Roberts and W. H. Rambaut. Vols. 5 and 9, *Ante-Nicene Christian Library*. New York: The Christian Literature Co., 1885. Book 1, chapter 20 sets forth the early church's rule of faith.

LaCugna, Catherine Mowry. *God for Us: The Trinity and Christian Life*. San Francisco: Harper San Francisco, 1991. An important contribution to the rehabilitation of the doctrine of the Trinity as a practical doctrine of the Christian life.

Luther, Martin. "The Freedom of a Christian." In *Career of the Reformer: I*. Edited by Harold J. Grimm. Vol. 31, *Luther's Works*. Philadelphia: Muhlenberg Press, 1957.

Moltmann, Jürgen. *History and the Triune God: Contributions to Trinitarian Theology*. Translated by John Bowden. New York: Crossroad, 1992. Moltmann has been at the forefront of revitalizing the doctrine of the Trinity for the church.

———. *The Trinity and the Kingdom: The Doctrine of God*. Translated by Margaret Kohl. New York: Harper & Row, 1981.

Powell, Samuel M. *Participating in God: Creation and Trinity, Theology and the Sciences*. Minneapolis: Fortress Press, 2003.

Smith, Timothy L. *Revivalism and Social Reform in Mid-Nineteenth-century America*. New York: Abingdon Press, 1957. An important statement about the essential connection between social reform and American revivalism.

Thomas Aquinas. *Summa Theologiae*. Edited by Thomas Gilby. The Blackfriars English translation ed. Garden City, NY: Image Books, 1969. Part 1, question 3, article 5 discusses whether God can be contained within any concept (genus). A significant statement about God's transcendence.

Tillich, Paul. *The Protestant Era*. Translated by James Luther Adams. Chicago: University of Chicago Press, 1948. Tillich sets forth the Protestant principle in this book.

Ware, Kallistos. *The Orthodox Way*. Crestwood, NY: St. Vladimir's Seminary Press, 1994. Argues for the need of converting our minds if we are to know and love God.

WORSHIP

The Practice of Worship

The diminished sense of the importance of communal worship is associated with a diminished sense of the importance of mediation and the means of grace such as the sacraments. This observation leads us to consider the tendency in American culture to represent worship as an act of abstract spirituality. By *abstract spirituality* I mean the notion that worship is mainly an act of inwardness and that it does not require physical or public acts. This sort of spirituality is abstract because it wrongly separates the spirit from the body. A spirituality that was only about the body and that left the spirit out of consideration would be just as abstract in the other direction.

Abstract spirituality has several causes. As already argued, one is excessive individualism. To the extent that communal worship loses its normative status and individual modes of worship are valued, worship will tend to become a matter of pure inwardness—it doesn't make much sense for an individual, engaged in solitary worship, to go through ritualized and bodily actions, which tend to have a public character. Another cause lies in the history of Protestantism. In its reaction to late medieval Roman Catholic piety, the Reformers, to varying degrees, sought to trim worship of ornamentation and pomp and to simplify the physical appearance of worship buildings. The theological convictions associated with this policy have been etched deeply into the Protestant American religious heritage, especially in the evangelical and charismatic portions of that heritage. In other circumstances, this iconoclastic temperament might have had no deleterious effects. But in combination with the American inclination toward individuality and informality, Protestant iconoclasm has reinforced the tendency away from the bodily and public side of worship. The inclination toward informality found expression in America's revivalistic tradition. Here the ideal of dramatic conversion meant that religious experience and moral reformation took precedence over ecclesiastical doctrine. The ideal of spontaneity meant that the practiced routines and rituals of traditional worship came to be dislodged by practices that were every bit as ritualized but that had the appearance of freedom from human contrivance. In the charismatic tradition, the immediacy of the Spirit of God and the ideal of extraordinary acts of God in worship rendered the ordinary means of grace and the planned rituals of worship either less important or, in extreme cases, undesirable. The manifestation of these sentiments today can be seen in the seeker-sensitive approach to worship, in which many of the customary features of Christian worship are pared away in the interests of reaching out to people for whom these features either mean nothing or impede a positive reception of the Christian message. Although worship in this approach may have an embodied character (since it is public and does consist of some public activity), its embodiment does not take a traditional form.

What would a theology of embodied worship look like? First, it would reject abstract spirituality by affirming our bodily nature. In this way it would ground worship in the doctrine of creation. It would take with full seriousness the fact that our created nature includes this bodily aspect. Worship, accordingly, would not contradict our bodily nature but would instead incorporate it. Of course, a theology of embodied worship cannot be based on the doctrine of creation alone. It must also take into account the doctrine of sin and the effects of sin on our bodily nature. Nonetheless, such a theology would do justice to the importance of both inwardness in worship and bodily practices. It would remind us that it is our entire selves—body and spirit—that are redeemed and not our spirits only. The essential participation of the body in worship testifies to its ultimate redemption in the resurrection. In this way, a theology of embodied worship will be associated with a sound theological anthropology.

Such a theology will also be based on the insight, expressed by Augustine, that God has made us for God's self and that our hearts are restless until they find rest in God. Concretely understood, this means that we find our good only in the knowledge and love of God. We are made for God and to love God. As a result, to live authentically and fully as a human being is to be a hearer and doer of God's word. It is to hear the voice of God calling to us and to respond with faithful obedience. Worship is one of the principal forms that our faithful obedience takes and is one of the principal contexts in which God's word is heard. This is the truth expressed in the belief that worship is beneficial for us. It is beneficial for us because we have been made for God. Worship—acknowledging God and honoring God—is humankind's highest good. That is why the heavenly scenes in the book of Revelation are scenes of worship. In heaven, beings enjoy creatures' highest good.

A consideration of theological anthropology leads us to see why Christian worship typically involves symbols, symbolic gestures, and other material aids to worship. The main reason for these things is the sacramental principle, as discussed previously. But Christian meditation on human existence helps us see the truth and importance of the sacramental principle. Human beings are not only creatures, but also bodily creatures. As a result, we come to know and relate to realities in ways congruent with our bodily nature. We come to know God and to relate to God in sensuous and bodily ways through the mediation of physical things around us. That is why even the most spartan worship ceremonies still use some material aids to worship, such as music, pulpit, and the reading of Scripture. It is simply not possible for human beings to intuit God in a purely spiritual fashion. We approach God as embodied spirits, and our coming to God must be in agreement with our nature. Likewise, even those churches most anxious about empty formalism in worship nonetheless employ some ritualized gestures, such as bowing the head in prayer and standing for the reading of Scripture. In this way they testify, even if unwittingly, to the importance of worshiping God with our entire selves. Finally, even the most iconoclastic churches make use of some symbols in the course of worship, even if such use is limited to a single cross located somewhere in the church building or an image of a dove on church stationery. By including these symbols these churches implicitly acknowledge the fact that, for purposes of recollection and proclamation, graphic signs of the Christian faith are useful if not necessary.

A sound theology will also help us see the way in which worship is associated with the sanctification of time and space. Minimally, worship means that at least one hour or so each week is devoted to God. Maximally, as in certain monastic communities, worship structures the entire day. In this way, worship reminds us that our time is a gift from God and that it is fitting to devote to God a portion of that time for the express purpose of giving thanks and rendering praise. Worship also signifies the hallowing of space. First of all, there is the fact that worship (usually) takes place in specified places and buildings, which are (in many traditions) consecrated before use. The architecture of church buildings illustrates more. Gothic cathedrals, for example, were built in the shape of a cross. The baptismal font was often near the entrance to the church, signifying the entrance into salvation. Consecrated ground lay nearby for burial. And so on. Even in the most informal churches, there is usually some sense that the place of worship is devoted to God's use, a sign of which is uneasiness if a proposal is made to use the worship area for commercial or recreational use. The phenomena of the multipurpose building, used for worship and any number of other events, and storefront churches seem to contradict the consecration of space, for here there is no space reserved for worship. Nonetheless, the presence of a cross and other symbols designates this space as at least a part-time place of worship with an appropriate sacral character. At least some sense of the sanctification of place remains.

A theology of embodied worship will also show forth the formative function of worship. It will show in detail the ways in which the components of worship help effect, over time, Christian character. It will be based on the premise that the Christian faith is more than cognitive belief and that it includes practices, including worship practices, as well. It will note the fact that, within the Christian faith, some things are learned only or best by doing. For example, it is no accident that communion is *served* to the congregation by *clergy*, in contrast to allowing the congregation to take the elements as in a buffet. The repeated serving and reception of communion will (if joined with sound teaching that helps the congregation understand), over time, instill in us the fact that clergy are ministers, that is, they are servants and the grace of God is something that we receive and not something that we take for ourselves. The physicality of the communion elements can reinforce for us the importance of the sacramental principle and the incarnation. Bowing the head and kneeling can remind us that God is in heaven and we are on earth—that God is the Lord and that we are God's servants, a useful concept in an age in which God is routinely conceived as a cosmic servant that exists for human well-being. The singing of hymns and songs will, over time, deeply ingrain their theology, perhaps more effectively than preaching, teaching, and catechism. That is why close attention to the theology ensconced in songs is of critical importance to the church. Examples could be multiplied, but the main point is clear: the Christian message and Christian practices are conveyed to us and internalized by us not only by didactic sermons and education but also by the routines of worship.

A theology of embodied worship will also remind us that worship is a service that we render to God. This conviction is grounded in the fact that, from ancient times, worship consisted in offering sacrifice. Worship was something people did for the gods. Of course, they always did so with the expectation of receiving blessings from the gods. Nonetheless, worship was an act of devotion in which the creature served the divine. A sound theology of worship will emphasize this point as a way of correcting the impression, widely assumed in our consumer-oriented culture, that the purpose of worship is to do something for me and that its value is gauged by the benefit that I derive from it. This impression is related to the view that the church is a voluntary association of like-minded people, congregating out of common need. This view encourages us to see the church as one instrument of self-help alongside others, each being used and valued according to our perceived needs. Of course, worship *is* beneficial for human beings. It is the fulfillment of our created nature. There is something desperately wrong with worship that is so barren that it provides nothing of benefit for the worshipers. But these observations do not diminish the point that, in our context today, what is needed above all is an insistence that worship is not primarily for me but is instead a service that I render to God. Such an understanding makes more sense of typical worship practices such as acts of praise and profession of faith. As 1 Peter teaches, the church as a whole is a holy priesthood, offering spiritual sacrifices to God. We will have a better grasp of this work of offering and of our role in it if we emphasize worship as a service that we render to God.

Finally, a theology of embodied worship will remind us that worship is not limited to ceremonies on Sunday. The people of God are called to offer spiritual sacrifices to God. These include praise (Hebrews 13:15) and thanks (Hebrews 12:28). But the sacrifices that we offer to God also include ourselves in the act of consecration. We are to present our bodies to God as living, holy, and acceptable sacrifices. This, Paul affirmed, is our spiritual service (Romans 12:1). The fact that consecration to God is an act of worship is grounded in Jesus Christ's act of self-sacrifice, which Paul expressly understood to be an offering to God and hence an act of worship (Ephesians 5:2). More generally stated, taking up our cross and following Jesus is worship. That is why Paul could say that the Philippians' gift to him was an offering and a sacrifice (Philippians 4:18). Good works, therefore, since they result from our consecration and our taking up the cross, are likewise acts of worship. Worship, then, is more than vocal praise and ritualized movements. It is, ideally, the totality of the consecrated life, in which everything is offered up to God as a holy sacrifice. This explains the prophets' exasperation with an Israelite society that was faithful in prescribed worship but failed to see that true worship entails the totality of our existence (Isaiah 1:11-17).

World-Transcendence and World-Participation

THE IMPULSE TOWARD TRANSCENDING THE WORLD

Recognition of the connection between worship and the conduct of life leads us to another aspect of the embodied nature of worship, namely, worship as an act of ethical and spiritual transcendence over the world. As I have noted previously, the Christian faith includes both cognitive and practical dimensions. It is both a knowing and a doing. As a practical matter, worship is a relation not only to God but also to the world. As I have also noted, there is, within the Christian faith, a twofold relation to the world—a relation of ethical transcendence and a relation of ethical participation.

In true worship we ethically and spiritually transcend the world. First, worship means acknowledging God to be the lord and denying lordship to everything else. As we give wholehearted worship to God, we conquer the world and its desire to elevate finite things to the status of divinity. In worship we distinguish between what is ultimate and what is relative, between that which rightly deserves our full allegiance and that which falsely claims our allegiance. To worship God and God alone is a decision to submit to God and the way of life that God has prescribed and to turn our backs on the fallen world's distorted view of life.

Second, worship is an act of ethical transcendence because it means the sanctification of life. The fallenness of the world consists in the refusal to acknowledge God and to order life under God's lordship. Worship signifies expressly that some things have been devoted to God and that, implicitly, all things should be so devoted. In worship, some things are expressly consecrated to God: space, time, implements of worship, and, at least during the time of worship, the worshipers. Worship signifies that, at least during this time, we acknowledge God's claim upon these things. They are devoted to the service of God. But meditation on this fact leads us to see that what is true of worshipers, time, space, and implements during worship should be true of everything at every moment. Everything—worshipers, time, space, material things—should exist continuously in a state of devotion to God. Worship is, therefore, a model of what all reality should be. As stated in Zechariah, in the eschatological future, even bells on horses and cooking pots in homes will be consecrated to God and thus be holy. But the kingdom of God is not yet present in its fullness. Consequently, the consecration and sanctification of all things—their devotion to God in and as an act of worship—remains for us a task. We are to live and act as though every moment, every place, every thing, and every person were holy and in a state of consecration to God. In this way, we ethically transcend the world, which wants to forget God. The world wants to live as though there is no God to be consecrated to. But by extending the consecration of worship to all things in anticipation of their sanctification in the eschatological kingdom, we overcome the world's desire to live without God.

THE IMPULSE TOWARD PARTICIPATING IN THE WORLD

However, it is important to remember that the world, although fallen, remains the good creation of God. Our ethical transcendence over the world does not mean our rejection of the world. As creatures, we continue to participate in the world and its structures. Worship is one of the ways in which we participate in the world. I have already discussed one of the ways in which this is true. Authentic worship is not an exercise in abstract spirituality, but instead an embodied activity. Worship encompasses bodily activities such as bowing, kneeling, speaking, and tasting. It includes ritualized gestures such as the sign of the cross and the greeting. It includes sensuous experiences such as tasting communion elements, hearing preaching and songs, seeing art and other material aids to worship, touching other worshipers in the greeting, and smelling incense. In all these ways and others, worship is an act of bodily creatures. Worship also affirms the goodness of our bodies. It is a proclamation that the human body and all other bodily things are fit vehicles for the worship of God. It is the declaration that, in spite of the consequences of sin and the fallenness of the world, the created world remains the domain of God and that it is capable of holiness.

Worship is an expression of our participation in the world in a second sense, namely, that in worship we take our place among the rest of creation in praise to God. Psalm 148 is instructive on this point. This psalm calls upon every created thing to praise God. Angels, sun, moon, stars, the waters above the heavens, sea monsters, fire, hail, snow, frost, wind, mountains, animals, and human beings are all to join together in the worship of God. It seems odd to us that inanimate things and irrational animals could praise God. But the point is that these things, by acting in accordance with their created natures, constitute praise to God. They do not consciously and verbally worship God, but their being and their typical modes of activity are the worship of God; for by acting in conformity with their created nature, they reflect the wisdom, goodness, and perfection of God. They thus proclaim the lordship of God. With human beings the matter is different. Because we are creatures of speech and intellect, worship for us must include the exercise of speech and intellect. But since our speech and our thoughts are under our control, we can refuse to use them for God. By such refusal we implicitly declare that we are not a part of the created world, which praises God. We want to lift ourselves above that world by pretending that our good lies elsewhere than in worshiping God. When we praise God, we humbly take our place among the rest of creation and acknowledge that we are not the ultimate reality of the cosmos and that our good lies in knowing and loving God. Consequently, to worship is to acknowledge our creaturely status and to act in agreement with that status. In this way, worship is an affirmation of our participation in the world.

WORSHIP UNDER THE CONDITION OF FINITUDE

Another aspect of the embodied character of worship lies in the fact that worship is always offered under the conditions of finitude. Perhaps the most obvious result of human worship amidst finitude is the mediated character of our knowledge of God. The necessity of mediation is not a result of sin. It is instead a consequence of our creaturely finitude. Our worship of God partakes of this finitude. Perhaps it will not always be so. The book of Revelation asserts that, in the eschatological future, the servants of God and the Lamb "will worship him; they will see his face" (22:3-4). That is why the new Jerusalem has no temple (21:22). Revelation is speaking symbolically of an unmediated knowledge of God. But in the meantime, on this side of the eschatological day, our worship is mediated. We do have need of temples and other physical implements. We need symbols to help us think of God. We need gestures and ritualized actions to help us recollect. We need sacraments to reinforce our faith. We need ministers to lead us and represent us. All this shows us why the practice of abstract spirituality—worship without mediation—is mistaken. Such spirituality is a denial of our finite and embodied condition. It is a grasping after the pure spirituality of angels. It is an overly realized eschatology—believing that already we have no need of temples, that already we see the face of God in a direct and unmediated way.

But it may be objected that, according to the doctrine of the Holy Spirit, we do have an unmediated experience of God. Isn't that what the Holy Spirit is—the immediate presence of God? This is an issue of great theological subtlety. On one hand, the Holy Spirit does seem to be the presence of God within us in an unusually intimate way. Indeed, the Spirit seems to know us better than we know ourselves (Romans 8:26-27). On the other hand, there is great danger in worship that focuses principally on the presence of the Spirit. The danger is that such worship will manifest a theology of glory that has forgotten the theology of the cross. This was apparently the situation in Corinth. So impressed were they with the gifts of the Spirit as a sign of realized eschatology that at least some of them believed they had transcended any need of Jesus—hence their practice of affirming, in the Spirit, "Jesus is cursed" (1 Corinthians 12:3). The way forward from this dilemma is to see that the Holy Spirit is in fact a principle of mediation. The Gospel of John is our most important source in this matter. This Gospel is clear that the Holy Spirit takes up the mediatorial role of Jesus Christ. Jesus mediates to his disciples the knowledge of God the Father. But, once the physical presence of Jesus is removed, the Holy Spirit continues that ministry of mediation. The Holy Spirit teaches disciples everything and reminds them of what Jesus said (14:26), testifies on behalf of Jesus (15:26), and will glorify Jesus by declaring to disciples his message (16:14). All this makes it clear that the Holy Spirit mediates the knowledge of Jesus to us just as Jesus mediated the knowledge of the Father. So, although the Spirit is the full presence of God within us, it would be a mistake to separate the presence of the Spirit from the mediated presence of Jesus and the Father. On trinitarian grounds we affirm that the Spirit is not the Spirit without the Father and the Son. The presence of the Spirit, no matter how immediate, is always the mediated presence of the Father and Son in the Spirit. Authentic worship, therefore, is not the enjoyment of the unmediated presence of the Spirit. It is instead allowing the Spirit to bring us into the presence of the Father through Jesus Christ.

Another manifestation of the finitude of worship lies in the fact that worship is offered by human beings with limited capacities. Paul testified to this fact with his observation that we do not know how to pray as we ought, so that we need the Spirit to intercede for us according to the will of God (Romans 8:26-27). Our inability to pray properly is not always a result of sin. It may also (as in this passage) result from our limited capacity to know. Many activities in worship, including the sermon and the prayers, labor under this same result of humankind's essential finitude. Our emotional constitution likewise has a bearing on our ability to worship. Those whose cares and anxieties intrude unavoidably on their thoughts can hardly help allowing them to affect the degree to which they can worship with wholehearted attention. Human and bodily experiences such as fatigue likewise affect our capacity to worship God with the eagerness and attention that are proper. As Acts reports, even a sermon by the foremost theologian of the first century can induce slumber, as the unfortunate Eutychus discovered (Acts 20:7-12).

The finitude of human worship also shows up in the tension between spontaneity and order. There has been, in the American churches, a long-standing discussion, often conducted with great rancor, on the question of the proper balance between freedom and spontaneity and order and decorum. Unable to agree, churches have organized around worship styles, ranging from High Church, liturgically oriented worship to informal charismatic worship. Not all of this is due to sin. Human beings find it difficult to find and sustain a balance. Moreover, because of the limitations of knowledge and wisdom, there is an inevitable diversity of opinion on what is most important about the form of worship. Because of these difficulties, worship is subject to a variety of problems, from the deadening tedium of empty formality to the artificial attempts at sustaining excitement and spontaneity of some forms of revivalism. Although we may expect, in the eschatological kingdom of God, a perfect harmony of order and spontaneity, in the midst of history we must accustom ourselves to mere anticipations of that harmony because of our finite condition.

The Practice of Worship in Community

Community

To students of religion, the concept *communal worship* is nearly redundant. Throughout human history, communal worship has been the norm, whether in the context of the family or of the nation. It is, in fact, individual worship that needs explaining. And yet, our culture testifies to a pervasive feeling that communal worship is at best optional and that individual worship—worshiping God in one's own way—is the norm.

This feeling arises in part from our culture's diminished sense of God's transcendence and an increased sense of God's immanence. When God is regarded as transcendent—holy and unapproachable—then it is natural to look to mediators (such as clergy, sacraments, sacred places) to help us connect to God. But when God is regarded mostly in terms of immanence and is thought to be not only present everywhere, but easily accessible by all, then there is no special need of mediators and mediating religious institutions. A possible exception to this phenomenon is the popularity—especially among teenage Christians—of worship services that emphasize contemporary music. The popularity of this movement means that attendance at these worship services can be quite large. These services certainly have an impressive communal aspect. At the same time, the fact that numbers of people are worshiping at the same time in the same place does not in itself imply that communal worship is taking place. Individualistic worship can occur alone and also in the midst of a vast crowd of fellow worshipers. Moreover, the intentional similarity between these worship services and rock concerts encourages the observation that the focus is on individual experiences instead of on congregational communion. Of course, congregations offering youth-oriented services are not the only churches that must face this problem. In the individualistic atmosphere of American culture, even highly liturgical worship may overlay a congregation, each member of which is approaching God as an individual. What is required for authentic communal worship is not only a congregation of worshipers, but also a communion among them such that they are worshiping as the one body of Christ and not as so many individuals who happen to be in the same location. This is the problem that Paul addressed in 1 Corinthians 12–14. The Corinthians were indeed worshiping as a congregation. But their worship was not truly the worship of a community. Each insisted on exercising his or her spiritual gift oblivious to the needs of the congregation. Their worship services were not that of a body, but of an aggregate of individuals. So, it is a welcome sign that young Christians are congregating for worship. But leaders must diligently pursue communion and unity in hopes that the worshiping community will indeed be a community and not an aggregate.

The feeling that communal worship is optional is occasioned also by the fact that American society has, since the 1960s, witnessed a decline in the public's trust in institutions of all sorts, including the church. Although the Christian churches never had as strong a grip on the public's spirituality as is sometimes imagined, its grip seems to be weakening in comparison with a generation or two ago. Americans increasingly seem comfortable with the proposition that no one—and especially no institution—has a monopoly on religious truth. With a decline in the church's prestige and influence goes a decline in the public's conviction that the proper way to worship God is under the auspices of the institutional church.

Finally, this feeling arises from our culture's orientation toward the consumer and the consumer's convenience. One implication of this consumer orientation is that church is thought to be an instrument useful for the realization of individual goals and as a voluntary association of like-minded people, united in the pursuit of similar goals. In this view, the church's worship is evaluated in terms of utility: it is valuable to the extent that it contributes to the individual's needs, whether spiritual or social. The assembly of worshipers occurs because people with similar needs find it useful to congregate.

A different aspect of the consumer orientation of worship is the phenomenon and popularity of television ministries. Although these ministries perform a valuable service, they do reinforce the tendency toward individualistic worship, in which required commitment and sacrifice are minimal and in which convenience is maximal. The problem with the television-consumer approach is that the worshiper is often reduced to being a purely receptive subject and is no longer an active participant in worship. It may be objected that the viewer's worship is still active, having been transformed from traditional forms of activity—singing, greeting, confessing, and so on—into purely inward forms such as affirming inwardly what is being portrayed on the screen. But this objection begs the question by assuming that this transformation is merely a change and not also a loss. What is needed today is a recovery of the importance of the people of God, seen to be a community, gathering to praise and petition God publicly. But this is unlikely to happen without an understanding of why this is a vital part of authentic Christianity.

A place to begin is 1 Peter 2. This chapter portrays the church as "a holy priesthood, to offer spiritual sacrifices acceptable to God through Jesus Christ" (v. 5) and "a chosen race, a royal priesthood, a holy nation,

God's own people, in order that you may proclaim the mighty acts of him who called you out of darkness into his marvelous light" (v. 9). In these verses the church is expressly likened to Israel, whose distinguishing mark was its worship of God and whose members were to live in a state of priestly holiness. But portraying the church as the new Israel does not in itself overcome the individualism and consumer orientation of our worship today. After all, the individualistic misinterpretation of the spiritual priesthood of believers (whereby each of us acts as our own priest in approaching God) is still quite popular. What is additionally needed is an understanding of the church as a called community—the *ecclesia*. First Peter affirms of the church that "once you were not a people, but now you are God's people" (2:10). This is offered as a commentary on the preceding assertion: God has "called [the church] out of darkness into his marvelous light" (v. 9). These two verses state that to be *called* is to become a *people*. It is not that individuals are called and then formed into a people. It is rather that God's call is a people-forming event and that individuals are to be incorporated into the formed people of God. If we ask about the purpose of this calling, the answer is stated in terms of worship: offering spiritual sacrifices (2:5) and proclaiming the mighty acts God (2:9). To be the *ecclesia* is to be called by God and thereby constituted a people for the purpose of worshiping God. These verses in 1 Peter show us convincingly that the people of God exist for the sake of worship and that worship has its natural context in the gathering—the *ecclesia*—of God's people. None of this is to say that there is something inauthentic about individuals worshiping God in their solitude, perhaps in prayer or adoration. But in our current cultural situation, in which individualism and consumerism are such powerful forces, it may be helpful to remind ourselves of 1 Peter's emphases.

There are other theological themes that support the centrality of the communal dimension of worship. One of these is the sacramental principle. It is a conviction, deeply embedded in the Christian faith, that human beings cannot of themselves come into the presence of God. In the Bible, this conviction is expressed in the Bible's affirmation that "no one has ever seen God" (John 1:18) and that God "dwells in unapproachable light" (1 Timothy 6:16). Even Moses, who above all humans was said to know God intimately, was able to see only God's back, not God's face (Exodus 33:17-23). The knowledge of God, then, cannot be a matter of direct seeing. Consequently, we require something to mediate the presence of God to us. This is the basis of the doctrine of the incarnation, which affirms that, in Jesus Christ, God has mediated to us the knowledge of God. That is why in John's Gospel Jesus asserts that "whoever has seen me has seen the Father" (14:9). In the knowledge of God, God is both the mediator and the object mediated. Now that the visible presence of Jesus has been taken away, the Holy Spirit mediates Jesus to us.

But the sacramental principle goes beyond the knowledge of God generally considered. It pertains as well to worship. In worship God becomes present to us by means of finite things instituted for that purpose. Take, for example, the Lord's Supper. In spite of the historical controversies over the meaning of this sacrament, all traditions are agreed on the general point that this sacrament mediates to us the presence of God, whether that presence is conceived of as the real presence of Christ's body or as Christ's presence to us through our recollection or in some other way. Likewise, virtually every Christian community has an official who presides over worship and has authority to administer the sacraments. This official may be formally regarded as a mediator, as in those churches with a strong concept of the priesthood, or only informally regarded as a mediator and in a weakened sense, as in evangelical and charismatic churches. But even in these latter churches, the pastor performs mediatorial functions, such as offering the pastoral prayer and authorizing the administration of the sacraments.

Meditation on the sacramental principle will disclose to us the importance of the communal dimension of worship and the fundamental problem with any tendency toward making the individual practice of worship the norm. An exclusive or near-exclusive emphasis on individual worship rests on the premise that authentic worship of God requires no mediation—no minister, no sacraments, and, therefore, no community. A recognition of the principle of mediation requires worship to be at least minimally communal.

But the mediating aspect of the worshiping community goes beyond the office of the minister and the administration of sacraments. It includes as well what I referred to previously as the formative function of worship. The formative function is the worshiping community's capacity to mold us into Christlikeness. This capacity is actualized in many ways, such as in the sermon, the reading of Scripture, confessions of sin and professions of faith, and music. In all these ways and others, we receive from the worshiping community influences that, if assimilated, help shape us into a Christian way of life.

Authority

The communal dimension of worship raises the contested issue of pastoral authority and communal discipline. Historically, there have been two central issues: first, the fact that the right to administer sacraments has been limited to ordained clergy, and, second, the fact that the sacraments have been one of the principal means of church discipline. It does not take much imagination to see that these factors in church authority are highly problematic in our culture today and why that is so. In a culture that sees little need for mediation in religion, the minister is not regarded as necessary and the sacraments are no longer thought to be a necessary means of bringing about the presence of God. As a result, the sacraments are not as operative in church discipline as they once were, and the role and importance of the ordained minister has been questioned. As these words are being written, a few Roman Catholic bishops are threatening to exclude Catholic politicians from the Eucharist if they are complicit in policies that are contrary to church teaching. But no one really expects this threat to change the behavior of these politicians; in today's climate, it is felt that one can still be a Catholic in good standing even if he or she is not able to participate in the Eucharist. Naturally, exercising discipline is even more difficult in those church traditions and denominations that place less emphasis on the Eucharist, for they thus lack an important instrument for holding their members accountable to Christian standards of behavior.

Other disputed questions today on the subject of authority and discipline include the authority of preaching and the role of clergy. Concern about the authority of preaching seems muted these days, at least in comparison with the frenzy of concern associated with the biblical theology movement of the 1950s and 1960s. In our postmodern climate, there does not seem to be much patience for Karl Barth's conviction that preaching is (when God chooses to make it) one form that the word of God takes. Preaching seems instead to be regarded as performing the sociological and ecclesiological function of contributing to the formation of disciples. For this purpose, to be sure, a certain authority of preacher and sermon is required—the authority of faithfulness to the ideal of the Christian life, of which preaching is an instrument. But the time does not seem propitious for a revival of concern about the authority of preaching regarded as a proclamation of the word of God. The office of the minister, however, continues to come into question as a result of the emphasis given in recent decades to the role of the laity in worship and in the larger life of the church. By now the slogan "every Christian is a minister" is well known. When every Christian is a minister, then inevitably the purpose and distinctiveness of an ordained ministry is called into question. In our current situation, in which institutions and hierarchical organizations enjoy much less confidence than in previous generations, the theology of ministry—and especially of its mediatorial function—will have to be continually revisited.

The Practice of Worship in a Fallen World

The church and its worship exist eschatologically. This means that the church and its worship are an anticipation of the fullness of God's kingdom. But, as an anticipation, the church exists at the same time under the conditions of sin. The church's worship is not unaffected by the fallenness of the world. Because of this, worship is subject to certain distortions.

Within the Bible, the most prominent distortion of worship due to sin is idolatry. This is the thrust of Romans 1:18-25, in which the entire Gentile world is indicted for its worship of creatures instead of the creator. It is a theme also enunciated repeatedly in the Old Testament prophetic tradition. But this prominence in the Bible may lull us into a false sense of security on the grounds that we today do not overtly offer worship to created things and do not bow down to images and idols. There are, however, other, more subtle forms of idolatrous worship. One is syncretism, joining worship of God to worship of other beings, on the principle that worship of one god supplements worship of another god. This was the problem with the Colossian church. For reasons not clear to us, they believed in the wisdom of supplementing devotion to Christ with devotion to other beings, a devotion apparently involving the worship of angels, visions, and ascetic discipline (Colossians 2). Against this Paul argued that the fullness of divinity dwelled in Christ (2:9), that disciples attain spiritual fullness in Christ (2:10), that in the cross God had disarmed all other spiritual powers (2:15), and that disciples have died to the spirits of the universe (2:20). Although we today are not likely to mix worship of God with worship of spirits and angels, there is a permanent temptation to supplement existence in Christ with other sources of spiritual well-being. Hence the adage that anything—money, pleasure, and so on—can be one's god and the object of one's worship. It is fear of syncretism that has generated the iconoclastic spirit in Christian history, whether in the eighth-century Byzantine church or the sixteenth-century Reformation. Admittedly, such iconoclasm has often gone too far and overlooked the importance of art and other material aids to worship. However, we should acknowledge that its fear has a basis in fact.

The other main distortion of worship due to sin is the phenomenon of Christians divided because of differences in worship. The most dramatic manifestation of this distortion is the division between Roman Catholics and Protestants, or, to be more specific, the fact that the Roman Catholic Church is not in full communion with Protestant churches and consequently does not sanction joint worship. All agree that this state of affairs is unsatisfactory. It contradicts the creedal affirmation of the church's unity. But under the conditions of sin, actual union, or at least communion and joint worship, has not been possible. A less dramatic manifestation of division has resulted in recent years from the increasing use of so-called contemporary music in worship and the adoption of greater modes of informality in worship. This phenomenon, born from a laudable interest in evangelism and the revitalization of the church, has regrettably produced a wealth of resentment and, in a few cases, actual division. Although the issue itself is simply one of strategy and is not a result of sin—after all, the church has in its history used a variety of styles of music—the inability of Christians to actualize the church's unity in this contentious matter surely results at least in part from the distorting effects of sin on us all.

Worship and Participation in God

Worship is a service that we render to God. However, this does not mean that worship is a merely human deed. It is true that human beings can do things that pertain to worship. We can congregate, sing, proclaim, pray, and so on. But as the Gospel of John affirms, those who worship God must "worship in spirit [or Spirit] and truth" (4:24). In theological language, worship must be trinitarian if it is to be authentic.

First, it is instructive to note that there is, in the New Testament, a trinitarian rhetoric that bears on worship. According to Ephesians 2:18, *through* Christ we have access *in* one Spirit *to* the Father. Although many New Testament passages abbreviate this pattern by omitting the Spirit, this text should function for us paradigmatically. It states that it is through Christ as we are in the Spirit that we may approach God the Father. Romans 16:27 offers a truncated version—"To the only wise God, through Jesus Christ, to whom be the glory forever"—as does Ephesians 5:20—"[give] thanks to God the Father at all times and for everything in the name of our Lord Jesus Christ." These and similar texts establish a pattern that can inform our understanding of worship in vital ways. All acts of worship, whether praise or thanks or petition, are to be offered to God the Father. But they are to be offered through Jesus Christ or in the name of Jesus. This is because we are the body of Christ and because Christ is the heavenly priest who leads our worship of God the Father. Finally, worship is to be offered in the Spirit. This means, first, that worship presupposes our sanctification by the Spirit. The church, called to worship, must be holy if it is to approach the holy God. It is in and through the Holy Spirit that we consecrate ourselves and our acts to God and thus become the holy people of God. It means, second, that worship is possible only as, in the power of the Spirit, we are drawn out of our mundane existence and our immersion in the fallen world. Without the Spirit, our prayers remain unconsecrated—mere human words. Without the Spirit, the sermon is a speech. Unless we are in the Spirit, we cannot, like John the Revelator, hear the loud voice like a trumpet (Revelation 1:10). In the words of Karl Barth, the Holy Spirit is the possibility and actuality of revelation. Without the Spirit, there is no revelation and no presence of God.

Second, it is because of the trinitarian structure of worship that worship is an ecstatic experience and that it is an act whereby we ethically transcend the world. By *ecstatic*, I mean that worship, although (as argued previously) a bodily act performed under the conditions of finitude, is an encounter with the living God. Admittedly, most worship today lacks the dramatic quality that biblical reports of encountering God portray. Nonetheless, the Christian church believes that in such mundane acts as hearing and tasting and singing, the worshipers encounter God the Father, through Jesus Christ, in the power of the Spirit. To worship is to be drawn from the mundane into the divine even while dwelling in the mundane. It is to transform the mundane until it is no longer mundane but is instead an instrument of God's grace, even while its outward form remains mundane. In worship we are lifted above ourselves and addressed by God. Here we find our true being as we become hearers and doers of the Word.

A third aspect of the trinitarian dimension of worship appears when we consider the idea of communion. In worship we have communion with God and with one another. But we get a bit more insight if we draw upon recent theological reflection that points to the grounding of communion in the trinitarian being of God. Today, we are encouraged to think of the trinitarian life of God as a life of communion, in which the trinitarian persons exist in and through one another. It is not that the persons exist in their own right and then enter into communion. It is instead that communion is the mode of being of the divine persons. Worship, then—our communion with God and with one another—is in fact our participation in God's trinitarian life of communion. In worship we live the divine life, at least if our worship is truly an act of communion. Naturally, under the conditions of sin it is never fully an act of communion, for sin divides. But our worship can nonetheless be an anticipation of the perfect communion that will be ours in the eschatological kingdom of God. Even as an anticipation, such fragmentary communion is a participation in God, a sharing in the fellowship between the Father and Son through the Spirit.

The implication of this insight is that our communion with one another should mirror the communion that is God's trinitarian life. The church is, in fact, this communion of saints. It is the togetherness, in the Spirit, of the people of God. That is why Paul was scandalized by the behavior of the Corinthians in their eucharistic meals (1 Corinthians 11:17-22). Division within the body of Christ means that the significance of the Lord's Supper has not been grasped, with the result that the Supper is consumed in an unworthy manner (11:27). The truth is that the Supper is both cause and sign of unity: "The bread that we break, is it not a sharing in the body of Christ? Because there is one bread, we who are many are one body, for we all partake of the one bread" (10:16-17). Differently stated, the church is never more the communion of saints than when it becomes one body by feeding on Christ.

We can fill out this trinitarian insight by emphasizing that the church is the body of Christ. Jesus Christ was the extension of God's trinitarian life into history. He was the coming of the triune God to humankind. The life of Jesus, including his communion with God the Father in the power of the Spirit, was the ensemble of trinitarian relations played out on the plane of history. But that means that the church, at least insofar as it is the body of Christ and enlivened by the Spirit, is likewise the life of the Trinity in history. The church likewise is the coming of the triune God to humankind. But this truth must be actualized in practice. The church must actually be an extension of God's trinitarian life. It does so by participating in that trinitarian life. But since that life is a life of communion, the church actualizes its participation in God by truly being a communion of saints. Worship is one of the principal means by which the church actualizes its participation in God. In worship, the church is drawn into the Son's communion with the Father, and each member extends this communion to the others. In turn, the church, through its evangelistic activity, offers this communion to the whole world. Worship, therefore, is the basis of evangelism. Evangelism has for its purpose the incorporation of all people into the people of God, who have been called to "offer spiritual sacrifices acceptable to God through Jesus Christ" and to "proclaim the mighty acts of him who called you out of darkness into his marvelous light" (1 Peter 2:9).

Concluding Meditative Prayer

We praise you, our God, who are worthy to receive glory, honor, and power, who created all things and from all things receives praise. May we be like the living creatures and elders in heaven who worship you forever and ever. You demand our worship, although it is by your Spirit that we worship. You command us to worship you and it is our pleasure and good to do so. We lift up our eyes to you, our God, high and lifted up, even though you are closer to us than any can be. You accept our words and acts of worship, even though no word is fit and no act adequate. Blessed are those who pray to you, lifting up holy hands without anger or argument. Blessed are those who offer to you an acceptable worship with reverence and awe. But we confess to you, our Lord, that we have forgotten and dishonored your name. We have failed to make the whole of life an act of worship. We have lifted up unworthy things as objects of our worship. Have mercy on us, our God, and preserve us safe from the spirit of idolatry. Remind us always of your greatness. Reform our bent toward forgetfulness. Make us, we pray, a kingdom of priests and fit us to offer spiritual sacrifices to you. Help us, our God, to join the chorus of creatures throughout your world that worship you. Give us voice to praise you. Grant, Father, that in the power of your Spirit we may participate in Jesus' glorification of you. May we always prove worthy of our calling, and may we forever worship you in Spirit and in truth. We pray for those who do not yet worship you as they ought and for those who, with stubborn heart, refuse to worship you. Draw them by your grace to the knowledge and love of you, and lead them into eternal life.

You, our God, whom the entire world worships, we praise.
We praise
    the Father, to whom all worship is given,
    through the eternal Son, our great high priest in the heavenly temple
        who lives forever to intercede for us,
    in the power of the Holy Spirit, inspirer and source of our worship, who
        sanctifies and bears our offerings to God.
We praise you, holy Trinity, beginning and end of our worship.

Sources Consulted and Recommended

Althaus, Paul. *The Theology of Martin Luther*. Translated by Robert Schulz. Philadelphia: Fortress Press, 1966.

Augustine. *Confessions*. Translated by R. S. Pine-Coffin. Baltimore: Penguin Books, 1976.

Built of Living Stones: Art, Architecture, and Worship: Guidelines of the National Conference of Catholic Bishops. Available at http://www.nccbuscc.org/liturgy/livingstones.htm.

Clapp, Rodney. "Tacit Holiness: The Importance of Bodies and Habits in Doing Church." In *Embodied Holiness: Toward a Corporate Theology of Spiritual Growth*, edited by Samuel M. Powell and Michael E. Lodahl. Downers Grove, IL: InterVarsity Press, 1999.

Collins, John N. *Are All Christians Ministers?* Collegeville, MN: The Liturgical Press, 1992. Discusses the important question of the status of ordained clergy in today's church.

St. John of Damascus. *On the Divine Images*. Translated by David Anderson. Crestwood, NY: St. Vladimir's Seminary Press, 1980. An enduring statement about the importance of the sensual dimension of Christian worship.

The Epistles of St. Clement of Rome and St. Ignatius of Antioch. Translated by James Aloysius Kleist. Vol. 1, *Ancient Christian Writers*. New York: Newman Press, 1946. The letters of Ignatius are among the first and most powerful statements about the monarchical bishop and his authority.

Holper, J. Frederick. "As Often as You Eat This Bread and Drink the Cup." *Interpretation* 48, no. 1 (1994): 61-73.

Meyers, Ruth A. "The Promise and Perils of Liturgical Change." *Anglican Theological Review* 86, no. 1 (2004): 103-14.

Morrill, Bruce T., ed. *Bodies of Worship: Explorations in Theory and Practice*. Collegeville, MN: The Liturgical Press, 1999.

Taves, Ann. *Fits, Trances, & Visions: Experiencing Religion and Explaining Experience from Wesley to James*. Princeton, NJ: Princeton University Press,

1999. A very clear exposition of some leading aspects of the American revivalist tradition.

Tillard, J. M. R. *Flesh of the Church, Flesh of Christ: At the Source of the Ecclesiology of Communion.* Collegeville, MN: The Liturgical Press, 2001. An important statement about the centrality of communion as the key to understanding both the church and its worship.

Torrance, James B. *Worship, Community and the Triune God of Grace.* Downers Grove, IL: InterVarsity Press, 1996. A provocative affirmation of the trinitarian character of Christian worship.

Waznak, Robert P. "The Catechism and the Sunday Homily." *America* 171, no. 12 (1994): 18-21.

DISCIPLINE

Discipline has many meanings. A word that encompasses them and that is prominent in the New Testament is *paideia*. From the rich range of meanings of *paideia*, my exposition will separate out two main ideas: discipline as formative practices that shape Christian character and discipline as corrective practices that seek to restore believers to the path of righteousness if they have wandered.

The Practice of Discipline

The Christian life is a demanding life. No understanding of God's grace should blunt the force of this observation. Although God's grace is required if we are to live as we ought, this grace does not obviate the necessity of striving. If we had any doubt about this, a review of the New Testament would soon convince us. Pertinent to this truth are those passages that liken the Christian life to athletic training, notably 1 Corinthians 9:25-27: "Athletes exercise self-control in all things; they do it to receive a perishable wreath. . . . So I do not run aimlessly, nor do I box as though beating the air; but I punish my body and enslave it, so that after proclaiming to others I myself should not be disqualified." Verses like this testify to the exacting character of the Christian life. We are to be like athletes who exercise self-control and punish the body so that the Christian life may be authentically lived. The need of discipline arises from our embodied status. Because we are creatures existing bodily, the satisfaction of appetites must be controlled, desires must be scrutinized, habits must be formed, and practices must be shaped.

Besides the need of self-control, the athletic metaphor reinforces the point that the Christian life is something that requires practice. Characteristics such as generosity and love are not the sorts of things that are acquired instantaneously and miraculously. Even if the motivation of our actions is suddenly transformed in a dramatic conversion, learning how to act appropriately as a Christian takes time to learn. We must observe others we regard as exemplars and imitate their actions. We must learn how to discern the particulars of moral situations so that we may know what appropriate action is. Above all, we must practice so that our practice of the Christian life does not atrophy. The Christian life does not consist only in the desire to love or the capacity to love. It consists in the practice of love. Lack of practice can well mean a diminishing of our capacity.

World-Transcendence and World-Participation

As I have noted, the Christian life contains two impulses, one toward spiritually and ethically transcending the world and the other toward spiritually and ethically participating in the world. These two impulses appear in *paideia*. On one hand, Christian discipline along with its *telos*, Christian character, are the means by which we overcome the world. On the other hand, Christian discipline is not an end in itself and does not aim at a strictly otherworldly goal, but instead aims at producing Christian character in the world and, in an important sense, *for* the world.

THE IMPULSE TOWARD TRANSCENDING THE WORLD

As a means of overcoming or transcending the world, *paideia* is principally self-denial. The world that is transcended in Christian discipline is the fallen, sinful world that lives in and through us. What must be overcome is the power of that world as it is manifest within us. So *paideia* is not about denying my physiological being or my psychological self. They need redemption, not denial. Instead, *paideia* is the denial of my participation in the fallen world and of the false self that has arisen under the power of sin. This false self must be crucified with Christ and buried with Christ into death. Two New Testament passages guide our consideration of the world-transcending character of Christian discipline:

> If any want to become my followers, let them deny themselves and take up their cross and follow me. For those who want to save their life will lose it, and those who lose their life for my sake, and for the sake of the gospel, will save it. (Mark 8:34-35)

> The grace of God has appeared, bringing salvation to all, training [from *paideuo*] us to renounce impiety and worldly passions, and in the present age to live lives that are self-controlled, upright, and godly, while we wait for the blessed hope and the manifestation of the glory of our great God and Savior, Jesus Christ. (Titus 2:11-13)

The first passage presents, in unmistakable terms, one of the central paradoxes of the Christian faith: that our clinging to life brings death, while the release of life that comes from self-denial brings eternal life. The paradox is at least partially resolved once we realize that the life that we are to deny and lose is not our true life. Our true life is found in Christ. The life that we are to deny—to crucify with Christ—is nothing more than the fallen world in the distorted guise of a human life. In denying *this* self we are losing nothing of true importance, even if (because it is the self that we have fashioned for ourselves) it is painful for us to lose it. The second passage gives us a bit more sense of what self-denial entails: living in a self-controlled *(sōphronōs)*, upright, and godly manner while renouncing (in Greek, "denying") impiety and worldly passions (or desires). We note here the prominence of self-control and desire. Self-denial, as the New Testament and human experience show, ultimately comes down to dealing effectively with desires that are not in conformity with godliness. In the moral world in which the New Testament was written, dealing effectively with desire was a matter of living temperately, that is, living with *sōphrosunē*.

In the Christian tradition, *sōphrosunē* is associated with asceticism and mortification—putting to death the deeds of the body. Asceticism, although not distinctively Christian, has been a perennially Christian response to the call to *sōphrosunē* and self-denial. Although asceticism has a unfavorable image these days, there is no denying that there are ascetic tendencies in the New Testament. Matthew 19:12 is instructive. Its mention of those who have made themselves eunuchs for the sake of the kingdom of heaven appears to refer to those, like Jesus, who have undertaken the celibate life on behalf of the gospel. Paul too seemed to favor celibacy ("I wish that all were as I myself am" [1 Corinthians 7:7]). More broadly, in 1 Thessalonians 4:4-5, Paul urged his readers to control their bodies (or, in an alternative translation, "acquire their wives") in holiness and honor and to avoid the passion of desire that characterized the Gentile world. Beyond the issue of celibacy, the New Testament writers certainly wanted Christians to live carefully. This point is evident from the sorts of things they condemned: greed and envy (Romans 1:29), fornication (1 Timothy 1:10), being a lover of self, being a lover of money, being a lover of pleasure, lacking self-control (2 Timothy 3:2-4), drunkenness (1 Corinthians 6:10), and licentiousness (Galatians 5:19), to name a few.

At the same time, the New Testament has a cautious attitude toward certain interpretations of asceticism. First Timothy expressly criticizes unnamed teachers who were forbidding marriage and were demanding abstinence from certain foods (4:3). In response to this teaching, the letter reminds us that marriage and food are among the good things of God's creation and may be rightly used with thanksgiving as they are sanctified by God's word and by prayer (4:4-5). Colossians likewise counters an ascetic teaching by declaring regulations about food and severe treatment of the body to be merely human inventions that, although appearing to possess wisdom, are in fact useless (2:20-23). We may conclude that the New Testament gives a qualified approval of ascetic practices. Christians must certainly live in a self-controlled fashion, but must always remember that what is being denied in self-denial and what is being spiritually transcended is not the world of God's creation, but instead the fallen world of sin.

In light of this, there is value in asking *why* self-denial and ascetic practices are instrumental in the formation of Christian character. The answer is that, although salvation is a gift of God's transforming grace, a transformed Christian character is not given to us all at once and without effort. Although God's grace is supernatural, its effect is not instantaneous. This is the important truth of Philippians 1:6: God "who began a good work among you will bring it to completion by the day of Jesus Christ." Using other terms, we may say that, since it is a part of our created nature to develop physiologically and psychologically, the obtaining of a Christian character is likewise a developmental process. This is the basic insight that underlies the modern Christian education movement. God's grace acts upon us but in ways that correspond to our created nature and not in contradiction to that nature. As already noted, even Jesus learned obedience through what he suffered (Hebrews 5:8). The developmental character of human nature seems inescapable, even with respect to the Christian life. As a result of this developmental character and because becoming a Christian means becoming free from sin, Christians must practice self-denial.

THE IMPULSE TOWARD PARTICIPATING IN THE WORLD

Paideia in the form of self-denial is an exercise in spiritually transcending the world. But it is important to remember that it is not a rejection of God's creation. One way of grasping this point is to note that although Christian discipline includes a disciplining of the body and its desires, the purpose of such discipline is not to escape from the body, but rather to consecrate the body. We are to present our bodies as instruments of righteousness (Romans 6:13) and as holy, living sacrifices (Romans 12:1). The purpose of mortification and ascetic practices is not to debilitate the body so that it no longer hinders the soul, but instead to make the body fit as a temple of the Holy Spirit (1 Corinthians 6:19). Christian discipline, then, is redemptive. It aims at restoring us to the condition of holiness by the purgative activity of self-denial and asceticism. Discipline is thus a way of participating in the world of God's creation, for it is an affirmation of the body and the embodied character of our existence. It affirms that the body is redeemable and that it can be a fit instrument in God's service.

The Old Testament reveals a broader way in which discipline expresses the Christian impulse toward participating in the world. Especially important here are the opening chapters of Proverbs, with their teaching about the benefits of receiving instruction. As Proverbs represents it, the goal of life is to become wise. Instruction (*torah*, the equivalent of *paideia*) is the necessary means of becoming wise. For those who obtain wisdom, there is no end of blessing: living securely, "without dread of disaster" (1:33); "[understanding] righteousness and justice and equity, every good path" (2:9); being delivered "from the way of evil, from those who speak perversely" (2:12) and from the adulteress (2:16-19); abiding in the land (2:21); enjoying length of days and abundant welfare (3:2); having favor and reputation in the sight of God and people (3:4); possessing long life, riches, and honor (3:16), and many more. Wisdom and instruction, in other words, enable one to live well in human community and to negotiate successfully the trials that attend human life. Proverbs presents a frank this-worldly portrait of wisdom and of the blessings of wisdom. Of course, we have to make allowance for the overly optimistic theology that we find in Proverbs, with its simplistic teaching that the righteous will be blessed and the wicked will suffer. Nonetheless, Proverbs is the Bible's testimony to the truth that instruction and discipline along with the character that they produce are congruent with the world of God's creation. Not even the distortions of sin can destroy the residual goodness of God's creation. Because of this, Christian discipline and character are at home in the created world, even if they are not at home in the world that human sin has fashioned. To undergo Christian discipline is to participate in the world that God has created and that God is recreating.

There is another sense in which Christian discipline is a mode of participating in the world. It is that Christian discipline has as its purpose our existence not only *in* the world, but also *for* the world. The Christian life is a life for others. But, as John Calvin astutely pointed out, "In seeking to benefit one's neighbor, how difficult it is to do one's duty! Unless you give up all thought of self and, so to speak, get out of yourself, you will accomplish nothing here."[1] If we are truly to love one another, then we must, in Paul's words, "Do nothing from selfish ambition or conceit, but in humility regard others as better than [ourselves]." We must "look not to [our] own interests, but to the interests of others" (Philippians 2:3-4). In this way, we will be following the pattern of Jesus Christ, who emptied himself and took the form of a slave (2:7). But this is not something that comes naturally to us. It requires the slow patient work of the discipline of formation. And this discipline aims at enabling us to love the neighbor. In this way, Christian discipline arises out of the impulse toward participating in the world. Discipline is not simply for our own development, but also for those whom God has created.

DISCIPLINE UNDER THE CONDITION OF FINITUDE

The embodied and practical character of Christian discipline has another implication, namely, that the process of discipline, both in its formative and corrective aspects, is subject to the limiting conditions of finitude. These limitations are not due to human sin, but simply to the fact that we are finite creatures. We find obstacles in the performance of *paideia*, obstacles that affect our attaining Christian character and living the Christian life. Three obstacles that are prominent are ignorance, weariness, and inattention.

Because of human ignorance, many aspects of formative and corrective discipline fail to be as effective as they might otherwise have been. For example, the pastor's teaching role is dependent on the pastor's knowledge and on the reliability of the sources available for preaching and teaching. These resources include the general state of scholarship. Every pastor labors under the limitations of his or her theological education. Attempts to expand on one's knowledge are praiseworthy, but ultimately we encounter the same sort of limitation—biblical and theological scholarship is the work of human beings who inevitably bring their intellectual limitations as well as their prejudices to their studies. This is an inescapable fact of pastoral life. Of course, such limitation does not justify laziness in the pastor's study. But it should remind us that pastors and the intellectual community that supports their work labor with manifest limitations of insight and imagination. The pastoral duty of exhortation suffers from human finitude in a different way. Such exhortation is a matter of providing the right and needed word at the right time. But we are often ignorant about the right time and circumstances and may well be perplexed about the right word. Ignorance likewise besets the congregation's intercession in the case of sin and the exercise of corrective discipline. As the letter of 2 Corinthians shows us, it is easy to misjudge how to deal with sin and misdeeds. What is the proper balance of harshness and leniency? How do we distinguish the sins that lead to death from those sins that do not? Any congregation that takes its formative and corrective responsibilities seriously will find common human ignorance as a consequence of our embodied condition and as an obstacle to the exercise of those responsibilities.

Ignorance also plagues the congregation's exercise of the gifts and offices of the Spirit. Sadly, the mere fact that these gifts and offices are from the Spirit does not ensure their intelligent employment. With the best of intentions, they can be exercised in an unhelpful or even counterproductive way. Finally, ignorance affects the practice of self-denial by making judgment difficult. Self-denial involves countless decisions about matters of food, drink, rest, dress, and the acquiring and use of consumer goods. Consideration must be given to the intrinsic good of these things, their instrumental value, and the spiritual dangers that they may represent. But such consideration requires knowledge—usually more than we possess through casual contact with the world. In the absence of an earnest attempt on our part to become informed, all or part of the spiritual dimension of these things may escape us. That is why the New Testament reminds us of the need to discern God's will in Romans 12:2 and Ephesians 5:10, for at least in the area of self-denial, it is not easy to know.

The effectiveness of formative and corrective discipline is compromised also by human weariness. The effectiveness of pastoral teaching and exhortation may be diminished either because of physical fatigue or because of the weariness that results from exasperation with a recalcitrant congregation and the mental stress of overwhelming situations. The same is true for the exercise of the gifts and offices of the Spirit—their effectiveness as tools of formative discipline are compromised by the other demands made on us as spouses, employees, and parents. In the frenetic society we have created, in which unrestrained busyness is the norm, the energy available for exercising one's gifts among the people of God is diminished. The discipline of devotional practices likewise suffers. We fail to mature as Christians as we ought because we lack the physical and emotional strength necessary to engage meaningfully in devotional practices and self-denial.

Finally, our finitude means that sometimes we do not concentrate on what God has called us to with the diligence that is desirable. The pastor's teaching and exhortation may suffer because of a lack of concentration. Because of a multitude of demands made on the pastor, he or she may fail to discern congregational needs and may be unable to sense the opportune moment. What is true of the pastor is true of all church members. Due to the distractions of life, we may be oblivious to the congregation's need of our gifts and may be unaware of our possession of the gifts. The same applies to devotional practices and self-denial—it is easy to take our eyes off the goal of Christian character because of the many demands upon us, many of them good. Yet the result is that we do not attend to the need of spiritual discipline and thus find ourselves spiritually flabby even though our lives are bursting with church activities.

The Practice of Discipline in Community

There are two convictions that pertain to the practice of discipline in community. They are that the church is the body of Christ and that the church is holy. Because of these convictions, the function and well-being of the entire body—and not only the function and well-being of the members—is a matter of theological and pastoral concern.

The church is the body of Christ. This means that the church has been given spiritual gifts and offices for the express purpose of "building up the body of Christ," so that we may "come to the unity of the faith and of the knowledge of the Son of God, to maturity" (Ephesians 4:12-13). Some of these gifts and offices (notably that of pastor) have become formal positions charged with forming and correcting believers. Others are informally exercised by members of the body. Regardless of the form they take, they serve the purpose of *paideia*—the development and maintenance of Christian character in the members. Discipline, therefore, is not to be thought of as something that only individuals engage in for their own growth. There is a genuine and necessary communal dimension to discipline.

The church is holy. This means that the character of the church's members is not a matter of indifference to the church as a whole. Although there is an important sense in which the church is holy because of its election by God and its being the bride of Christ, there is also an important sense in which the church's holiness can be compromised by the actions of its members. This is the point of Paul's metaphor in 1 Corinthians 5:6: "A little yeast leavens the whole batch of dough." Because of this, Paul urged strong measures to preserve the church's holiness. There has always been a strain of thinking within Christianity, according to which the church's holiness depends entirely on the holiness of its members, with the result that discipline within the church was not only a matter of pastoral concern, but also an issue of theological principle. This was the motivation that energized the Novatian movement in the third century. Concerned that the church was going soft on sin, members of this movement took a rather firm stance on the issue of repentance, insisting that (for serious sins) repentance after baptism was out of the question. The Montanist movement likewise tended to define the church's holiness in terms of the moral rectitude of its members. The church rejected these forms of rigorism in favor of a different understanding of its holiness but nonetheless retained some forms of internal discipline designed to bring about Christian character.

The church has always made provision for the formative aspect of communal discipline. This is seen above all in the office and role of pastor. In the New Testament, pastors have responsibility for instruction in matters of doctrine (1 Timothy 1:3) and practice (1 Timothy 4:6). This responsibility is taken with a maximum of seriousness: "Pay close attention to yourself and to your teaching ... for in doing this you will save both yourself and your hearers" (1 Timothy 4:16). The saving importance of pastoral instruction lies in its formative power: "The aim of such instruction is love that comes from a pure heart, a good conscience, and sincere faith" (1 Timothy 1:5). Although pastoral instruction is not the church's only means of inculcating love, a good conscience, and faith, it is a principal means.

Beyond instruction, the New Testament portrays the pastor as someone whose job is to exhort and reprove. Although this is rightly regarded as a task of each member of the church, the pastor has the special responsibility of exhorting and reproving "with all authority" (Titus 2:15). The pastor bears the apostles' authority, the authority that Paul described as the authority "for building you up" (2 Corinthians 10:8). Paul could be quite adamant about this authority. He commended the Thessalonians for receiving his preaching "not as a human word but as what it really is, God's word" (1 Thessalonians 2:13) and was not squeamish about invoking apostolic authority to buttress an exhortation to holiness: "Whoever rejects this rejects not human authority but God" (4:8). Not surprisingly, Titus 1:7 represents the bishop as God's steward, noting that the bishop "must have a firm grasp of the word that is trustworthy in accordance with the teaching, so that he may be able both to preach with sound doctrine and to refute those who contradict it" (1:9). The task of exhorting and reproving, then, is inseparable from the pastor's bearing apostolic authority to declare sound doctrine.

Besides the pastor, the church collectively exercises formative discipline in several forms. At the most basic level, each believer is God's instrument in the forgiveness of sins: "If you see your brother or sister committing what is not a mortal sin, you will ask, and God will give life to such a one" (1 John 5:16). Beyond this common task are the gifts and offices of the Spirit. The formative value of the gifts can be seen immediately by inspecting a typical list (Romans 12:6-7): prophecy, ministry (*diakonia*), teaching, exhorting, giving (or sharing), leading, showing mercy. Logically, each of these necessarily is directed toward other members of the body. But, as the Corinthians were slow to grasp this point, Paul made it a matter of explicit discourse: "To each is given the manifestation of the Spirit for the common good" (1 Corinthians 12:7). In other words, the gifts of the Spirit are ways in which each believer is to contribute to the maturation of other members. The same is true of the church's offices. Pastors, teachers, evangelists, and so on all exist to build up the body of Christ, a building up that (lest any should misunderstand) is identified with the formation of Christian character in the members (Ephesians 4:11-13).

More informally, we can observe in the New Testament a type of formative *paideia* less formally structured than the spiritual offices and gifts. I refer to the power of example. Although Christianity has rightly emphasized the importance of imitating Christ, the New Testament knows as well of the force that one believer can have on another through example. For instance, Paul expressly urged his congregations to imitate him (Philippians 3:17, 1 Corinthians 4:16), just as he in turn imitated Jesus Christ (1 Corinthians 11:1). Similarly, 1 Peter orders bishops to be models for their flocks (5:3); Timothy is instructed to be an example with respect to speech, conduct, love, faith, and purity (1 Timothy 4:12); and Hebrews exhorts its readers to imitate the faith of their leaders (13:7). But it is not only leaders and disciples with highly visible public ministries who are examples. Paul assured the Thessalonian congregation as a whole that they had "[become] an example to all the believers in Macedonia and in Achaia" (1 Thessalonians 1:7), and Hebrews commands us to imitate those in the past who have shown faith and patience (6:12). It is evident from these passages that the church looked upon at least some of its members as resources for knowing what the Christian life should be like. The recipients of these letters were being urged to conform their lives to the pattern of other believers. The importance of this point should not be missed. The church developed formal disciplines of formation, but it also relied on the informal means of personal example and influence. This is the context in which we should understand the concept of the saint. The saint is someone whose life has an exemplary quality. The idea of the saint is the idea of the power of personal example stretching across time, so that the saint's life has an exemplary power not only for contemporaries, but for future generations of the church as well.

In summary, it is important to note that, according to the New Testament, the church does not leave the formation of Christian character to chance or individual striving. It is vital for individuals to exert themselves in the task of discipline. However, there is a proper and necessary role for the church in the process of formative discipline. In part, this role is fulfilled by structured offices and tasks; in part it is fulfilled as at least some believers live the Christian life in an exemplary way and thus exert a formative influence on others.

The New Testament understanding of discipline has another side—corrective discipline. It is important to remember that this aspect of *paideia* is not punitive, but is instead supposed to be re-formative. This affirmation is based on those passages in the New Testament that speak of God's disciplining us: Hebrews 12:5-11, Revelation 3:19, and 1 Corinthians 11:32. The point of these passages is that corrective discipline is a sign of being children of God. Those who are not children of God are, in the words of Romans, given up to the destructive effects of sin. Those who are children of God receive correction in the hope that they will amend their lives. It is in this spirit that the church's corrective discipline should be administered, as the relevant passages in the New Testament (such as 1 Corinthians 5:4-5 and 2 Corinthians 2:5-8; 7:2-13) indicate.

The New Testament declares that the church has both responsibility and authority with respect to the discipline of its members. This authority is so extensive that the church even has an instrumental role in forgiving sin. As John's Gospel states, "He breathed on them and said to them, 'Receive the Holy Spirit. If you forgive the sins of any, they are forgiven them; if you retain the sins of any, they are retained'" (20:22-23). In Matthew's Gospel this authority is described as Jesus' delivering the keys of the kingdom to the church (see 16:19 and 18:18).

More specifically, corrective discipline exercised by the community takes several forms in the New Testament. We read of unruly members being publicly rebuked (1 Timothy 5:20), being shunned by the rest of the community (1 Corinthians 5:9-11; 2 John 10-11; 2 Thessalonians 3:14-15; and Titus 3:10), and being excommunicated, that is, being handed "over to Satan for the destruction of the flesh" (1 Corinthians 5:5 and 1 Timothy 1:20). Matthew 18:15-20 also specifies a procedure for resolving disputes in the church. From these passages, it is clear that the church collectively took a hand not only in forming its members, but also in reforming them as need arose. For our purposes, the important thing to note is that the New Testament is not squeamish about asserting the role of the community in correcting its members. There is a twofold reason for this assertion. First, there is the practical concern that the unruliness of some members will spread to others, and thus the number of people whose faith is endangered will increase. This is the concern of passages such as 2 Timothy 2:14-18. Second, there is a concern associated with the church's holiness. As noted above, the church is the holy people of God. However, its holiness should not be taken for granted, but rather actualized in each member. Sinful behavior by some compromises the church's holiness. That is why Paul insisted that the sinful member in Corinth be expelled. His presence was like a bit of leaven whose presence would contaminate the entire dough.

The communal dimension of *paideia* has always been found, in some form, in the church. Monasticism, especially in its coenobitic (that is, communal) form, can be regarded as an organized, long-term experiment in the formation of spiritual character. The monastery was a community whose principal purpose was spiritual perfection—the development of

Christlikeness. Although composed of individuals who entered into the monastic life voluntarily,[2] its life was not individualistic. In fact, it was highly regimented because experience had shown that monastic life apart from a structured communal life (as in the eremitic form of monasticism) resulted in eccentric behavior and unsound judgment. As it developed in the Latin Middle Ages, monasticism had, for instance, strict rules of governance. An abbot presided over the monastery and had virtually complete authority, as well as responsibility for the monks' souls. Built into the list of monastic virtues was obedience to the abbot, not only for the smooth operation of the monastery, but also because utter obedience was regarded as a sure way to achieve humility. The regimentation extended to the details of daily life, at least in Benedictine monasticism and its offshoots. The amount, type, and performance of daily worship was specified, as was the amount and type of physical labor and leisure time. Measures for corrective discipline were likewise precise. Although the abbot was given wide latitude in running the monastery, the rules of monastic life were intentionally specific, leaving little to chance or aberrant interpretation. The idea behind communal monasticism was that, with a willing subject, Christian character could be developed reliably if not inevitably and that the requisite virtues could be instilled by placing people in an atmosphere highly conducive to spiritual development. Above all was the conviction that this atmosphere must have a corporate character and that the disciplined life take place in a communal context in which actions and attitudes are scrutinized and shaped.

The early church knew of another, somewhat less formal communal means of shaping Christian character—the idea of the saint. In the 1500s, the Reformers rebelled, with some good reasons, against the medieval cult of the saints, and even today many Protestants are more than a bit repelled by Roman Catholic popular devotion insofar as it involves venerating saints. However, we do not have to embrace every aspect of popular devotional practices in order to appreciate the exemplary role that the idea of the saint has played. We get insight into this role if we attend not to the activities that are ascribed to saints in heaven, but instead to the qualities that qualify them as saints. In the post–New Testament church, those regarded as saints were typically martyrs, that is, those who had testified to their faith by suffering publicly for Jesus— either to the point of death or (in the case of the "confessors") through suffering torture, imprisonment, or some other form of punishment. If one thing about the early church is clear, it is that martyrs were held in the highest regard, for it was they who were considered to be living most like Jesus. Monks were likewise imitating Jesus, but even the monastic life could not compare to martyrdom with respect to Christlikeness. The important point for us is that the church, in esteeming the saint/martyr, was honoring those who excelled in the task of being like Jesus. In this sense, the early saints played an exemplary and hence formative role. We know of this role because the church wrote and preserved a great many accounts of the martyrs. Their lives became teaching tools in the quest for Christlikeness. Moreover, the use of martyrs as spiritual exemplars was an express act of the church as a community, even if it was acting in a somewhat informal way.

The early church also developed formal procedures for the corrective side of *paideia*. This took the form of repentance (discussed in chapter 4). In contrast to later practice, repentance in the early church was (at least for very serious sins) a highly public matter. Those who were repenting were expected to appear weekly at church with clothing and demeanor appropriate for those in a state of contrition. Their progress in repentance was monitored by priests, and they were not admitted to communion until their repentance was judged to be complete.

Protestant churches have not been without modes of communal formative discipline. At least in its conception, this was the impulse behind the Lutheran idea of the spiritual priesthood of believers. Although often understood in a highly individualistic way (every believer stands before God alone in an unmediated relationship and acts as his or her own priest[3]), Martin Luther's idea was that every believer is a priest on behalf of others in the community. In other words, Luther was attempting to soften the distinction between laity and clergy by regarding every Christian as possessing priestly duties, including forgiving sin and praying on behalf of one another. This conception of the Christian's calling points us to a communal yet informal (because it is not organized) mode of formative discipline. It sees the church as an interacting network of believers, with each taking responsibility for the spiritual well-being of others.

What for Luther was something informal and presupposed became in the ministry of John Wesley something carefully organized and supervised. It was not merely presupposed as something common to Christians but was made the object of intense discussion and planning. In the early days of the eighteenth century revival, Wesley became convinced that the new methods being successfully used, such as field preaching, had to be supplemented with other methods if converts were to be conserved. He saw that, although large numbers of conversions were taking place, losses were abundant as well because of a lack of nurturing structures. His answer was to create what he called class meetings. These weekly meetings of eight or so people were rigidly structured. Each had a leader who was charged with the task of visiting each member between meetings. But this was not just a friendly visit. The leader was responsible for gauging the members' progress or lack of progress in the way of salvation. Members who persistently fell into serious sin and neglected the prescribed means of grace and discipline were not allowed back into the class meetings. Of course, they were still eligible to attend the local Church of England parish church and receive its ministry. Exclusion from the class meeting was not exactly like having Paul hand you over to Satan for the destruction of the flesh. Nonetheless, exclusions did occur, and their purpose was to ensure that the class meetings were populated by people eager for salvation.

The meetings themselves were also rigidly structured. They were not mainly prayer meetings or Bible studies or times of fellowship and support. They were instead devoted to one purpose—accountability. Each week the members had to relate to the others the temptations they had encountered, sins they had committed, and so on. By modern standards, they were a bit weak on nurturing converts and would-be converts. But Wesley was convinced that conserving the results of revivalistic preaching required forming people into small groups in which they would be forced to be accountable on pain of exclusion. In this way, the class meetings exercised both a formative discipline function and a corrective discipline function. Of course, we must not think that the class meetings were full-service churches. Wesley understood that they had an important but limited function. For other avenues of formative discipline, he relied on the church's ordinary ministry of preaching and sacraments. Nonetheless, the point remains that Protestants have developed their own forms of communal formative discipline. Although traditionally critical of some of the forms that Roman Catholic formative discipline took, Protestants have recognized the fact that the church is called to act collectively in the formation of Christian character.

The Practice of Discipline in a Fallen World

The Christian life is an eschatological existence—the life of God's kingdom in the midst of a fallen world. This fact explains the necessity of discipline. If the kingdom of God were here in its fullness—if Christ had already put every enemy under his feet—then the Christian life would be one of effortless spontaneity. As it is, practices of formative and corrective discipline are necessary. Although the New Testament frequently reminds us of the contrast between life in Christ and life in the world (for example, in 1 Peter 4:1-4; 1 Thessalonians 1:9; 1 Corinthians 6:9-11; Romans 12:2; Ephesians 5:8; and Titus 3:3), and even though we have been crucified with Christ and have died to the elemental principles of the world (Colossians 2:20), this crucified former life shows an annoying and persistent capacity to rise again. Because the Christian life is an eschatological existence, our life in Christ coexists with the power of sin. The result is temptation and the possibility of falling away from Christ. This result is distressingly prevalent. Each of us knows and has succumbed to the power of temptation, whether in trivial or grave forms. The problem of clergy sexual abuse, which crosses denominational lines and appears to be considerable, puts a public face on this power.[4] The reality of this power necessitates striving and especially discipline—both formative (as, for instance, when seminaries and denominations undertake educational efforts to prevent clergy sexual abuse) and corrective (as when denominations subject offending clergy to judicial proceedings).

Whereas the finitude resulting from the embodied character of our life means that the practice of discipline suffers from various inescapable limitations, the eschatological character of our life means not just limitations, but also distortions due to sin. No aspect of Christian *paideia* is exempt from the distorting power of sin. It is because of this eschatological dimension that the Christian life must be a life of continuous repentance.

The first point to be made pertains to the communal dimension of discipline—to the fact that Christian character is formed in and through human relationships in which the pattern of Christian living is given concrete and imitable form. Under the conditions of finitude, the work of formation is never complete and always marked by imperfection. But in a fallen world, a community not only will fail to bring about the full measure of *paideia*, but also will, to some extent, malform its members. In extreme cases, the community may be so influenced by the fallen world that it has utterly lost its Christian character and consequently gives birth not to Christian disciples, but to their opposite. Or, the community may assume a demonic character by aggrandizing power to itself and abusing its authority. In these cases (which almost always attract the label "cult"), community identity and authority are had at the expense of the member's autonomy. More ordinarily, Christian communities malform their members in less overt ways, just as families can hardly avoid misshaping children and stunting their maturity.

Beyond this general point, it may be helpful to review the various forms that discipline takes and note a few of the ways in which they are subject to the distortions of sin.

It is not difficult to see the threats to pastoral teaching and exhortation. Two are prominent: on one hand, it has happened in Christian history that a minister has used the pastoral office as an instrument of his or her personal agenda instead of placing it in the service of God; on the other hand, it has also happened that pastors have lacked the courage or godliness required to preach the word of God rightly. The first of these is to be distinguished from the results of ignorance mentioned in the previous section. No pastor can possibly know everything that should inform preaching, teaching, and counseling. We must humbly accept our human limitations. But it is a different thing altogether to convert the ministry of the word into a soapbox for one's idiosyncratic opinions. This use of the pastoral office, although perhaps common, is sinful in the strict sense of the word, for in so doing we (in the words of Romans 1) fail to acknowledge God and instead exchange the glory of the immortal God for images of creaturely realities. We substitute our conceptions for God's revelation. The second failure is classically represented by Elijah, who, fearing for his life at the hands of Jezebel, fled into the desert (1 Kings 19). All of us are subject to this fear. That is why we must, with Paul, pray that we may speak the word boldly (Ephesians 6:19-20).

The power of example is likewise subject to the distortions of sin. Just as Christlike examples within the congregation are a formative influence, so un-Christlike examples are a de-formative influence. It is axiomatic that most people are followers. For that reason, it is essential that the Christian community lift up as exemplars those who are truly like Christ. Regrettably, exemplars are not always Christlike. This happens when the church becomes confused about Jesus Christ and forgets that the path of discipleship is the path of humility and self-denial. The church in America has a particularly odd tendency to anoint socially prominent converts (for example, athletes and celebrities) as exemplars, even before they have made much progress in developing a Christian character. Another aspect of the distortion of the power of example is seen in the disappointing way in which, in some of the less cautious moments of

Christian history, saints went from being examples of holiness to objects of religious devotion in their own right. Here the exemplary aspect of formative discipline is not so much distorted as lost altogether.

The distorting power of sin is evident also in the Christian's need to strive in such areas as devotional practices and self-denial. There is a perennial temptation to emphasize striving in such a way as to lose sight of God's grace. Whenever this happens, the result is the transformation of the Christian life into a legalistic righteousness, whose measure is obedience to a moral code and whose inevitable result is pride. It is against this view of the Christian life that theologians such as Augustine and John Calvin erected powerful theologies of grace. It is true that their theologies are in some ways one-sided and invite misunderstanding. But the uncompromising fervor of their writings is a warning against the ineradicable tendency to turn the Christian life into something that we do and to forget the grounding of this life in our participation in God's trinitarian life. Of course, discussion of the legalistic distortion of Christianity compels us to recognize the opposite distortion, antinomianism, which is the view that the Christian life lacks all relation to law and to striving. Although never articulated as a formal theology, its practical effects are evident throughout Christian history whenever believers fail to live out the ethical imperative of the gospel.

It is difficult to imagine formative discipline in the form of devotional practices being subject to the distortions of sin. And yet, such is the pervasiveness of sin that these practices are not exempt. Take prayer, for example. Although prayer seems beyond corruption, the New Testament provides an example of prayer grounded not only in ignorance, but also in selfishness. I refer to the request by James and John (Mark 10:35-40) that they sit on Jesus' left and right when he came into his kingdom. This request does not strike us as having been preceded by much searching for God's will. On the contrary, they had come to Jesus with a firm and decided desire and had already identified it with God's will. Regrettably, a great deal of praying in Christian history has been of this sort. Further along the line of distortion are those occasions when prayer expresses not only a purely selfish wish, but also a belief in magic. This happens whenever a theory of prayer is offered that in some way makes the words spoken in prayer critical to the value of the prayer. A sentiment like this is sometimes heard in certain versions of the health-and-wealth gospel, according to which asking for specific items from God is required if one is to receive them.

Discipline and Participation in God

So far in this chapter we have looked at the embodied character (and the implications of that embodied character) of Christian *paideia*, its communal setting, and the ways in which discipline is distorted under the conditions of sin. But it is also important to note the ultimate context of discipline—our participation in God's trinitarian life.

The connection between *paideia* and the Trinity is not immediately evident. After all, the persons of the Trinity do not need to engage in practices for the purpose of developing their divine character, and they do not exercise corrective discipline toward one another. But the foundation of discipline in the Trinity is easier to see if we focus on self-denial as the central aspect of discipline.

Self-denial is at the heart of the Christology of Philippians 2:6-8:

> Though he was in the form of God,
>   [he] did not regard equality with God
>   as something to be exploited,
> but emptied himself,
>   taking the form of a slave,
>   being born in human likeness.
> And being found in human form,
>   he humbled himself
>   and became obedient to the point of death—
>   even death on a cross.

If we meditate on the significance of this passage, we conclude that humility and self-denial are not foreign to God. We often, and rightly, speak of God's power. But we miss the Bible's full teaching about God if we emphasize only power. We should see that God's power is so great that God remains God even in the greatest humility. God can become what is not God without ceasing to be God. The doctrine of the Trinity tells us that it is part of God's nature to be obedient and submissive, just as it is part of God's nature to be powerful and to command. But we should not contrast obedience and power, submissiveness and command, as though somehow in God two contradictory attributes were paradoxically and inexplicably joined. Least of all should we assign a division of labor, by which the Father is powerful and the Son obedient in some sort of inequality of power. On the contrary, we should see that it is the one God whose trinitarian life embraces both the power to command and the power to be humble. Father, Son, and Spirit are the movement and life of God whereby God is able to pass over into utter otherness while remaining God. Otherness is not otherness to God. It is not foreign to God. So, when Philippians states that Christ emptied himself, it does not mean that he ceased to be divine. It means that in Christ, God passed over into that which seems to be the opposite of God. This passing over was truly an act of self-denial. Its historical effect was the life of the man Jesus. And yet, this supreme act of self-denial was not the end of his divinity. His self-negation was not a cessation. It was rather divinity in another and, for us, unexpected form.

This trinitarian understanding of self-denial helps us see that the call to deny ourselves and take up the cross to follow Jesus is not simply a call to service and suffering. It is also a call to participate in God's nature. The self-denial that is at the heart of the Christian life is not just a command issued by God. It is a reflection of God's nature. Consequently, as we deny ourselves in acts of Christian discipline, we are not only becoming godly, but also sharing in the communion between the Father and Son in the Spirit that constitutes the trinitarian life of God. This truth tells us why it is wrong to regard Christianity as a religion of law. In commanding us to deny ourselves, God is not asking us to become something alien to the divine nature. If God were commanding us to become something alien to the divine nature, this command would be arbitrary. However, in denying ourselves, we are commanded and invited to enter into the trinitarian life of God. With this understanding, we see that God's command is not arbitrary, but in fact corresponds to our created nature, whose end is fellowship with God. This is why we can practice self-denial with confidence, knowing that Jesus has already walked this path and emerged at its end with undiminished fellowship with God. And this is why in the Gospels Jesus states that those who lose their lives for his sake will save those lives—our true life is to be drawn into fellowship between the Father and the Son. Self-denial does not mean losing this fellowship. On the contrary, it is the only means of obtaining this fellowship, for in no other way can we participate in the trinitarian life that encompasses humility and self-denial. It is instead the life based not on self-denial, but on self-assertion that is an obstacle to living in God. It is this self-constructed life that we must zealously protect from all existential threats because it is so precarious. It is this life that must be crucified with Christ. The path to the resurrected life and to fellowship in God is found in the way of Jesus—the way of humility and self-denial.

Finally, the trinitarian ground of self-denial and discipline has the practical value of helping us remember that the Christian life—even the life of striving and self-control—is a life that relies on God's grace. The Christian life of discipline undoubtedly involves hard work. Yet this hard work is possible only because of our participation in God's trinitarian life. It is not simply the result of human exertion. Our human exertion is the work of God within us. It is the life of God acting in and through us as our communion with God is actualized more and more. Consequently, the result of our life is not pride, but instead the humility that comes from knowing that the good that we have accomplished is the good that God has accomplished. In the final analysis, Christian discipline is about humility more than it is about accomplishment.

Concluding Meditative Prayer

We praise you, our God, whose everlasting self-denial brought forth Jesus Christ, the savior. You are a God who is controlled, but not by others. Your acts are measured, although we cannot measure them. They are definite, but not defined. You deny yourself but are not negated. You correct us, but with love. Blessed are those who are disciplined by you and deny themselves. We confess to you, our Lord, our sloth and refusal to accept discipline and your divine training. We have lived for pleasures and have forgotten that you denied yourself and journeyed into the far country to save us. We acknowledge that we do not desire your discipline and shrink from your correction. We confess our addiction to ourselves. Preserve us, we pray, from profligacy. Deliver us from a dissolute life. Remind us of your love and sacrifice for us. Give us that discipline of life that will make us true athletes of faith. We pray for perseverance as we bear our cross and deny ourselves. We pray that you would make the church, your body, a community that trains us in righteousness. We pray for those who have not yet taken up the cross. Draw them to yourself and reveal to them the power of self-denial.

You, our God, the everlasting exemplar of self-denial, we praise.
We praise
> the Father, by whose will Jesus went to the cross,
> through the Son, who emptied and humbled himself and who
>> learned obedience through what he suffered,
> in the Spirit, in whose power we take up our cross and follow Jesus.

We praise the Holy Trinity, Father, Son, and Spirit, the beginning and end of all spiritual discipline.

Notes

1. *Institutes*, 1:695 (3:7.5).
2. At least originally. In time, monasteries came to be the dumping ground for unwanted and extra children of the nobility.
3. Greg Ogden's book, *The New Reformation: Returning the Ministry to the People of God* (Grand Rapids: Zondervan Publishing House, 1990), illustrates the problem. His purpose is to supplement the well-known aspect of the spiritual priesthood of believers (that each of us is his or her own priest before God) with the other aspect, that we are priests for one another (pp. 11-12). The problem is that he represents the first as a legitimate and original aspect of the doctrine, when in fact it was no part of Luther's original conception. See Paul Althaus, *The Theology of Martin Luther*, trans. Robert Schulz (Philadelphia: Fortress Press, 1966), 314.
4. *Sojourners Magazine* (July-August 2002) cites a study by Richard Blackmon at Fuller Theological Seminary showing that "12 percent of the 300 Protestant clergy surveyed admitted to sexual intercourse with a parishioner; 38 percent acknowledged other inappropriate sexualized contact" and that according to "a 1990 study by the United Methodist Church, 41.8 percent of clergywomen reported unwanted sexual behavior by a colleague or pastor [and] 17 percent of laywomen said that their own pastors had sexually harassed them." Available at www.sojo.net/index.cfm?action=magazine.article&issue=soj0207&artcle= 020741d.

Sources Consulted and Recommended

Abbott, Walter M., S. J., ed. *The Documents of Vatican II*. New York: The America Press, 1966. "Dogmatic Constitution on the Church," "Decree on the Bishops' Pastoral Office in the Church," and "Constitution on the Sacred Liturgy" all deal with the church's holiness.

Althaus, Paul. *The Theology of Martin Luther*. Translated by Robert Schulz. Philadelphia: Fortress Press, 1966.

Athanasius. *The Life of Saint Antony*. Translated by Robert T. Meyer. Vol. 10, *Ancient Christian Writers*. New York: Newman Press, 1978.

Benedict. *The Rule of Saint Benedict*. Translated by Cardinal Gasquet. The Medieval Library. New York: Cooper Square Publishers, 1966.

Brown, Peter. *The Body and Society: Men, Women, and Sexual Renunciation in*

Early Christianity. Lectures on the History of Religions. New York: Columbia University Press, 1988.

Calvin, John. *Institutes of the Christian Religion*. Translated by Ford Lewis Battles. Edited by John T. McNeill. Vol. 20, *Library of Christian Classics*. Philadelphia: Westminster Press, 1960. Book 3, chapter 7 is on self-denial.

Cyprian. *The Lapsed. The Unity of the Catholic Church*. Translated by Maurice Bévenot. Vol. 25, *Ancient Christian Writers*. New York: Newman Press, 1956.

Frend, W. H. C. *The Donatist Church: A Movement of Protest in Roman North Africa*. Oxford: Clarendon Press, 1952.

Gregory of Nyssa. "The Life of Saint Macrina." In *Ascetical Works*. Vol. 58, *The Fathers of the Church: A New Translation (Patristic Series)*. Washington, DC: Catholic University of America Press, 1967.

Lossky, Vladimir. *The Mystical Theology of the Eastern Church*. Crestwood, NY: St. Vladimir's Seminary Press, 1998.

Malherbe, Abraham J. *Social Aspects of Early Christianity*. 2nd ed. Philadelphia: Fortress Press, 1983.

Meyendorf, John. *The Orthodox Church: Its Past and Its Role in the World Today*. 4th rev. ed. Crestwood, NY: St. Vladimir's Seminary Press, 1996. On the church's holiness.

Schaff, Philip, ed. *Nicene and Post-Nicene Fathers of the Christian Church, First Series*. 14 vols. Peabody, MA: Hendrickson Publishers, 1994. Vol. 4 contains Augustine's anti-Donatist writings and his reflections on the church's holiness.

Tilley, Maureen A. *The Bible in Christian North Africa: The Donatist World*. Minneapolis: Fortress Press, 1997.

Trevett, Christine. *Montanism: Gender, Authority, and the New Prophecy*. Cambridge: Cambridge University Press, 1996.

Watson, David Lowes. *Covenant Discipleship: Christian Formation Through Mutual Accountability*. Nashville: Discipleship Resources, 1991.

CHRISTIAN VIRTUES

In chapter 7, we had a look at the kinds of disciplines—both formative and corrective—that bring about Christian character. The subject of this chapter is the sorts of virtues and practices that are the result of those disciplines and that collectively constitute Christian character.

It may be helpful to address the question of why this subject of Christian virtues should be an urgent matter for the church today. The answer is that, in the context of the American church, it is important for the church's mission and witness that the contours of the Christian life be specific and not vague. In today's religious culture there is a tendency to define religion in terms of inwardness—to see religion as something that humans engage in as a means of either self-actualization or maintaining emotional equilibrium. Although the Christian church is certainly in favor of self-actualization and emotional equilibrium, it sees the danger of defining religion strictly in these terms. Briefly put, in these circumstances, religion becomes protean, assuming so many forms that it is no longer something definite, and everyone has a religion of some sort. The danger is that in this situation the Christian faith will likewise become so individualized that it is no longer something definite, but instead becomes a nebulous set of beliefs and practices, a selection of which may be chosen by individuals in their pursuit of actualization and equilibrium. The need today is to present the Christian faith as something definite and identifiable because, as a practical matter, for most people today the principal and most effective form of the church's witness will be its practice of the Christian faith. The church's practice of the

Christian life and faith may well be the most convincing way in which the truth of the gospel can be demonstrated in today's religious situation. Of course, this argument does not obviate the need for other types of demonstration, including traditional strategies such as the intellectual defense of the faith. But in the waning days of Christian America, when the church's moral and spiritual integrity has seen better days, we can assume that for the typical American religious consumer, the truth of the Christian faith will be shown most convincingly by the church's becoming the community in which love and the ancillary virtues are practiced.

The Practice of Christian Virtues

It is not my purpose in this section to provide a catalog of all the essential Christian virtues and practices. The New Testament offers numerous lists of virtues and vices but does not attempt any systematic presentation. Similarly, Aristotle's discussion of the virtues is far from systematic or comprehensive. Instead, I wish to discuss some typical virtues and practices and also those that the New Testament regards as the most important.

The rule that Paul offered for the Christian life is "to lead a life worthy of the calling to which you have been called" (Ephesians 4:1). Everything that the New Testament has to say about the virtuous life follows from this basic rule. As an example of some leading Christian virtues and practices that result from this rule, let us look at Ephesians 4–5. Some of these are, it is possible, uniquely Christian. Others are not but are nonetheless undergirded with distinctively Christian warrants. The combination of virtues and warrants yields generalized statements about the Christian life that permit extensions into practices and virtues not specifically listed.

First, this passage expresses the warrant that "we are members of one another" along with a cluster of related counsels: to give up lying and instead to speak truthfully; to make sure that our anger is not accompanied by sin; and to moderate our anger (4:24-26). These counsels are obviously far from a comprehensive list of virtues that follow from our being members of one another. Still, they are representative. Moreover, they remind us of the communal dimension of Christian virtues. They are grounded in the fact that the church is the body of Christ. Another counsel follows, with an accompanying warrant: refrain from stealing and instead work honestly. The warrant is contained in the purpose of this counsel: so that the former thief may have something to share with the needy (4:28). This passage and the previous are good examples of virtues and practices that, although distinctively Christian, are not uniquely Christian, but which are grounded in Christian warrants. Paul was not the first person in human history to advise people to moderate anger, to speak the truth, and to labor instead of stealing. This tells us that a virtue can characterize the Christian life without our having to suppose that only Christians embody this virtue. At the same time, Ephesians supplies us with notably Christian reasons for embodying these virtues: we are members of one another (through our participation in the body of Christ), and we must attend to those with material needs. The first of these tells us not only that Christians are to speak the truth and be cautious in expressing anger, but also that their caution is grounded in the necessity of preserving the unity of the body of Christ. If we are truly members of one another, then harm to my neighbor in Christ is harm done to the body as such and to all its members, including Christ. That is why Paul could argue that division among church members meant that Christ himself had been divided (1 Corinthians 1:13). The second warrant reminds us that for Christians it is not enough to propose labor as a socially acceptable alternative to theft, for that leaves open the question of how the money earned from labor is to be used. The Christian faith insists that this latter question is as pressing as is the need for an alternative to theft. Not surprising, 1 Timothy provides the same rationale in its counsel for the wealthy: "They are to do good, to be rich in good works, generous, and ready to share" (6:18).

The next counsel and warrant is a consequence of our being members of one another. We are to forgo evil talk and instead speak only those words that build up. The warrant is contained in the purpose of this counsel: so that our words may give grace to those who hear (Ephesians 4:29). This reminds us of Paul's argument in 1 Corinthians 14 to the effect that the rule guiding the exercise of spiritual gifts is that they should build up the congregation. We again note that the virtue of speaking only what is good and useful is hardly one that only Christians urge. But we also note that the warrant has a distinctively Christian ring. Ephesians is concerned for the well-being of the church, just as in 1 Corinthians Paul was concerned about the way in which the exercise of spiritual gifts might benefit others in the body of Christ. In Ephesians 4:29, the purpose of the rationale is not to impress others with the graciousness of our speech, but instead to impart to them the grace of God. This passage is therefore concerned with the consecration of our speech. We are to consecrate our speech to God so that it becomes a divine service and thus fit to accomplish God's purposes. Accordingly, Ephesians 5:4 enjoins replacing obscene, silly, and vulgar talk with thanksgiving. In doing so, human speech is consecrated once again to its highest good, the praise of God, and delivered from being profaned by forgetfulness of God.

Next comes the command to give up bitterness, wrath, anger, wrangling, slander, and malice, replacing them with being kind, tenderhearted, and forgiving. The basis of this command is the conviction that God has forgiven us (4:31-32). Here see a connection between virtue and our participation in God's trinitarian life. In this counsel, we are expressly urged to imitate God (5:1). But we miss the point if we think of God merely as a being to be emulated. Such a view would inform us of the content of the Christian life but would leave us wondering how it is possible to live such a life. After all, who can be like God? The Christian faith, however, affirms that we can act as God acts only because and to the extent that we are drawn into the trinitarian fellowship and love between the Father and the Son in the Spirit. This again reminds us that the virtues are not simply human accomplishments, but are instead grounded in the trinitarian life of God. Being kind, tenderhearted, and forgiving are not only moral ideals but also actions of God instantiated in Jesus Christ. They reflect the trinitarian movement of God in Jesus Christ toward us through the Holy Spirit. For us to embody these virtues means that God's trinitarian movement toward the other is continued in us, that we are taken up into the same trinitarian movement of kindness and forgiveness. The church in which kindness and forgiveness are practiced is thus not only an imitation of God, but also a reality in and through which the Trinity lives in its outgoing movement. Logically and by way of summary, the command to be kind, tenderhearted, and forgiving is followed by the command to live in love just as Christ loved us (5:2).

There follows the admonition to banish fornication, impurity, and greed because they are utterly inconsistent with being one of God's holy ones (5:3). The important thing here is to note the connection between appropriate conduct and its grounding in the holiness that comes from being called. Just as ancient Israelites were to live in a state of heightened ritual purity because they were the holy people of God, so Christian disciples, who are a holy priesthood, are to conduct themselves in ways consistent with that holy priesthood.

Besides these specific injunctions, the passage offers a variety of generalizations from which additional specifics of Christian conduct can be inferred. Above all is the notion of putting off the old humanity and putting on the new (4:22-24) and the contrast between living in the dark and in the light (5:8-13). These metaphors speak of the Christian life as involving a change of great magnitude, a change that is capable of empirical specification, as the other verses in these chapters show. A bit more specifically, Ephesians counsels us to "take no part in the unfruitful works of darkness, but instead expose them" (5:11), to discern God's will (5:10, 17), and to be wise instead of foolish (5:15-17). These generalized sorts of counsels collectively tell us that the Christian life is to be distinguished from the life of sin. I will return to this point shortly in connection with the impulse toward world-transcendence.

The important point to infer from this exposition of Ephesians 4–5 is that the Christian life is one of great specificity. It possesses definite moral content, which rests on distinctively Christian warrants. This is not to say that there are no moral perplexities in Christianity. The long-standing debate in the first century over eating meat sacrificed to idols provides an illustration. Paul's proposal, which allowed eating such meat unless one had express knowledge of its pagan use (1 Corinthians 10:24-30), was clearly not acceptable to the author of Revelation, who flatly condemned such eating (Revelation 2:14, 20). This contrast is a testimony to the fact that Christians do not agree on all matters, even on important matters. Perhaps recognition of this fact is why Ephesians 5 urges the reader to "try to find out what is pleasing to the Lord" (v. 10) and to "understand what the will of the Lord is" (v. 17). Sometimes God's will is not evident. Nonetheless, the potential for disagreement does not disturb the conviction that on a great many matters the Christian life can be described quite precisely and with a great deal of agreement. Paul and other New Testament writers had a firm sense about what the Christian life entailed and what it excluded. This sense explains the New Testament's proclivity toward compiling lists of virtues and vices. From these lists we gather that virtues and virtuous practices such as the following characterize the disciple: love, joy, peace, patience, kindness, goodness, faithfulness, gentleness, self-control, purity, knowledge, compassion, and humility (Galatians 5:22-23, 2 Corinthians 6:6, and Colossians 3:12). Many more characteristics could be adduced from other lists. The composite list of evil characteristics is even longer. Let the list in Romans 1:29-31 suffice: wickedness, evil, greed, malice, envy, murder, strife, deceit, craftiness, gossip, slander, hating God, insolence, haughtiness, boasting, inventing evil, rebellion toward parents, foolishness, faithlessness, heartlessness, and ruthlessness.

What emerges from the New Testament's list-making is the sense that the Christian life stands for something morally. It is not morally indifferent. It is this point that early Christians, at least those converted from paganism, seemed to have had difficulty grasping. The reason for their difficulty is that ancient religions in the Roman world (with the exception of Judaism) make few moral demands on their adherents. The gods demanded sacrifice and honor but otherwise did not much concern themselves with the moral life of mortals. Hence the rather steep learning curve for early converts to Christianity, who had to be told—repeatedly—that fornication, honesty, speech, and many other practices were matters of intense interest to their new God.

The moral definiteness of the Christian life—the fact that it necessarily includes certain virtues and virtuous practices and excludes a large number of other practices—brings us to a consideration of the world-transcending impulse within Christianity. One of the outstanding features of the New Testament's moral teaching is its clear sense of difference between the Christian life and the moral lives of pagans. Of course, we have to make allowances for the tendency of members of a group, such as in the church, to make overly general statements and caricatures of those outside the group and to portray them as more debauched than perhaps they are. Nonetheless, New Testament writers are unanimous in wishing to draw the sharpest of contrasts between the new life of the believer and the old life of sin.

The theological basis of this contrast is the conviction that in Jesus Christ the new age of God's kingdom has dawned, bringing with it the transformation of life. Therefore, "you must no longer live as the Gentiles live." Why? Because, being part of the old age of sin, "they are darkened in their understanding, alienated from the life of God because of their ignorance and hardness of heart. They have lost all sensitivity and have abandoned themselves to licentiousness, [and are] greedy to practice every kind of impurity" (Ephesians 4:17-19).

World-Transcendence and World-Participation

THE IMPULSE TOWARD TRANSCENDING THE WORLD

In light of this contrast between the new and the old, several virtues and virtuous practices highlight Christianity's impulse to transcend the fallen world. Above all, the threat of persecution calls forth patience, which is grounded in hope (Romans 5:1-5). As the book of Revelation shows, the early Christian sense of confronting the demonic powers in the form of the Roman Empire threw into sharp and concrete relief the contrast between the new and the old. Certainty about the reality of the kingdom produced hope. But the demonic threats from the Roman Empire demanded patience and endurance. To be patient, for first-century Christians, was not simply a matter of waiting for the fullness of God's kingdom, but also of enduring the possibility and sometimes the reality of Roman persecution. Patience was not only an attitude of mind, but involved as well identifiable practices in the face of danger. Paul spoke of this when he praised the Philippians for "standing firm in one spirit, striving side by side with one mind for the faith of the gospel, . . . [being] in no way intimidated by [their] opponents" (Philippians 1:27-28). Patience was thus a virtue that concretely signaled overcoming the world.

But there were other virtuous practices that signaled overcoming the world. For Paul, maintaining the unity of the body of Christ was one of them; for its opposite, the spirit of division, was a sure sign of the power of the flesh. This was his complaint about the Corinthians. Their divisive and factious behavior indicated unfailingly that they still belonged to the old age of sin, which Paul signified with the term *flesh* (1 Corinthians 3:1-4). In order for them to "be united in the same mind and the same purpose" (1:10), they must leave behind the old order of sin and become spiritual, that is, they must become mature. Then, Paul argued, they would possess God's wisdom and would see that their factions were contrary to the gospel (3:18-23). Like Revelation, 1 Corinthians is arguing that a specific virtuous practice—unity of mind and purpose—represents a victory over the sinful power of the world.

Another example comes from James. In an important passage on the subject of wisdom, this letter contrasts the fruits of the wisdom from above with the fruits of earthly wisdom. The contrast consists in specific practices. Those who possess the wisdom from above are pure, peaceable, gentle, willing to yield, full of mercy and good fruits without partiality and hypocrisy. Those inspired by earthly wisdom exhibit envy, selfish ambition, disorder, and wickedness of every kind (James 3:13-18). Although not using Paul's language about the flesh or Revelation's focus on Rome, James is likewise affirming that specific Christian virtues have a world-transcending character. In particular, they are ours by virtue of our leaving behind the wisdom of this world and obtaining God's wisdom. Like patience in Revelation and unity in 1 Corinthians, the fruit of godly wisdom was not only attitudes of mind, but also discernible practices. In particular, possession of such wisdom would end the favoritism shown toward the rich and the denigration of the poor (2:1-13), result in careful speech (3:1-12), and eliminate conflicts (4:1-3).

A final example comes from 1 John, which portrays the old age of sin with the metaphors of death and darkness. In 1 John, the fact that we love fellow disciples signifies that we have overcome the darkness and walk in the light (2:10-11) and that we have passed out of the realm of death into light (3:14). However, the letter reminds us, love is not just a sentiment, but necessarily becomes concrete in specific acts of goodness toward the neighbor (3:16-17). Love, which consists of virtuous practices, is both a means of transcending the world and a sign that we have transcended it.

These examples confirm the judgment that the impulse toward spiritually and ethically transcending the world takes concrete form in distinctively Christian virtues and practices. One of the tasks of the church in every generation is to discern, in its moral environment, those things that represent the world that we must overcome as well as the virtuous practices that must be emphasized if we are to overcome the world. In American culture, we could point to the way in which violence is woven into our society, to the increasing acceptance of relationless and responsibility-free sensuality, and to the way in which all sorts of good things have been turned into commodities and consumer goods. In the face of phenomena like these, the church is called upon to develop those virtuous practices that will enable us both to conquer the world (by separating us from sinful practices) and offer a testimony to the fallen world of the possibility of the better life available in the new age of the Spirit. In chapters 9 and 10 I will offer a brief sketch of the sorts of virtuous practices that are called for in our situation.

THE IMPULSE TOWARD PARTICIPATING IN THE WORLD

Having argued that Christian virtues mean our transcending the world, it is necessary to add that they are not contrary to the world of God's creation. The "world," as I have argued, has an ambivalent character for Christians. It is, in one sense, God's creation and, in another sense, the fallen universe of sin. The Christian faith proclaims that, no matter how extensive the power of sin and thus how fallen the world, this world remains the creation of God and vestiges of its created goodness remain. Accordingly, Christian virtues are not simply against the world. As expressions of our embodied condition, they are of the created world and for the world's redemption. They are against the world only insofar as the world rises up against God and allows the power of sin to distort human nature.

The theological basis of this conviction has already been stated—the doctrine of creation. But it is profitable in this context to focus upon one aspect of the doctrine of creation, the idea of wisdom. In the Bible, wisdom is more than a human achievement. It has a transhuman quality because human wisdom is grounded in God's wisdom. Although the Bible knows that God's wisdom far transcends ours (Isaiah 40:13-14), it also insists that human wisdom is a gift from God (Proverbs 2:6), who is supremely wise. It is also important to note that, among humans, wisdom is not the sole possession of Israel. In fact, as scholars have noted, much of the wisdom expressed in Proverbs can be found in the wisdom literature of other ancient Near Eastern cultures. In previous theological generations there was some anxiety about this observation because it seemed to compromise the Bible's grounding in revelation. But in fact Proverbs does not claim to be based on revelation. We surely did not need God to reveal to us that "the wicked accept a concealed bribe to pervert the ways of justice" (Proverbs 17:23). This sort of observation is universal. It is true that the fear of Yahweh is the beginning of wisdom (Proverbs 1:7), but in Proverbs the wise person is set in contrast not to the pagan, but to the fool. Wisdom in the Bible has an international character about it. Job, for instance, is not an Israelite, but rather lives abroad in Uz. Although the Bible does not offer a theoretical account of how those outside Israel can be wise, it simply takes the possibility for granted.

This means that there can be something like a common human wisdom of a practical sort, rooted in God's creation embedded in the created order. As Christians acquire this wisdom, they, like humans generally, participate in the structures of wisdom in God's creation. Of course, a full account of wisdom must include the New Testament's insistence that human participation in wisdom is quite fallible and subject to the distortions of sin. Nonetheless, it is utterly appropriate for Christians to affirm the possibility and in fact the reality of people outside the church exhibiting a measure of common wisdom. As Thomas Aquinas put the matter, God's grace perfects nature, but it does not replace nature. On the contrary, the natural order has its own validity and autonomy within the providence of God, so that pagans are able to attain to a measure of common human virtues such as wisdom.

It is on this basis that we can affirm that Christian virtues, even when they are not unique to Christians, are a mode of our participation in the world. They represent one of the ways in which we share in the common structures of God's creation. This explains the fact that so much of the New Testament's moral teaching lacks a uniquely Christian character. Much of what the New Testament enjoins upon us is just the sort of advice that moralists of every age have urged. The Pastoral Epistles, for example, with their emphasis on moderation and self-control, reflect in a rough way the view of the philosophical schools in the Roman period. In this way, we are not forced into the artificial and untenable assertion that every bit of Christian ethics and spirituality rests on a unique revelation. This could be true only if, along the lines of Gnosticism, the creator and the redeemer were not one God, but two gods who opposed each other. In fact, however, in creation and redemption we have to do with the one God, who, in Jesus Christ, has created the world and effected its new creation. Because it is the same God who creates and re-creates, whose original wisdom in creation is Jesus Christ (1 Corinthians 1:24), Christian morality is not in utter contradiction to the world, but, as noted, only as the world has turned away from God and walks in the darkness.

The result of this analysis is that we should affirm those moral aspects of the surrounding culture that are consistent with the gospel and that contribute to healthy human society while maintaining a prophetic witness toward those aspects that are not consistent and that contribute to an unhealthy human society. Moreover, the act of affirming the surrounding culture should not be done grudgingly, as though the Christian faith were in danger of collapse if we acknowledge the presence of wisdom outside the church. On the contrary, such an affirmation is an act of praise to the God who in wisdom has made all things (Psalm 104:24) and an offering of thanksgiving for the residual goodness that we find in creation in spite of human sin.

VIRTUE UNDER THE CONDITION OF FINITUDE

The final aspect of the embodied character of Christian virtues and practices is the fact that we embody them under the condition of finitude. The immediate implication of this fact is that our virtue is always incomplete. We cannot develop the full range of virtues to the extent and depth that would be ideal. This incompleteness is not due to human sin. It is instead rooted in the limitations that attend our existence: limitations of knowledge, of time, and so on. The cultivation of virtues requires, for example, time. We are not born virtuous and cannot become virtuous simply by learning about virtue. The virtues must be observed in exemplars, and they must be practiced. But our time in life is limited to such an extent that the possibility of completely acquiring and adequately cultivating all the virtues is closed off to us. Moreover, as Aristotle observed, the process of moral deliberation has a built-in ambivalence that is inescapable. To be generous is to give the right amount, at the right time, in the right way, and to the right people. So, as he noted, there are many more ways to miss the proper action than to hit it. And what is true of the individual's moral life is true all the more of the moral life of communities. A community's good may be difficult to discern. If it is discerned, the means of attaining the good may be obscure. If the means are clear, intractable obstacles may stand in the way of realizing the good. Moreover, even if human motives are right, human judgment is severely limited by ignorance, by the effects of fatigue on our thinking, by our incapacity for sustained attention to problems. Although perhaps human virtue and judgment will be perfected in the fullness of God's eschatological kingdom, until then our moral life will be attended by finitude and its inevitable ambiguities.

The Practice of Christian Virtues in Community

Chapter 7 addressed the question, "What is the role of the Christian community in providing and supporting the disciplines that make Christian character possible?" In this section, we are asking the question, "In what sense can the community be said to be virtuous?" In more traditional language, we are asking about the church's holiness.

Our point of departure is the creedal affirmation "I believe in the holy church." Behind the creeds lie biblical affirmations such as 1 Peter 2:5 and 9 (which describe the church as a holy priesthood and a holy nation), Ephesians 2:21 (which describes the church as a holy temple), and ultimately the Old Testament's understanding of Israel. The connection with Israel is important in grasping the meaning of the creedal affirmations, for the church is holy in just the sense in which, in the Old Testament, Israel is holy. This holiness is a result of election. The critical text is Deuteronomy 7:6: "You are a people holy to the LORD your God; the LORD your God has chosen you out of all the peoples on earth to be his people." This linking of holiness and election means that, in a very important sense, Israel is always and irrevocably holy, even when it acts in decidedly unholy ways. To say that it is holy is not to make an empirical observation about its behavior. It is instead to make the theological affirmation that Israel has been collectively chosen to be in relation to God.

At the same time, Israel's election has quite definite moral implications. The clearest representation of this conviction is Leviticus 19:2-4: "You shall be holy, for I the LORD your God am holy. You shall each revere your mother and father, and you shall keep my sabbaths.... Do not turn to idols or make cast images." In the following verses Israel received commandments regarding care of the poor (Leviticus 19:9-10), theft and lying (v. 11), justice (v. 15), and so on. The point is that the holiness of Israel that rests on election must be realized in the ethical practice of every Israelite. Israel stands in a permanent relation of consecration to God. This consecration is one side of its holiness. But the holiness that results from consecration demands that Israel translate its holiness into ethics.

We will not go wrong if we interpret the church's holiness in a similar way. On one hand, the church's holiness rests on God's election: "He chose us in Christ before the foundation of the world to be holy and blameless before him" (Ephesians 1:4). The church, like Israel, has been placed in a relationship of consecration before the holy God. On the other hand, this factual holiness must be realized in the conduct of the church's members: "Be renewed in the spirit of your minds, and... clothe yourselves with the new self, created according to the likeness of God in true righteousness and holiness" (Ephesians 4:23-24). When, with the creeds, we recite, "We believe in the holy church," we are affirming the church's election by God and its status as a consecrated people. We are also committing ourselves to actualizing this holiness in our conduct by means of virtuous practices. There is, therefore, the closest of connections between Christian virtues and the church's holiness. The connection is not an identity, for the church's holiness is not—fortunately—simply equivalent to the holiness of its members. The connection is instead a spiritual and ethical imperative: "As he who called you is holy, be holy yourselves in all your conduct" (1 Peter 1:15).

The value of setting our discussion of Christian character in the context of the church's holiness is that it helps us see what is theologically at stake in the discussion of virtue. In classical virtue theory, the rationale for living the life of virtue was that such a life corresponds to human nature. To live virtuously is to actualize every human capacity and thus to live in the best way possible for human beings. There is much in this view that is commendable. Yet it falls far short of what Christians want to say about the life of virtue. In particular, Christians affirm that the rationale for virtue is not simply that it yields the good life, but also and more important that it is our faithful and obedient response to the God who is forming a holy people and who has incorporated us into that holy people. Theologically considered, the theory of virtue is not principally a theory of human being (although human nature has a part in this theory). It is instead an account of life as it ought to be lived in response to God's grace and God's call upon us to become members of the holy body of Christ.

The Practice of Christian Virtues in a Fallen World

The church lives under the conditions of sin. Although called to holiness, it is not unaffected by the power of the fallen world. Can the church lose its holiness? The Bible has two things to say in response to this question. On one hand, the church is holy because it has been called by God and consecrated by God. Like Israel, the church's holiness rests on its election before the foundation of the world, to use the language of Ephesians. On the other hand, the defilement (that is, the loss of holiness) of God's people appears, according to the Bible, to be a distinct possibility. Ezekiel 23 is an indictment of Israel and Judah because of their idolatry, which is expressly said to have defiled them (vv. 7, 13). The same point seems to be made in 1 Corinthians 5, in which Paul addressed the case of the man who was living with his former stepmother. In an attempt to bolster his command to have the offender expelled from the community, Paul used the metaphor of yeast: "A little yeast leavens the whole batch of dough" (v. 6). The offender is here likened to a bit of yeast. His sin will infect the entire congregation, just as a bit of yeast will cause the entire lump of dough to rise. But Paul's concern is not so much with the man's potential influence on the congregation as it is on the church's holiness. We know this because he went on to compare the church to the Passover bread, which must be free of yeast. His point was not that the sinful man would exercise a bad influence on the others (although that may very well have been a matter of concern), but that the presence of the sinful man ruins the consecrated character of the church just as yeast ruins the sacral character of the Passover bread. In summary, we may say that the people of God are holy by virtue of being elected and also that their holiness can be diminished by sin. This twofold observation corresponds to the conviction that the people of God are holy (expressed by Deuteronomy's theology of election), that they must actualize that holiness in conduct (expressed in Leviticus 19), that serious failure in conduct jeopardizes that holiness (Ezekiel 23), but that ultimately election trumps conduct (for, as Paul stated in Romans 11:29, the gifts and calling of God are irrevocable).

Consideration of 1 Corinthians 5 leads us to ask about the holiness of individuals within the church. Two points deserve mention. First, the individual's conduct is not irrelevant to the church's holiness. This uncovers for us an aspect of the Christian life—the fact that we should live in a worthy manner because otherwise we are diminishing the church's holiness. Second, the mere fact that the church as such is holy by virtue of election does not mean that each individual within the church can rely on that holiness as though the individual did not need to actualize that holiness in his or her conduct. As the Bible is well aware, the destiny of the church, grounded in election, is one thing. The destiny of the individual is quite another.[1]

The question of the individual's holiness raises the further issue of the distorting power of sin in the individual's quest for virtue. The first point to be considered is the relation between sin and vice, the opposite of virtue. I have already argued in this chapter that many of the virtues that Christians are to embody may also be found outside the Christian community, even if there is a distinctively Christian rationale for embodying these virtues. It is now time to state more specifically the relation between virtue and the Christian life. An illuminating biblical text on this subject is Romans 1:18-32. Paul's argument in this passage is that pagan vices—enumerated in great detail—result from the fundamental sin, which is their failure to honor God (v. 21) and to acknowledge God (v. 28). This passage tells us two things. First, sin is not identical with vice. Paul's argument is not that the pagan world has fallen into vice and additionally failed to honor God. It is instead that it has failed to honor God and therefore it has fallen into vice. Sin—refusal to honor God— has as its result the life of vice. Second, there is a close connection between sin and vice. Vice is, so to speak, the empirical form that sin takes. Pagans, having alienated themselves from God, necessarily plunge into vice.

The distinction between sin and vice is important because it reminds us that humankind's highest good is not merely to enjoy right relations within human community by cultivating social virtues, but also and above all to enjoy right relations with God. In other words, what is at stake in this distinction is the fundamental point of the Christian view of human existence. Humans are made not only for one another, but also and principally for God. This insight is one of the enduring contributions of Augustine: our hearts are restless until we find God precisely because we have been created by God and for God. Our authentic being consists in standing in God's presence with love and praise. If we were made only for one another—if the highest good were to be found in and through human community—then sin and vice would be identical. As it is, however, our good is incomplete without the knowledge and love of God. As a result, human life without this knowledge and love is disordered even if one's relations with and behavior toward other human beings is judged acceptable by one's moral community. That is why Martin Luther and Søren Kierkegaard were so insistent that moral rectitude is not the same as the righteousness that God demands. Although they saw the importance of moral virtues for human community, they also saw the human tendency to assume that conformity to human codes of conduct is the extent of God's demand on us—the tendency to collapse our relation to God into our relation to other members of the human community. It is this tendency that, in the spirit of Augustine, we must resist, unless religion is to be regarded as just a human phenomenon. We may say, then, that moral rectitude and virtue are necessary conditions of the authentic Christian life but are not sufficient conditions—they are not the sum total of that life.

This last consideration leads us to see that Christian virtues, although sometimes empirically identical to virtuous practices outside the Christian community, are different not only in rationale (for example, they often rest on different warrants), but also in intentionality. By this I mean that moral virtue was classically understood to mean those characteristics that arise out of humankind's social nature and that signify our functioning well within human community. There is a great deal of truth in this, and Christian theology has no wish to contradict that truth. But we grossly underestimate the nature of Christian virtues if we see them as having for their setting only human community, even if that community is the Christian community. Instead, we should see that virtues are also directed toward God, even if humans are unaware of their directedness toward the transcendent. They arise not only from our social nature, but also from the fact that we are created for fellowship with God. Once again, it was Augustine who first saw this with clarity when he interpreted the cardinal virtues of classical culture as just so many different forms of love, whose highest object is God. Properly understood, then, virtues have an ecstatic character—becoming virtuous is not only becoming human (as Aristotle and other classical philosophers argued), but also being drawn outside our humanity toward the knowledge and love of God.

In a fallen world, every aspect of the moral life can be distorted. Prominent among these are ends, means, norms, and motivations. Philosophers long ago recognized that the moral life is largely about the sorts of ends that are desired and sought. Aristotle understood that some people were so depraved that they consciously chose evil ends, but such people seemed to Aristotle to be comparatively rare. More common, according to Aristotle, was confusion about the ends proper to human well-being. Is human goodness a matter of material prosperity? Rewards and reputation from one's peers? Physical pleasure? In spite of this confusion, Aristotle seemed to believe that, at least in the Greek communities he was familiar with, there was broad consensus on the end to be pursued. The Christian tradition, however, has had a more somber assessment of the matter. We have serious doubts about humankind's capacity to know and to choose the appropriate ends. It is our observation that human communities often choose ends that are manifestly wicked.

The moral life is also about means toward desirable ends. As Aristotle observed, virtue consists not only in right action, but also in performing right action in the right way. This requires prudence, the intellectual virtue that governs the choice of means to desirable ends in human affairs. Aristotle was realistic enough to know that the choice of proper means was far from easy. Christians, however, are of the opinion that Aristotle's assessment seriously underestimated the problem. The church speaks from its own experience. In the laudable interest of protecting its members from heresy, for instance, the church has chosen means that today seem both overly zealous and destructive. Concern for salvation likewise induced the church to sanction internal crusades (such as that against the Waldensians). Concern for missions led missionaries to piggyback onto colonialization more than we now judge to have been advisable. And so on. As we are all too well aware, eagerness for a desired end can be used to justify a disappointingly large range of evil means.

Discussion of norms brings us to consider more particularly the distorting effects of sin upon moral communities. Moral communities, such as the family, church, and nation, play a formative role in the individual's acquisition of virtue both by transmitting and also by establishing moral norms. In a fallen world, history shows that communities' norms often fall far short of what is truly good for human well-being and what is God-pleasing. More insidious is the fact that, because individuals are shaped by those communal norms, the norms come to be regarded as self-evidently valid. When everyone in a community holds a norm to be valid, then it becomes part of the moral landscape and may cease to be an object of critical reflection. Instead of being scrutinized, it becomes one of the assumed and unquestioned principles by which we reason morally. Slavery offers us an example. In the Hellenistic and Roman periods, slavery was taken for granted as a fact of life. Even the New Testament does not question the validity of slavery, focusing instead on subjecting owners and slaves to Christian moral expectations. The efforts of apologists for slavery in the antebellum South show us how easy it is for a practice contrary to God's will to become a self-evident truth. This is a testimony to the nearly infinite human capacity for self-deception. This fact also tells us why it is not sufficient to ground morality in conscience alone. Although conscience plays an important role in moral deliberation, conscience is shaped by communal norms, and, as these are affected by sin, judgments based on conscience are distorted.

But even when ends and means are well chosen and communal norms are comparatively sound, the power of sin is not exhausted. In its most subtle form, sin can vitiate the moral worth of our actions by corrupting our motivation. But if ends are good, means are appropriate, and norms are sound, then how can our motivation be flawed? The key to grasping this point is to see what makes Christians uneasy about virtue as it was understood by classical writers such as Aristotle. On one hand, Christians applaud Aristotle's insight into the formative role of moral communities, his well-stated emphasis on ends that actually promote human good, and so on. But Christians still feel that Aristotle's ideal moral agent is motivated by one fundamental but flawed consideration, namely, that which is judged to be good for that moral agent. This consideration is not completely misguided. Aristotle is certainly correct that moral practices and decisions should be guided by a conception of what is good and that the overall good must include what is good for individuals. Self-interest is a legitimate moral factor. But Christians will nonetheless feel that the moral life that we are called to on the basis of God's revelation in Jesus

Christ cannot be accommodated within a morality whose chief consideration is one's self-interest. In other words, the fact that we are members of the body of Christ means that self-interest becomes a secondary issue. That is why Paul could tell the Corinthians that it was better to allow themselves to be wronged by fellow believers than to dispute with them in public law courts (1 Corinthians 6:7), that they should not exercise their freedom if doing so meant harming the faith of other believers (1 Corinthians 8:9), and that the exercise of spiritual gifts must be guided by the needs of the church as a whole (1 Corinthians 14:12). But why is it a sinful motivation to act in a self-interested way? It is not because self-interested motivation necessarily results in acts of gross wickedness. It is instead because acting principally from self-interest—making it the ultimate principle of morality—falls far short of the glory of God, which (as John's Gospel reminds us) is the cross of Jesus Christ. Self-interested motivations may very well result in behavior that is morally upright when judged by human standards. If it does, Christians should be the first to applaud, for morally upright behavior is a good thing. But sin is not only and not even mainly acts that are obviously wicked. Sin is as well something good that falls short of the life that is revealed in Jesus Christ. This is the point of the temptation stories in the Gospels of Matthew and Luke. When the devil tempts Jesus to throw himself from the heights of the temple in order to convince the crowds, the devil is not asking Jesus to do something manifestly evil. Jesus is instead being asked to choose a path that differs from the path that God has ordained—the way of the cross. This explains why Christianity is not just another morality. It *is* a distinctive moral life and moral community. But the Christian faith insists that a morality that is ignorant of its divine ground and that fails to follow that pattern of Jesus is incomplete and, indeed, in the grip of sin.

It is important to note an effect of sin that particularly affects the Christian church. This effect relates to the two ethical impulses of the Christian life, the impulse toward transcending the world and the impulse toward participating in the world. The authentic Christian life is the harmonious balance of the two. However, in a fallen world, it is all too easy to fall into imbalance. When too great an emphasis is placed on the impulse toward world-transcendence, the result is a harsh and bitter form of Christianity that seems to value sectarianism for its own sake. In this form, sheer difference from the world is the highest good, with no sense of the fact that the world remains God's good creation with a residue of that goodness even amidst sin. In this hypersectarian mood, the world is thought to be so totally under the power of demonic forces that the disciple's only recourse is to flee the world. Not surprising, this mood often finds the apocalyptic streams within the Bible congenial, for they reinforce the tendency to think of the church's relation to the world in starkly dualistic terms. Because of the demonizing of the world, adherents of this mood often go to extremes in rejecting the world, even to the point of rejecting *adiaphora*, that is, practices that Christians have traditionally not regarded as being matters of great spiritual importance. In this view, *everything* has spiritual importance—anything that does not directly improve one's spiritual life is held to be sinful. The problem with this approach is that its laudable moral earnestness is joined to a hatred of the world. This hatred is grounded in an incapacity to remember that the world, even in its sin, is still the arena of salvation and grace and that the goal of Christ's work is the reconciliation of all things in Christ (Colossians 1:20). In their own way, extreme forms of this mood are infected by the sin that Paul described in Romans—failing to acknowledge and honor the creator. This shows us that sin is often a matter of eccentricity. By this I mean that sin distorts and corrupts that which is good by drawing it away from its center in God.

The opposite distortion comes from too great an emphasis on world-participation. This is found whenever the people of God accommodate themselves to the world and uncritically assimilate its beliefs, values, and practices. The Bible is full of examples, notably Israel's persistent tendency to join the worship of local deities (the Baals) to its worship of Yahweh. A New Testament example is the temptation faced by the Colossian church to supplement its faith in Christ with worship of other cosmic powers. The practical effect of this supplementation was their assimilation of religious practices of a highly ascetic nature. But the Bible is not the only source of examples. In every generation, the church faces the temptation of identifying the kingdom of God with some human reality or ideal. These days the temptation is unlikely to take the form of the overt worship of other gods. But the temptation is real nonetheless. Moreover, this is a permanent temptation that the church will never escape as long as its existence is an eschatological existence. We will always be affected by the leading ideas of our time. Because of our embodied condition, we inevitably think and practice with general trends in the surrounding culture. To the extent that a distinctively Christian culture is cultivated in the church, this tendency can be resisted when resistance is called for, but (under the conditions of sin) it will always be difficult for the church to discern just which aspects of the surrounding culture should be resisted. What makes this issue even more complicated is that the decision as to whether a segment of the church has accommodated itself to the world depends on one's view of the Christian faith. For example, in the opinion of fundamentalist churches, those Christians who understand the doctrine of creation in conjunction with the theory of biological evolution have flagrantly and sinfully assimilated themselves to the world. Other churches have a different assessment of the matter. Accommodation to the world, then, is sometimes in the eye of the beholder. Nonetheless, the temptation toward assimilation is real and dangerous. Its result is inevitably the union of Christian ideals with cultural ideals in such a way that the prophetic witness of the church withers. If it is true that the overemphasis on world-transcendence is grounded in a loss of the doctrine of creation, then we may say that the overemphasis on world-participation signals a failure to honor and acknowledge God as judge and redeemer. This latter overemphasis means forgetting that the kingdom of God cannot be identified with any human institution, movement, idea, belief, or practice—even those of the church. Just as God remains transcendent even in and through the incarnation, so God's ways transcend human ways. This transcendence means that God stands in judgment over all human conceptions of and attempts at constructing the good life. It also means that the good life is found only in God.

The Christian life, then, must be a balance of the two impulses toward transcending the world and participating in the world. Admittedly, under the conditions of sin this balance remains an ideal. Nonetheless, to speak of salvation is to speak of our striving after that balance. The kingdom of God is precisely that balance, for on one hand it is that act of God whereby we transcend the world and its sin while, on the other, it is the transformation of the world and the redemption of God's creation.

The church is the eschatological anticipation of that kingdom. The church is to be the place in which the desired balance is sought and in which means of grace begin to bring about that balance. This means that the church is to be a community of healing. In it, disciples are to be trained in the discernment necessary to know what in the world should be spiritually transcended and where we should participate. In it, the virtue of humility and the practice of repentance are cultivated in light of the difficulty of this discernment and in light of the church's rather poor record in practicing discernment. But the church is also to be a community of testimony. First and above all, it is a testimony to the power of forgiveness and to the possibilities of God's grace in the process of seeking the desired balance. It is also a testimony against the world's sin—not against the world, but prophetically for the world against its sin.

Christian Virtues and Participation in God

I have already argued that virtues have an ecstatic character. They point toward God and, when well embodied, draw us out of our humanity and direct us toward God. It is now time to complete this thought by noting the fully trinitarian character of virtue.

If the Bible is correct that love is both the highest and the summation of God's commands, and if Augustine was right to interpret all the virtues as different forms of love, then the connection between virtue and the Trinity is evident. Virtues are not only directed toward God, but also grounded in God's trinitarian life of love—in the fellowship between the Father and the Son. As we love and thus engage in the other virtuous practices, we are participating in that trinitarian life by the power of the Spirit.

If it is by the power of the Spirit that we participate in God's trinitarian life, then the life of virtue is not simply a human accomplishment achieved through effort. Consequently, we miss the truth if we think of God merely as an example of goodness that we should emulate. The Christian life is not only an imitation of God, but also our living in God through the power of the Spirit. But it is not only the Christian life that is grounded in God's trinitarian life. All human virtue is grounded in God. This means that every human being in some way participates in God, just as indeed every creature in the universe does. It is humankind's sin that it does not realize that whatever virtue it has obtained is found in and through God. Christian virtue, then, does not differ from human virtue outside the church in the sense that the former is godly virtue and the latter ungodly virtue or in the sense that the former is the result of grace and the latter the result of human effort. On the contrary, we should see all virtue, wherever it is found, as grounded in God. Christian virtue differs from worldly virtue by being a higher and fuller actualization of our participation in God. As Christian writers in the patristic era stated it, whereas all humankind participates in the *logos*, Christians do so in a more elevated way by virtue of our incorporation into the body of Christ.

In history, the trinitarian life of love has been embodied in Jesus Christ and in the new creation. Jesus Christ, who is the image of the God who is love, has begun to renew us in that image. The practice of love and, with it, the other virtues is in this way both the imitation of Christ and also our existence in the new creation.

Concluding Meditative Prayer

We praise you, eternal ground of all that is good and end of every virtuous deed. We praise your goodness and the consummate embodiment of your goodness, Jesus Christ. We praise you for the gifts and gift of your Spirit, who makes us share in your perfect virtue. Blessed are those who are perfect as the heavenly Father is perfect and whose lives are an imitation of God. We confess to you, our Lord, our lack of virtue and the paltry results of our attempts to be virtuous. We acknowledge the weakness of our comprehension and the sluggishness of our deeds. We confess our great need of you and your goodness. Grant that we may walk worthily of our calling and lead us by your Spirit into the paths of righteousness. Preserve us, we pray, from confidence in our own good. Save us from pride in our moral deeds. Deliver us from ignorance of your will and your ways. Keep us mindful of your perfection and our imperfection, but also of your grace, which brings us close to you. We pray for ourselves, whose virtue is weak. We pray as well for all those in your world who do not know you as the source of virtue and as eternal virtue itself. Bring them, we pray, to know and to love you. May we be for them a city set on a hill and a light that shines forth the light of the world.

You, our God, who are love, wisdom, and every other virtue in the perfection of your eternity, we praise.
We praise
    the Father, who sent Jesus into the world as the model and embodiment
        of virtue,
    through the Son, who is the image of the eternal God and the incarnation of
        all goodness,
    in the Spirit, whose gifts give us the virtue of God.
We praise the Holy Trinity, Father, Son, and Spirit, the eternal ground and source of virtue.

Note

1. I am aware that the various streams within the Christian tradition have a variety of views on the subject of election, holiness and the relation between the individual's holiness and that of the church. Limitations of space prevent the full exposition that this important issue deserves.

Sources Consulted and Recommended

Aristotle. *The Ethics of Aristotle: The Nicomachean Ethics.* Translated by J. A. K. Thomson. Rev. ed. London: Penguin Books, 1976.

Augustine. *The Catholic and Manichaean Ways of Life. De Moribus Ecclesiae Catholicae Et De Moribus Manichaeorum.* Translated by Donald A. Gallagher and Idella J. Gallagher. Vol. 56, *Fathers of the Church.* Washington, DC: Catholic University of America Press, 1966.

Jones, L. Gregory. *Emboding Forgiveness: A Theological Analysis.* Grand Rapids, MI: William B. Eerdmans Publishing Company, 1995.

Kierkegaard, Søren. *Fear and Trembling and the Sickness unto Death.* Translated by Walter Lowrie. Princeton, NJ: Princeton University Press, 1968.

Luther, Martin. "The Freedom of a Christian." In *Career of the Reformer: I,* edited by Harold J. Grimm. Vol. 31, *Luther's Works.* Philadelphia: Muhlenberg Press, 1957.

Meeks, Wayne A. *The Moral World of the First Christians.* Library of Early Christianity. Philadelphia: The Westminster Press, 1986.

————. *The Origins of Christian Morality: The First Two Centuries.* New Haven: Yale University Press, 1993.

Powell, Samuel M., and Michael E. Lodahl, eds. *Embodied Holiness: Toward a Corporate Theology of Spiritual Growth.* Downers Grove, IL: InterVarsity Press, 1999.

Thomas Aquinas. *Summa Theologiae.* Edited by Thomas Gilby. The Blackfriars English translation ed. Garden City, NY: Image Books, 1969.

Volf, Miroslav, and Dorothy C. Bass, eds. *Practicing Theology: Beliefs and Practices in Christian Life.* Grand Rapids, MI: William B. Eerdmans Publishing Company, 2002.

WORKS OF LOVE: GENEROSITY AND JUSTICE

C hapter 7 described some of the disciplines that produce Christian character. Chapter 8 set forth a theological account of Christian virtues and practices in a general way. Chapters 9 and 10 discuss important and representative virtues and provide some concrete illustrations of points made in preceding chapters.

Matthew 23 is a sustained diatribe against the scribes and Pharisees. In 23:23, Jesus states that they have neglected the weightier things of the law—justice, mercy, and faithfulness—while being scrupulous about tithing herbs from their gardens. In this chapter, I wish to focus on two of those weightier things, justice and mercy. Mercy, in Matthew's Gospel, means generosity, as we learn from 6:2-4, where mercy denotes the giving of alms to the needy.

This saying of Jesus is part of a larger theme in Matthew's Gospel, in which Jesus establishes a connection to the prophetic tradition of the Old Testament. This is seen more clearly in two episodes (9:10-13 and 12:1-8), during which Jesus quotes from Hosea 6:6: "For I desire steadfast love [translated *mercy* in Matthew's Gospel] and not sacrifice, the knowledge of God rather than burnt offerings." So, when in Matthew 23 Jesus regards mercy and justice as the weightier things of the law, he is giving voice to a common theme among the prophets, classically expressed in Amos 5:23-24:

> Take away from me the noise of your songs;
>> I will not listen to the melody of your harps.
> But let justice roll down like waters,
>> and righteousness like an ever-flowing stream.

The purpose of this chapter is to show that the practice of generosity and justice arises naturally out of an understanding of the embodied, communal, and trinitarian dimensions of the Christian faith. As mentioned previously, the Christian practice of generosity means first of all the sharing of material goods with those who need such goods. The definition of justice requires a bit more discussion. In part, it pertains to a society's judicial process—ensuring that everyone is treated fairly. In the Bible, this aspect of justice is usually mentioned in connection with the inability of the poor and others lacking power to receive the legal rights due them. In part, justice pertains to the distribution of goods within a society—ensuring that everyone in a society receives the goods that are due them. But even though justice and generosity are defined quite differently, they are connected by the fact that each pertains to right practice toward our neighbor, especially in the realm of material goods.

Because justice is a matter of social organization and policies and not simply a matter of individual decision and action, the practice of justice differs from the practice of generosity. It necessarily involves the attempt to change society's laws. That is why the Old Testament often linked its idea of justice with its hoped-for future messianic king:

> His authority shall grow continually,
>> and there shall be endless peace
>> for the throne of David and his kingdom.
> He will establish and uphold it
> with justice and with righteousness. (Isaiah 9:7)

Because of the social nature of justice, such a king would be necessary, for only such a king would combine righteousness with the exercise of power necessary to achieve justice.

The Practice of Generosity and Justice

The practical aspect of generosity and justice hardly needs much emphasis—unlike faith and love, there has never been any tendency to spiritualize them in such a way that an interior attitude is thought to be a satisfactory substitute for practice. The problem is not that we will reduce generosity and the quest for justice to sentiment or subjective intention, but that we will fail to see that they are ways in which love is made actual and concrete. Without generosity and justice, love remains a feeling or an attitude. It was against this error that 1 John asked, "How does God's love abide in anyone who has the world's goods and sees a brother or sister in need and yet refuses help?" (3:17), and stated that "those who do not love a brother or sister whom they have seen, cannot love God whom they have not seen" (4:20). So, although it is true that love is the ultimate principle of the Christian ethical life, it is also true that when love is considered apart from the concreteness of generosity and justice it remains abstract.

World-Transcendence and World-Participation

THE IMPULSE TOWARD TRANSCENDING THE WORLD

As noted previously, the embodied character of the Christian faith means that we stand in a twofold relation to the world, a relation of ethical transcendence and participation. Generosity and justice each represent our transcendence over the fallen world. Generosity is our victory over sin as it manifests itself in a number of vices: greed and envy (Romans 1:29), love of self, love of money, and ingratitude (2 Timothy 3:2-3). Each of these vices is an expression of a tendency to elevate our interests above those of others and is ultimately community destroying. We know that this was for Paul a serious matter because it is the chief lesson that he drew from the incarnation: to have the mind that was in Christ is to "do nothing from selfish ambition or conceit . . . in humility [to] regard others as better than [ourselves]," and to "look not to [our] own interests, but to the interests of others" (Philippians 2:3-5). Only this mind is community creating. To be greedy and envious is to want someone else's good for *myself* alone. If we love money, then money and not the welfare of others becomes our highest good. That is why 1 Timothy 6:17-18 insists that those with money must use it for the good of others. Possession of wealth tends to make our own good prominent in our thinking and to diminish our concern for others. To be ungrateful is to regard *myself* as inherently deserving and to regard the other person as an instrument of my well-being. To practice generosity means that we have, however provisionally, been freed from preoccupation with our own good and enabled to act on behalf of the other's good. This is, according to the Christian faith, the foundation of community—not enlightened self-interest, but life for others. Moreover, it is only in such a community that thoroughgoing generosity is possible.

Unlike generosity, the practice of justice is a victory, not over the evil and selfish inclinations of the heart, but over the corporate domain of sin. The corporate aspect of sin means that world-transcendence is more difficult in the case of justice than of generosity. It is possible to imagine someone extinguishing greed and envy and practicing generosity consistently. This would represent a complete ethical transcendence over the fallen world—complete though not permanent, since greed and envy could always resurface. Nonetheless, consistent and faithful generosity does represent the possibility of complete transcendence over sin. It is different with the practice of justice. The corporate nature of injustice means that, no matter to what extent the individual may practice justice, the organization of society remains such that injustice prevails to some extent. Local acts of justice by individuals are a partial but not a complete victory. So, although the individual's practice of justice represents his or her transcendence over the world, there is an important sense in which the fallen world has not yet been transcended. Even the individual who practices justice remains embedded in a social organization that in some degree yields injustice. A small businessowner, for instance, may practice justice by paying employees a living wage. But the owner may have little control over suppliers and distributors whose practices may be unjust. A city politician may promote just policies locally but will have little control over state and federal laws. It has been a great contribution of theological movements such as the Social Gospel and Liberation Theology to show us that our ethical transcendence over the world is incomplete, not only because of our individual failure to practice the Christian faith consistently, but also because we participate in the fallen world in ways that are subtle and, seemingly, intractable.

THE IMPULSE TOWARD PARTICIPATING IN THE WORLD

The practice of generosity and justice signifies not only our transcendence over the fallen world, but also our participation in the world. This participation takes not only the negative form of our unwitting and unwilling participation in unjust social organization, but also our participation, as creatures, in the world of God's creation. The need and practice of generosity, especially insofar as it involves satisfying material needs and is a bodily practice, is a sign of our participation in the material world and of our essential creatureliness. Every act of generosity should be a reminder to us that we are material beings with material needs. Generosity thus discloses our essential solidarity with the world of living beings, the world that God found to be good. Our participation in this world is disclosed as well by the fact that generosity necessarily involves physical acts of giving and receiving. Of course, in our situation today, the giving and receiving may be quite impersonal—writing a check that is delivered by a postal system to an agency whose members we do not know, who then distribute goods that we do not see to people in need whom we will never meet. Even so, generosity necessarily involves the physical act of giving in some minimal form. There is no such thing as a purely inward and spiritual act of generosity. Generosity inevitably involves our participation in the creaturely realm of physical acts. Generosity is also a mode of participating in the world because it is a means of building human community. At least ideally, generosity establishes relationships of friendship and reciprocity. By acting generously we proclaim that we are members of the human community and not beings that are exempt from its needs and constraints.

We can see the sense in which the practice of justice is a mode of participating in the world if we note that, in order to practice justice, we must reject an otherworldly attitude that regards salvation as a liberation from the created world. The practice of justice implies the belief that the world is both God's creation and the object of God's redeeming activity. It implies as well that instances of justice in history are anticipations of the perfect justice that will occur in the kingdom of God. The practice of justice is an affirmation of the book of Revelation's vision of a new heaven and a new earth and of Revelation's picture of a future in which God dwells with humankind on a transformed earth. It is important to make this point because one of the residual effects of apocalypticism is the conviction that this world is so totally under the domination of Satan that it is beyond redemption. As a result (according to this convictions), any efforts toward large-scale justice are thought to be mistaken, given the inevitability of the earth's destruction, and harmful, since such efforts detract from the more important task of seeking individual conversions. To practice justice and to see justice as a promise of God's eschatological kingdom is to reject this negative consequence of apocalypticism and to affirm the world's goodness and the reality of its participation in God's new creation.

GENEROSITY AND JUSTICE UNDER THE CONDITION OF FINITUDE

Our embodied existence and our participation in the world mean that generosity and justice are practiced under the condition of finitude and that their realization is constrained. In the case of generosity, this point is most easily seen by considering its concreteness. As noted previously,

172

generosity is one of the ways in which Christian love is made concrete. But the concreteness of generosity implies the limits of its practice. Aristotle's analysis is helpful here. Generosity consists in giving the right amount, to the right people, at the right time, and in the right way. But Aristotle saw that it was difficult to measure up to generosity understood in this way. There are many ways of missing the mark and few ways of hitting it. Above all, generosity requires deliberation about the circumstances: the right amount, the right recipient, the right time, and the right way. But human deliberation is a fallible matter—not because of our sin, but because of our finitude. We do not know all the relevant circumstances, and our judgment may be flawed by any number of unavoidable factors. Consequently, generosity must be practiced with humility and with the awareness that practice invariably falls short of its ideal result.

The matter is more complex in the case of justice. First, it is easy to find disagreement about appropriate ends in the practice of and quest for justice: What is a fair distribution of society's goods? What is a living wage? What constitutes minimally decent working conditions? Second, it is just as easy and perhaps easier to be confused about appropriate means to those ends: How should we frame laws so that the effects of injustice are ameliorated? How can we influence the political process to ensure passage of those laws? What means of enforcement should we advocate? As with generosity, fallible human deliberation and prudence are required for the practice of justice. Not surprising, Christians can and do disagree on these matters. The finitude of our deliberative powers makes such disagreement inevitable, even with respect to the ends to be sought. Christians will not agree, for instance, on what constitutes a living wage. This disagreement is not always based on human perversity or obstinacy. It sometimes results from the finitude of our perspectives—the fact that each of us assesses matters, even ethical matters of the greatest importance, from value calculations that differ from others. So, although all Christians will (we trust) agree that grinding poverty is a great evil that should be eliminated, they will not agree on the level of material goods that are due to society's members. Because these differences result, at least in part, from our finite condition, there is no reason to believe that greater spiritual devotion will overcome them. Dialogue and sustained reflection may bring the various opinions closer to agreement, but honest disagreement is an inevitable consequence of finitude.

The limitations of finitude appear also in the essentially tragic character of moral practice. By *tragic*, I mean that moral issues almost always involve some conflict of values that cannot be harmoniously and fully resolved. The conflict involves a choice, not between the good and the evil, but instead between two goods. The resolution must take the form of elevating one good above another. It thus inevitably involves some sort of moral compromise. Affirmative action gives us an example. If rules are put in place that create opportunity for one class of people, then to some extent opportunity may be diminished for another class of people. A society may, with good reason, decide that the resulting good outweighs the harm done to the second class, but this decision is in fact the selection of one good over another. A progressive income tax is another example. The policy of taxing the more affluent at higher rates than the less affluent results from a decision in which one good (the benefits of a reduced taxation to the less affluent) is elevated in importance above another good (perhaps a belief in the intrinsic fairness of a uniform rate of taxation). Needless to say, such arrangement of goods is subject to all sorts of miscalculation. In fact, there is no arrangement of goods that is so intrinsically rational and beneficial that it would receive universal acceptance. It is an essential part of our finite moral lives that we must make these sorts of controversial decisions that necessarily involve the subordination of some goods to others.

These consequences of our finite condition mean that the church should never identify its efforts and their results with the kingdom of God. By the grace of God they may be anticipations of that kingdom, but they can never be its full reality. Our efforts, no matter how well-intentioned and well-executed, will always have the mark of finitude about them. They will suffer from the sorts of limitations that we would never associate with God's kingdom, even though the church is the body of Christ. Its being the body of Christ, experience shows, is no guarantee of its wisdom and competence. This fact, however, is no excuse for inactivity. As anticipations of God's kingdom, the church and its efforts are supremely important, for they are the continuation of Jesus' proclamation of the kingdom. They also represent our faithful response to God's grace and our obedience to God's command. But it will always be important to maintain a distinction between the work of the church and the work of God. The church consecrates its efforts to God as a prayer and trusts God to make use of those efforts.

The Practice of Generosity and Justice in Community

Generosity and justice are by definition communal practices. Neither can be practiced by solitary individuals. Each requires others to whom one is generous and for whom one seeks justice. But a fuller analysis of their communal character is possible if we attend to the theology that underlies them.

Christian theology teaches that there is an important sense in which sin is corporate—it transcends the individual. Without denying that individuals are sinners and commit acts of sin, the church has also asserted that sin is not fully understood if it is portrayed only in terms of individuals and their deeds.

The corporate character of sin has been variously represented in Christian thought. In the Bible, it appears in the conviction that the heavenly powers are fallen. Early in the biblical tradition, Yahweh was thought to be surrounded by a host of heavenly powers (as in 1 Kings 22:19) in a sort of divine council. Later (in apocalyptic literature), these powers came to be regarded as rebellious and subject to God's judgment (see, for example, Isaiah 24:21-23). In the New Testament, this conviction appears in Paul's admonition that "our struggle is not against enemies of blood and flesh, but against the rulers, against the authorities, against the cosmic powers of this present darkness, against the spiritual forces of evil in the heavenly places" (Ephesians 6:12). This helps us understand Paul's insistence that, in the cross, God has disarmed these powers and triumphed over them (Colossians 2:15). It also helps us see why Revelation represents the Roman Empire as a demonic reality. The great beast that rises from the sea and is intent on destroying the people of God receives its power from the dragon, Satan (Revelation 13:2). In contrast to Paul's positive assessment of the empire in Romans 13:1-7, Revelation detects cosmic evil at the base of Rome. Sin, as represented in these passages, is not only a human phenomenon, but also a cosmic and transpersonal reality. It has a corporate dimension that stands behind the sinful acts of individuals. Although it does not cause those acts (since human beings are still responsible), those acts are not fully comprehensible without the background of cosmic sin.

The corporate character of sin appears in another form in the New Testament, namely in Paul's understanding of Adam and the effects of Adam's sin. Although Paul's remarks are brief and not fully clear, it is clear that he believed that sin, death, and condemnation had come upon humankind as a result of Adam's sin (1 Corinthians 15:21-22 and Romans 5:12-21). Paul's language is striking: "Because of the one man's trespass, death exercised dominion through that one" (Romans 5:17) and "by the one man's disobedience the many were made sinners" (5:19). Much theological effort has been expended over the centuries in the attempt to elucidate Paul's meaning. But at the very least we can say that he is expressing the idea that sin is prior to the individual's act—that even before we begin to act we participate in a fallen system marked by sin, death, and condemnation. Sin, we may conclude, has in Paul's thought a communal character insofar as human beings bear the image of Adam, "the man of dust" (1 Corinthians 15:49).

Salvation likewise has, in the Bible, a corporate dimension. It is important to reinforce this point due to the pervasive impression among Americans that the goal of salvation is the individual's going to heaven to be with God. Not only is this picture overly spiritual (leaving out the destiny of the world), but it is also excessively individualistic. The biblical ideal of salvation, in contrast, includes the renovation of cosmos (Romans 8:21) and the reconciliation to God of all things in heaven and earth (Colossians 1:20). In themselves, these affirmations do not constitute a corporate understanding of salvation. However, they do remind us that Paul understood salvation to encompass much more than simply human redemption. These passages, therefore, discourage any attempt to think of salvation in strictly individualistic terms. For Paul, the object of Christ's redeeming work is nothing less than the entire world. The corporate dimension of salvation is more fully portrayed in some of the symbols used in the Bible. First of all is the symbol of the kingdom, as in Isaiah 9 and which was the subject of Jesus' proclamation. But there is also the symbol of the eschatological banquet, first enunciated in Isaiah 25:6 and then used often in the parables of Jesus, and Revelation's symbol of the city, New Jerusalem. Kingdom, banquet, and city all point to a corporate understanding of salvation, in which the goal of redemption is an eschatological gathering of people. As Luke's Gospel puts it, "Then people will come from east and west, from north and south, and will eat in the kingdom of God" (13:29).

Theology in the last 150 years has sought to recover this communal understanding of sin and salvation and to overcome overly individualistic accounts. Of course, developments in theology have not permitted a simple repetition of the biblical representation of sin and salvation. The rise of modern science has rendered the notion of cosmic, fallen spiritual powers problematic. The development of social sciences, especially sociology, means that theologians have a somewhat broader conception of human good than they had previously. Prominent among these efforts at recovery have been Liberation Theology and its American precursor, the Social Gospel.

The Social Gospel was a response to a host of social problems that plagued America, especially American cities, in the late nineteenth and early twentieth centuries. It was also a reaction to the tendency of American Christianity to represent sin only as the evil acts of individuals and salvation as the conversion of sinners. Against this individualistic interpretation, theologians of the Social Gospel insisted that both sin and salvation must be thought of in terms that include the social dimension of human existence. In their situation, that meant speaking out against and trying to change dehumanizing industrial conditions as well as the causes of unemployment and alcohol abuse. They saw that some sinful behavior could not be curbed only by convincing individuals to amend their ways. That is why there was continual agitation to prohibit the production of alcohol. Although, in retrospect, this was a flawed strategy, it was consistent with a communal doctrine of sin. The point was to eliminate, where possible, the sources of sinful behavior. These theologians were not rejecting the spiritual dimension of sin and salvation. Although some in the movement were socialists, none were philosophical materialists. At the same time, their theology did have a revised eschatology, one that incorporated an optimistic and progressive view of history. But this was not its only feature. Its eschatology included as well a vision of human community in which not only souls, but every dimension of human being, was redeemed. This eschatology then translated into practical action intended to bring about, in American society, conditions of justice that would approach that eschatological vision.

The theology of the Social Gospel was not without problems. Nonetheless, it does represent a serious effort to recover the Bible's sense of the corporate aspect of sin and salvation and to join this sense to a program of practical action. A more recent attempt to recover this sense is Liberation Theology. Although Liberation Theology has experienced some changes in the last forty years, there are several constants in this tradition. First, it regards poverty as a legitimate target of the church's evangelistic ministry, on the grounds that salvation concerns the totality of human existence. In this way, it connects soteriology firmly to the doctrine of creation. Second, it understands poverty to be caused by social and political factors, not only by individual greed and laziness. Accordingly, it has made use of social scientific analysis and Marxist class-analysis in order to see better how poverty comes to be. Third, like the Social Gospel, Liberation Theology has made a prominent place for the practical dimension of the Christian faith in its insistence on the centrality of praxis. In the concept of praxis, the cognitive and reflective aspect of faith is joined to the practical dimension, expressing itself in the form of action that promotes justice.

In summary, we can say that the Christian tradition and its biblical roots recognize a dimension of sin that goes beyond individual misdeeds, a dimension that is operative upon individuals and affects their capacity for living well. It likewise recognizes a dimension of salvation that is more than the redemption of human souls and that includes the redemption of every aspect of creation. Christian concern about justice is grounded in this vision of salvation, of its eschatological consummation, and of the moral imperative to contribute to the creation of a just society, even if its justice is fragmentary and a mere anticipation of the ideal justice of the eschatological kingdom of God. Of course, this corporate dimension of sin and salvation has been variously conceived in Christian history. It will always be necessary for Christian intellectuals to think seriously and creatively, amid changing social contexts, about the nature of justice and about the best means of contributing to it. Nonetheless, faithful Christian thought will always hold fast to its bedrock conviction about the corporate nature of both sin and salvation.

This historical prelude has served to show that the church's quest for justice is grounded firmly in the Christian faith, its eschatology, and its communal implications. But can we also say that generosity is grounded in the Christian ideal of community? The answer can be found if we attend to the following points.

Second Corinthians 8–9 is an attempt by Paul to persuade the Corinthians to make good on their promise to support the offering of money that Paul was collecting for the church in Jerusalem. Paul had two examples of generosity that he hoped would move them: the churches of Macedonia (who had "overflowed in a wealth of generosity" [8:2]) and Jesus Christ, who, "though he was rich, yet for your sakes he became poor, so that by his poverty you might become rich" (8:9). Although Paul did not elaborate on this point, he was implicitly saying that Christian generosity has a christological ground. Just as we are to love as Christ loved (Ephesians 5:2), so we are to be generous because, and as, Christ was generous. But, because the church is the body of Christ, christological arguments are also ecclesiological arguments. That is, because the church is Christ's body, it carries on the ministry and practices of Christ, including generosity. Generosity, therefore, for the Christian is not simply a social virtue to which we are obligated because we are social beings. It is an implication of the fact that the church is a community of a particular sort—the body of the Christ whose incarnation was an act of generosity on our behalf. The church, having been founded on an act of divine generosity, is to be the community whose nature consists in being generous to others, as in the example of the Macedonian churches.

This point is articulated more fully in Paul's teaching about the gifts of the Spirit. One of these (Romans 12:8) is generosity. Superficially understood, this passage teaches that the Holy Spirit enables some to be extraordinarily generous. But this understanding misses the context of Paul's teaching about the gifts. As the argument in 1 Corinthians 12 makes clear, the purpose of the gifts is to bring about the well-being of the body of Christ. Each gift, including generosity, contributes essentially to the soundness of the church. This teaching likewise shows us why the Christian practice of generosity is not simply a human social virtue. It presupposes not just any sort of community, but community of a definite sort, and takes its meaning from the character of that community. This fact explains why Christians must practice generosity with humility and why Jesus criticized those whose generosity was practiced ostentatiously. In the ancient world, generosity was a public event, for at least part of its purpose was to gain prestige and honor for the giver. But in the church, the purpose of generosity is utterly consumed by its orientation to the good of the entire body.

These christological and pneumatological points help us understand the New Testament's rather pragmatic advice about wealth and labor. According to 1 Timothy, the rich "are to do good, to be rich in good works, generous, and ready to share, thus storing up for themselves the treasure of a good foundation for the future" (6:18-19). Ephesians 4:28 teaches that "thieves must ... labor and work honestly ... so as to have something to share with the needy." The rationale of these exceedingly practical prescriptions about money have persuasive power only if one's use of money is regulated by the conviction that the church is the body of Christ. First Timothy urges generosity, but not so that the giver may be honored by the community in the manner of ancient patrons (although admittedly it does add a rationale for generosity that is based on self-interest). Ephesians teaches that the importance of earning money lies in the fact that it gives us the capacity to share with those in need. In each case, the church is being taught to consider money as a means of generosity for the well-being of the community instead of considering generosity a means of public praise.

The Christian practice of generosity, therefore, is implied by the fact that the church is the body of Christ and by the ecclesial context of the gifts of the Spirit. The Christian practice of justice requires a more complicated exposition. This is because, as already noted, justice pertains to social laws and customs, and the quest for justice involves the attempt to change these customs and laws. However, the problem is that, outside Matthew, Mark, and Luke, nowhere in the New Testament is the quest for justice mentioned. In other words, although justice did figure into the message of the prophets and of Jesus, in the documents that most directly reflect the life of the church—the Johannine literature, Paul's letters, and so on—there is seemingly no interest in justice. Indeed, some New Testament passages seem to run contrary to an interest in justice. These include the admonitions that slaves should be good slaves (such as Ephesians 6:5-7, 1 Timothy 6:1-2, and 1 Peter 2:18-21) and that disciples should remain in whatever station of life they occupied when they converted (1 Corinthians 7:17-31). If these passages were the sum total of Christian thought on social issues, the result would be quite the opposite of progressive. Additionally, the Johannine literature, with its razor sharp distinction between church and world, has a strongly sectarian emphasis that does not encourage disciples to show even generosity to those outside the community. If the world outside the community is not an object of generosity, it is difficult to see how Johannine Christianity would have any interest in justice. Finally, the apocalyptic orientation of early Christianity means that, when an interest in justice is expressed, it takes the form of a desire for God's eschatological vengeance on the wicked, as in Revelation 6:9-10.

For these reasons, the Christian practice of justice cannot be simply read off the text of the New Testament, as generosity can. However, there are mitigating factors that help us understand the New Testament's lack of interest in justice. One is the fact that the church in the first century was a minuscule portion of an enormous, despotic empire. Even if early Christians had sought to actualize the prophets' concern for social justice, they were in no position to do so. In their context, decisions about taxation, for example, were made faraway by a process not subject to popular change. Christians did not have the same political status in the Roman Empire that the prophets had in ancient Israel. Moreover, as the Johannine literature reveals, the main order of business for the early church was survival. It was necessarily inwardly focused because it was a small, threatened community in a hostile environment. Although we may wish that the early church had spoken out forcefully about social issues, it is understandable that it did not. We must also come to terms with the fact that the apocalyptic orientation of the church likely affected its outlook on social issues. This is expressly the point of 1 Corinthians 7:29: Paul urged his readers to remain in their various conditions—whether slaves or unmarried—"in view of the impending crisis" (7:26) and because "the appointed time has grown short" (7:29). Decisions about issues such as slavery and marriage could be put on hold because the present age was thought to be near its end. Although apocalyptic thought appears periodically in Christian history and is not dead today, most Christians today have adjusted themselves to the reality of a protracted length of time before the end of history. The theologically responsible thing to do is to see the New Testament, first in its canonical context (that is, in taking seriously the prophets' witness to justice) and, second, in its social and theological context (that is, as the product of an inwardly focused, apocalyptic group). Thus a way will be cleared for a Christian doctrine and practice of justice. Today, with the tools of New Testament scholarship and the social sciences available, we are in a position to appreciate the prophetic interest in justice and its eschatological setting. As a result, the pursuit of justice today takes its meaning from Jesus' proclamation of the eschatological kingdom of God and its prophetic antecedents.

What, then, is the role of the community in the practice of justice? We can point to four functions. First, the Christian community, in its history, has thought extensively about justice. The Christian tradition is an ongoing dialogue on matters of substance such as justice. This tradition looks backward to its founding document—the Bible—as it has been interpreted by faithful reflection. But it also incorporates insights drawn from ancillary disciplines such as sociology and philosophy. The Christian theory and practice of justice, therefore, is not something left to individual predilection. Responsible Christians, in their thought and action, will draw upon this tradition and submit to its wisdom.

Second, the Christian community is to be an anticipation of the kingdom of God. Of course, it anticipates the kingdom under the condition of finitude and in a fallen world. This is why the church is not identical with the kingdom but is instead an anticipation. But as an anticipation, the church is to be the place where we strive to ensure that God's will is done on earth as it is in heaven. This means that, with regard to its internal life, the church must exemplify justice. Christians individually and congregations and denominations collectively must act justly. In this way, it will be a witness to the world of the possibilities of God's grace.

Third, the church's mission includes the task of bearing prophetic witness, in the name of God's kingdom, against injustice. The church has been entrusted with the gospel of the kingdom, a message of "good news to the poor ... [of] release to the captives, [of] recovery of sight to the blind, to let the oppressed go free" (Luke 4:18). Although this is not the whole of the gospel message, it is an essential part. In this regard, the church takes up the mantle of the prophets and speaks for God in the world. Also like the prophets, the church has the task of speaking up on behalf of those who otherwise have no voice and bringing their need of justice to the public's attention.

Fourth and most ambitious (and dangerous), the church is called upon to act in the world for the sake of justice. The form of this action will vary from one context to another, but will always involve the church in the attempt to change society so that justice prevails. In the American context, this means not only consciousness-raising and advocacy, but also attempts to change public law. This is the most ambitious task because, as the theologians of the Social Gospel saw, the issue of social sin is not fully addressed until its causes are addressed. It is the most dangerous task because it involves the church in the political process, in which compromise is necessary and results are never guaranteed. The advocates of Prohibition believed that they were striking a deathblow to sin by eliminating the production and trade of alcohol. Regrettably, the result was an unforeseen rise in crime and the organization of crime. Any involvement in politics inevitably involves settling for what is possible and forsaking what is ideal.

The Practice of Generosity and Justice in a Fallen World

The finite character of our deliberative knowledge is not the only problem that the practice of generosity and justice has to contend with. More serious is the fact that we practice these virtues as part of our eschatological existence between sin's past and God's future. The eschatological character of our practice of generosity appears very simply in the possibility of wrong motives. If our redemption were complete, if the kingdom of God were here in its fullness, if sin had finally been overcome, then the question of motive would never arise. A good act would be a good act. But as Jesus noted, it is possible to act in a generous way with sinful intent (Matthew 6:2-4). This means that, no matter how saintly we may be, we are never far from the corrupting effects of sin. One of the effects of sin is to transform overtly good actions into sin by the corruption of our motives. But the way in which sin achieves this is subtle, for even in corrupting our motives, sin convinces us that we are acting with good motives. Sin is effective not only in getting us to act with wrong motives, but also, and more insidious, in blinding us to the fact that our motives are impure. That is why self-examination and perpetual vigilance are required in the Christian life. Our subjective certainty of the purity of our motives is not always a reliable sign of their purity.

Eschatological existence means that we are not immune from the effects of sin. It means also that we continue to participate, however unwillingly, in the fallen world. Eschatological existence means that we live as citizens of the kingdom of God and also as inhabitants of the world. Although our membership in the kingdom of God means that we have turned our backs on the fallen world, it cannot erase the fact that, in subtle ways, that world continues to appear in our lives and to shape our lives in ways that may not be apparent. With respect to justice, this reality manifests itself in the fact that we necessarily participate in forms of social and economic orga-nization that, to one degree or another, produce conditions of injustice. I say necessarily because there is no possibility of escape from these forms of organization. Even utopian communities that seek to insulate themselves from the world cannot be completely self-sustaining. Even they must obtain raw materials from outside the community and must abide by civil laws, at least those that are reasonably just, even though these laws may create or reinforce certain forms of injustice. Perhaps the best example of this point is the way in which, in the context of affirmative action programs, we have learned how the present distribution of social goods reflects past conditions of injustice. Those who are currently affluent owe—in some measure—their affluence to opportunities and privileges that came at the expense of certain classes of people. Other examples are possible. The point is that we can hardly avoid participating in structures that foster injustice. To be a Christian— to live eschatologically—is to live with the knowledge that, even though we are members of God's household, we nonetheless cannot escape entanglement with the fallen world.

There are more overt consequences of practicing and pursuing justice in a fallen world. One is complacency, which may be defined as reducing justice to generosity and ignoring the need of large-scale justice. Complacency may occur because of an unbalanced theology, as in the case of those whose apocalypticism convinces them of the impossibility of redeeming the world; or because of selfishness, as with those who are so preoccupied with their own well-being that they have no vision for the well-being of others; or by convenient ignorance, as with those who over-look the way in which they benefit from organized injustice.

Another overt consequence is publicly and consciously identifying with organized injustice. Regrettably, the Christian church has a very poor record on this issue. The church has rather consistently allied itself with social institutions that have actively oppressed a great variety of people. In the American context, the church's support of slavery and its rather tardy advocacy of women's rights are prominent examples. This is not to say that the church has not had its reasons for joining itself to these institutions. Sometimes these reasons have been embarrassingly bad (as in the idiotic theology that underlay slavery). Sometimes these reasons have been under-standable but probably based on false premises (as in the Roman Catholic Church's fear of communism that led it to resist progressive movements in the nineteenth century). The lesson to draw from this is that, like the indi-vidual, the church must engage in perpetual self-examination.

A third consequence of practicing justice in a fallen world is the temp-tation to use improper means to good and just ends. The church's record here, too, is not uniformly good. From the crusades to the recent scandals involving pedophilia, the church has manifested a tendency to select strategies that, in retrospect, are wrong and harmful. Admittedly, it is dif-ficult to know, in the midst of a great moral debate, just which strategies are best, but this fact simply points to the need of a wiser and more Christian process of decision making.

A fourth consequence is despair. Eschatological existence means coex-istence with the world and the present evil age. Under these conditions, it is easy for Christians to lose hope. Already in the first century this was an issue: "Where is the promise of his coming? For ever since our ances-tors died, all things continue as they were from the beginning of cre-ation!" (2 Peter 3:4). In view of the apparent intractability of sin and the endurance of the fallen world and the fruitlessness of the church's paltry efforts, the expectation of justice and the kingdom of God may easily wane. But to live eschatologically is also to live as a participant of and witness to the kingdom of God, which, we believe, has come to humankind in the life, death, and resurrection of Jesus and which con-tinues to appear wherever God's grace finds a faithful response. To live eschatologically is to overcome despair with hope in the God who makes all things new, even if with God "one day is like a thousand years" (2 Peter 3:8). It is to know that "hope does not disappoint us, because God's love has been poured into our hearts through the Holy Spirit"

(Romans 5:5). It is to say with Paul, "If we hope for what we do not see, we wait for it with patience" (Romans 8:25).

Generosity, Justice, and Participation in God

Every virtue is grounded in the God who is love. When we practice generosity and justice, which are concrete forms of love, then we participate in God.

But this abstract formulation needs amplification. The God who is love is Father, Son, and Holy Spirit. This means that, if we are to understand generosity and justice rightly, we must see how they are defined by the trinitarian life of God. The way forward in this matter is to see that generosity and justice characterize the Father's saving act in Jesus Christ and the Holy Spirit. It is not that human generosity and justice are somehow reflected in the eternal perfection of God's nature. It is instead that human generosity and justice find their fulfillment in being like the act of God toward us through Jesus Christ in the Spirit. The christological ground of generosity points toward this trinitarian understanding. The ground of Christian virtue is not Jesus Christ in his humanity, but instead the fact that in Jesus Christ and in the Spirit, God has come to us and that this coming is an act of generosity and an act that manifests God's justice. The same is true of the fact that generosity is a gift of the Spirit. This gift must be seen in its trinitarian context whereby the Spirit gives the church the means to carry on the ministry of Jesus.

In the life, death, and resurrection of Jesus, the triune God has entered into human history and approached humankind. As the body of Christ and in the power of the Spirit, the church is an extension of God's entry into history and an extension of God's coming to humankind. And just as Jesus Christ was an act of God's generosity and an act that manifested God's justice, so the being and activity of the church is to be an act of God's generosity, manifesting God's justice. Of course, the church is and acts under the conditions of finitude and sin, so that we cannot simply identify the church's activity with God's activity. Nonetheless, the church—the human, finite church beset by sin—is the extension of God's ministry in Jesus Christ. The Christian practice of generosity, therefore, should be seen as the imitation of God. It is a repetition of God's paradigmatic act in Jesus Christ, and, when faithfully performed, it is a fresh act of God through the power of the Spirit. The practice of justice is likewise done as a repetition of God's paradigmatic act of justice in Jesus Christ and as an act enabled and inspired by the Spirit of God. In this way, to practice generosity and justice is to practice the love that 1 John enjoins on us, the love that enables us to know the God who is love.

Concluding Meditative Prayer

We praise you, God of mercy and justice, for your gifts to us and your righteous demands upon us. We praise you for being a God who commands justice for the widow and the orphan. We praise you for being both just and the one who justifies us. We praise you for your kingdom, the rule of justice and mercy. We praise you for generously giving us all that is yours: your only Son, the Spirit of life, and all good things. It is your nature to give yourself, but your giving does exhaust you. There is no end to your giving. Blessed are those who receive your generosity with thanksgiving and who practice your justice. We confess to you, our Lord, our unworthiness to benefit from your generosity. We acknowledge the infrequency of our thanks. We confess our failure to embody your justice and our inclination to rest content with injustice. Preserve us, we pray, safe from ingratitude and unjust deeds. Help us to be rich in good works, generous and ready to share, thus storing us for ourselves the treasure of a good foundation for the future. Give us wisdom and courage so that we may act justly and thus anticipate your kingdom. We pray that you would hasten your kingdom of justice and peace. Make us mindful, we pray, of your Son, who gave himself for us. Make us worthy of your gifts.

You, our God, who gives without limit and who executes justice, we praise. We praise
> the Father, who in generosity and kindness gave the Son for our justification,
> through the Son, who although rich, gave himself for us and whose kingdom is the rule of justice,
> in the Spirit, holy Gift, whose fruit is generosity and justice and all good things.

We praise the Holy Trinity, Father, Son, and Spirit, source and eternal image of generosity and justice.

Sources Consulted and Recommended

Aristotle. *The Ethics of Aristotle: The Nicomachean Ethics.* Translated by J. A. K. Thomson. Rev. ed. London: Penguin Books, 1976.

Boff, Leonardo. *Faith on the Edge: Religion and Marginalized Existence.* Translated by Robert R. Barr. San Francisco: Harper & Row, Publishers, 1989.

——. *When Theology Listens to the Poor.* Translated by Robert R. Barr. San Francisco: Harper & Row, 1988.

Byers, David M., ed. *Justice in the Marketplace: Collected Statements of the Vatican and the United States Catholic Bishops on Economic Policy, 1891–1984.* Washington, DC: United States Catholic Conference, Inc., 1985.

Dorr, Donal. *Option for the Poor: A Hundred Years of Vatican Social Teaching.* Maryknoll, NY: Orbis Books, 1983.

Hopkins, Charles Howard. *The Rise of the Social Gospel in American Protestantism 1865–1915.* Vol. 14, *Yale Studies in Religious Education.* New Haven: Yale University Press, 1967.

Jennings, Theodore W. *Good News to the Poor: John Wesley's Evangelical Economics.* Nashville: Abingdon Press, 1990.

Madron, Thomas W. "John Wesley on Economics." In *Sanctification and Liberation: Liberation Theologies in the Light of the Wesleyan Tradition.* Edited by Theodore Runyon. Nashville: Abingdon Press, 1981.

Marquardt, Manfred. *John Wesley's Social Ethics: Praxis and Principles.* Translated by John E. Steely and W. Stephen Gunter. Nashville: Abingdon Press, 1992.

Smith, Timothy L. *Revivalism and Social Reform in Mid-Nineteenth-century America.* New York: Abingdon Press, 1957.

Tillich, Paul. *Love, Power, and Justice; Ontological Analyses and Ethical Applications.* New York: Oxford University Press, 1954.

CHAPTER TEN

WORKS OF LOVE: CARING FOR CREATION

The subject of this chapter is our ethical and spiritual relation to the created world and the practices associated with that relation. A few words about the chapter's title may be helpful. Why should our relation to the created world be classified as a form of love? In what sense is the physical world an object of love? It is true that in common conceptions of love, in which love is a relation between persons, it doesn't make much sense to think of the created world as something that we could love. But the Christian tradition knows of another conception of love—willing the good for someone (or something) else. In this case, love is not so much a sentiment as the ensemble of actions that are intended to actualize something's good or to benefit it. With this conception, we can see how love of the created world is possible. It consists in acting in such a way that the created world (or at least that portion of the created world that we directly affect) achieves the good for which it was created. Of course, further discussion is necessary for us to discern what this created good is, which actions are consistent with that good, and how those actions cohere with our other ethical responsibilities. Nonetheless, from a Christian standpoint there is nothing odd about professing our love for the created world, keeping in mind Augustine's caution that, properly speaking, we are to love finite things only in and because of God. This prevents our regarding anything finite as something worthy of veneration for its own sake. In view of humankind's occasional tendency to deify nature, perhaps this is a point worth remembering.

Another preliminary point that needs mentioning is the way in which this subject compels some distinctive theological maneuvers. What I mean is that, unlike the other subjects of this book (baptism, faith, worship, and so on), care of the created world has little biblical warrant. Whereas there are numerous biblical passages that address justice, none directly and substantively speaks of our responsibility to God for the created world. Indeed, a few passages seem to suggest that the world was created mainly or even only for our benefit. The Christian tradition similarly has had, until recently, virtually nothing to say about this issue. The absence of direct support for care of creation in Christian sources has in the past led some to the view that the Christian faith is at best indifferent to humankind's effects on the world and that, at worst, it encourages a rapacious attitude toward the world. The response to this indictment is rooted in the contextualized nature of the Christian faith. By this I mean the fact that Christians always inhabit definite intellectual situations and that, inevitably, we find ourselves addressing issues of pressing importance in our situation with intellectual tools drawn from our situation. Christian thinking is always done within a given and necessarily limited intellectual horizon. That is why the writers of the New Testament failed to condemn slavery in principle. So thoroughly ingrained in ancient society was slavery that the possibility of its demise was virtually unthinkable. We may be disappointed at their shortsighted vision, but it helps to remember that future generations will marvel at our shortsighted moral vision. This insight helps us see why neither the Bible nor previous generations of Christian writers have discussed the care of creation. On one hand, until recently, there was no environmental problem to provoke thinking and concern. The earth was big enough and the human population small enough that pollution and use of resources was not experienced as a problem. On the other hand, it is only with the rise of modern science, especially the biological sciences, that we are in a position to appreciate both the fragility of the natural world and the interconnections between all living things and the physical environment. So, it is no failing of the Christian tradition that it has not expressed itself more fully on this subject. Throughout most of history, the main order of business was not loving and preserving the world, but trying desperately to preserve human life. Today, however, in the affluent nations, the importance of caring for the world is a matter of concern.

One lesson to draw from these observations is that the Christian faith must be rethought in every era. Although it is true that there are enduring convictions that the church cannot give up, each era brings issues that are both pressing and unprecedented. In each generation the church must adapt its practices in ways that are creative, effective, and faithful to its convictions. Another lesson to draw is that the practices of the past—no matter how long-standing and pervasive—are not necessarily normative. They must be repeatedly judged in the light of circumstances and knowledge as well as in the light of the Christian faith. Just as slavery, in ancient times accepted and practiced by Christians, is now regarded as a sub-Christian institution, so the attitudes and practices of previous generations of Christians may need to be revised in light of current conditions.

The Practice of Caring for Creation

Since neither the Bible nor the Christian tradition developed practices encompassing caring for creation, theology today must proceed by synthesizing other practices that have been developed. Among these are moderation (discussed in chapter 7), wisdom (discussed in chapter 8), and justice (discussed in chapter 9).

Among the causes of environmental problems, immoderate appetites probably ranks low. We are all aware of statistics to the effect that the average American consumes five or ten times the amount of resources and energy that inhabitants of the global south consume. It is true that, collectively, the level of consumption in developed countries is a substantial part of our environmental problems. But a theological discussion of the virtue and practice of moderation must begin with the observation that getting individuals, one at time, to reduce their consumption is not an effective strategy for solving environmental problems. But this does not mean that moderation is pointless. After all, Christians were counseled to live moderately centuries before environmental issues became problems. Christian moderation is not a proposed solution to a problem. It is instead a faithful response to the gospel, a response that happens to have a positive if small effect on environmental problems. That effect is twofold. First, moderation means that resources and energy are being consumed at a reduced rate. Second, moderation characterizes Christians as the sort of people who are mindful of their relation to material goods.

The bodily dimension of moderation appears in the fact that it is associated with specific practices, just as profligacy and excessive consumption can be identified by specific practices. As with other moral virtues, becoming a moderate person is a matter of unlearning profligate patterns of action and learning moderate patterns. And what is true of individuals is true of communities. Communities and their institutions can undergo a learning process in which patterns of organizational behavior are changed.

The Bible speaks rather generally about moderation. Negatively, it tells us to avoid the love of money and the desire to become rich (1 Timothy 6:9-10). Of course, the biblical rationale for this counsel has nothing to do with environmental concerns. Love of money is a danger because it may lead us away from the Christian faith—we are reminded of the connection between greed and idolatry (Ephesians 5:5). The desire for wealth is to be avoided because it exposes us to temptations and harmful desires. The purpose of these admonitions is to impart to us elements of a Christian character. Their pastoral aim is to keep disciples on the path of life and to help them avoid obstacles on that path. This pastoral aim is fully valid today. But we may also observe that the qualities enjoined on us will also characterize disciples as the sort of people who are mindful of the wider implications of their patterns of consumption. The Bible is trying to draw our attention away from our inherent desire for wealth and to show us the spiritual dangers of this desire. If we extend this pastoral concern a step or two farther, then we can see in the Bible a desire that disciples not devote their wealth to the enjoyment of pleasures. Attention to this counsel will help form disciples who are careful about consumption and the spiritual dimension of consumption. In this way, Christian disciples will be people with characteristics consistent with a deep care for the created world.

It is in this spirit that we can interpret passages that urge us not to be slaves to desire and pleasure (Titus 3:3). It is possible to interpret them quite narrowly. In this case, these passages signify nothing other than a negative attitude toward bodily pleasures and a concern about their disruptive effects on the Christian life. But we can also see in this sort of text a desire that our lives be oriented beyond ourselves. A life in which the satisfaction of desires is paramount is a life that is oriented to a narrow horizon of meaning. It sees life in the thinnest of terms—a matter of needs and their satisfaction. Although it is true that we are beings with needs, the Christian faith is predicated on the conviction that the satisfaction of needs is not the ultimate purpose of being human. We are made for God and for others. Being a slave to desire and pleasure is wrong, not because satisfaction of needs is wrong, but because if we are slave to desire then we cannot be a servant of God. Being a slave to desire means that our existence is disordered, for we have lost our orientation to God and, thereby, to others. So, passages such as Titus 3:3 are in fact urging the same truth that is expressed in 1 Corinthians 10:24: "Do not seek your own advantage, but that of the other." Like Titus 3:3, this text directs our existence away from a preoccupation with itself. To the extent that Christian disciples embody this sort of counsel, they will be people of moderation who, in their patterns of consumption and desire-satisfaction, will be mindful of the fact that their lives are interwoven with the lives of others in many ways. They will be aware that their consumption of goods and satisfaction of needs has a spiritual dimension and that their behavior has implications that go beyond themselves. Of course, as I have already noted, moderation and mindfulness are not solutions to the problems of the environment. But they are aspects of Christian character that are required if we are to become people who care for the created world and who honor the creator.

More positively, the Bible commands contentment (1 Timothy 6:8 and Hebrews 13:5) and, more strongly, self-sufficiency and independence (Philippians 4:11 and 1 Timothy 6:6). The idea of self-sufficiency in the ancient world was used extensively in philosophical circles to designate a moral ideal according to which the person who has achieved the good life needs nothing besides virtue for happiness. In this conception, the possession of external goods adds nothing to happiness and their absence does not detract from happiness. The New Testament writers probably did not wish to recommend everything implied by the philosophers' use of "self-sufficiency." But Philippians 4:11, in which Paul expressed his indifference to circumstances, shows us how close Paul was to the philosophers in this respect. This attitude is possible only if we have internalized the injunctions to glorify God with our bodies (1 Corinthians 6:20) and to do everything to God's glory (1 Corinthians 10:31). These injunctions assert that our true being lies in our orientation to God. If God is our highest good—if we are fulfilling our created purpose to be worshipers of God—then our circumstances can become comparatively unimportant. The significance of being content is that it directs our ethical and spiritual attention away from our own good—narrowly conceived—and points us to our highest good. Like the negative commands to avoid the love of money and pleasure, it instills in us the conviction that our good is not identical to our material surroundings, for "is not life more than food, and the body more than clothing?" (Matthew 6:25).

We should acknowledge that being content with what we have is a relative matter. As our society has become more affluent, we have experienced luxury inflation. Goods such as the telephone and indoor plumbing that were once regarded as helpful but inessential have become an essential part of our lives, replaced by other goods such as the cellular telephone that moved into the "helpful but inessential" category. There is every reason to expect that in the future the cellular telephone will be thought of as an indispensable part of life. So, being content with what we have takes concrete form in particular cultural situations. First Timothy 6:8 commands us to be content with food and clothing, but this falls far short of what we today regard as essential for life. The observation that being content is relative to historical circumstances is important if we are to minimize unedifying and rancorous debates about the extent of Christian simplicity. Is an SUV for a large family a luxury or, if not a necessity, at least so practical that its purchase is justified? When can we morally justify replacing a computer in these days when the pace of obsolescence is increasing? These sorts of decisions, with their inherent ambivalence, constitute the subject of moderation. There will always be the danger of Christians obsessed with acquiring material goods and enjoying sensual pleasures. But there is also the problem of Christians regarding every concession to the modern world as a capitulation to sin. Prudence and the practice of moderation suggest that there is a virtuous middle ground between, on one hand, obtaining the latest gadgets and goods either from an acquisitive habit or an excessive desire for novelty and, on the other hand, an inordinate anxiety about acquiring things that truly make life easier. What is above all needed is a recognition of the communal dimension of virtues such as moderation—recognition of the value of seeking the community's collective wisdom as we determine the contours that a moderate life will assume.

Wisdom is another aspect of Christian character that forms the basis of care for creation. But to see this it is necessary to advert to the Old Testament conception of wisdom. In the Old Testament, wisdom is, above all, a characteristic of God displayed in the created order. To say that God made the world with wisdom (Psalm 104:24) is to say that each sort of thing in the world plays its role in the whole—hence Psalm 104's enumeration of the habitats and behaviors of the various animals, including humankind. The divine wisdom embedded in the world is a matter of the world's being a whole in which the various parts fit together. This notion of wisdom as things fitting together carries over into the book of Proverbs. Here human wisdom is portrayed as acting in ways that fit with the created world, whether in its human or nonhuman aspects. In other words, wisdom is a set of embodied practices. There is, in this theology, a way of being human that conforms to the order of the cosmos. This is the path of wisdom. There is also a way of being human that contradicts this order. This is the way of foolishness. It is important to see that, in the Old Testament's wisdom theology, wisdom and foolishness are not decided simply by their consequences. Consequences are important in the life of wisdom, but there is a larger context for understanding wisdom and foolishness. That larger context is the cosmic moral order. The wise person fits into it; the foolish person does not. The Christian who is wise and who meditates upon the nature of wisdom, will see himself or herself as a part of a larger created whole and as ethically fitting into that whole to the extent that he or she practices wisdom. To repeat a point already made: wisdom in itself is not the answer to every environmental problem. But it is a characteristic of the Christian life that is a prerequisite if the people of God are to be people who care for the created world. This care assumes that we see ourselves as integral parts of a whole that affects us and that we affect. It assumes that we grasp the point that some modes of behavior conform with the world's moral order and some modes contradict it. With wisdom, we are able to practice moderation, for we see our lives in the context of God and of God's created world and not only in the context of our immediate needs and desires. Wisdom lifts our attention beyond ourselves to larger realities and it brings home to us the ethical implications of our participation in those larger realities.

A third aspect of Christian character that underlies our care for the created world is the practice and pursuit of justice. In chapter 9, I discussed justice in terms of relations with the human community, without defining the extent of that community. It is natural, when considering justice, to think of one's immediate community. But there are larger considerations that bear on caring for creation. For one thing, there is our responsibility for preserving the created world in such a condition that it will sustain future generations of human beings. This issue falls under the question of distributive justice: how should society's goods be distributed, if society is defined to include not only those currently alive but future generations as well? For another, we have a responsibility to God the creator, and this responsibility has partly to do with our behavior toward the created world. Therefore, as the Bible recognizes, there is an important connection between wisdom and justice. The wise person is the one who sees the right order of things, whether in human affairs or in the larger created world, and recognizes disorder when it occurs. The just person acts to bring about or preserve this order. In the Bible, justice is completely a matter of what has often been called social justice—fair distribution of resources and equity in legal procedures. But, with our current environmental problems, we do no violence to the Bible or the Christian tradition if we see that human justice in relation to God—our responsibility to God—includes not only just relations in human community, but also caring for God's creation. Moreover, just as, in the Bible, justice means that the community must be specially sensitive to the needs of those who lack the power to protect and speak for themselves, so today the church is called on to be an advocate for the created world, which is likewise unable to protect itself against abuse by humankind and which lacks a voice for its sufferings.

World-Transcendence and World-Participation

THE IMPULSE TOWARD TRANSCENDING THE WORLD

How is care for God's creation an expression of our ethical transcendence over the world? Clearly, it does not mean our transcendence over the physical world of God's creation. Nowhere in the Bible or the Christian tradition is there any suggestion that the created world is something that we must overcome. The transcendence that care represents is a transcendence, however partial, over the attitudes and practices that underlie and, in part, cause environmental problems. It is important to keep in mind that the causes of environmental problems are many and complex and that Christian devotion and virtue are not the complete solution to these problems. Even if every member of the human race were a practicing Christian of the highest order, we would still (given current technology and rates of population growth) have environmental problems. Nonetheless, the development of a Christian character, with virtues such as moderation, wisdom, and justice, is a victory over the sort of life that has contributed to environmental problems and that stands in the way of a resolution.

This observation rests on the conviction that, at bottom, humankind's problems either are rooted in sin or are exacerbated by sin. In other words, humankind's problems are not only technical problems with technological solutions. Some problems, such as disease, are mainly technical problems and admit to strictly technological solutions. But even here human sin and foolish behavior contribute to the problem. Many problems are caused almost totally by humankind's tendency toward shortsighted and selfish behavior. Environmental problems are largely in this latter category. Patterns of waste, degradation, and poor management of resources, learned over generations when there was a seemingly limitless supply of resources, have been blindly carried into the present era when the limitations of nature have become evident. Obstinacy, ignorance, prejudice, and inertia combine to prevent an expeditious solution to these problems.

Therefore, when we care for God's creation, we are overcoming the sinful and foolish tendencies that have contributed to and largely caused environmental problems. Each act of caring for creation is an instance of God's kingdom encroaching on the fallen world. Each such act anticipates the eventual triumph of the kingdom of God, when the new creation will be brought to consummation. Each signals, in a preliminary way, the overcoming of sinful tendencies within us and within the corporate structures that we live in.

THE IMPULSE TOWARD PARTICIPATING IN THE WORLD

It is easier to see how care for creation represents our ethical participation in the world. In caring for God's world, we declare our solidarity with the rest of creation. We acknowledge our creaturely status (assuming that we do not see our care as the work of outside managers assigned the task of overseeing a domain that is fundamentally alien to us). In care we acknowledge that the physical world is the context of our life and that, being bodily creatures, our lives are radically dependent on the world. In short, care means that we see ourselves as a part of the world that God created—not spirits temporarily lodged in it, but integral parts of it. It is because we are integral parts of creation that prudential reasons for environmental concern can be effective strategies. What I mean is that, besides theological rationale for care, humans may be moved to action by the fact that our continued existence and well-being depend on the health of the world. Natural disasters and environmental catastrophes have a way of convincing us, when arguments do not, of our radical dependence on and participation in the world.

Beyond this sort of prudential concern, care also proclaims our belief in the goodness of God's creation. This is an important point because if there is only a prudential basis of our care, then we have not yet escaped the full grasp of sin. In this case we would care only because, and to the extent that, it promoted our well-being. Although this approach may be an effective strategy in rousing humankind to action, it falls far short of the Christian understanding of our responsibility. Although Christians have no hesitation in affirming that the physical universe is available to be used for our good, we also insist that the world has a relation to God that is, in some sense, independent of human beings. After all, the universe existed for billions of years before humankind came along, and there are portions of the universe that will never be experienced by us. There is no basis in the Christian faith for asserting that the natural world exists only for us. In biblical language, this means that the entire created world is good. It is a whole whose parts cohere, each part playing its role (except humans, who have sought to rewrite the script so as to make ourselves both director and lead actors). The capacity to affirm that the world is good (despite the presence of sin within it) is the benefit of wisdom. As previously discussed, it is wisdom that enables us to transcend our narrow, human-centered view of reality and gain a larger perspective.

Affirmation of the world's goodness and of our essential participation in the world is important for another reason. In every era of Christian history there have been some who have regarded the world as a lost cause. They typically find support in the apocalyptic tradition within the Bible. Second Peter, for instance, teaches that the heavens and all the earthly elements will be dissolved by fire, to be replaced by new heavens and a new earth (3:10-12). However, a more comprehensive look at the Bible indicates that destruction is not the symbol that describes the effect of God's kingdom. The new heavens and earth spoken of in Revelation 21:1 must be understood analogously to the new creation at work in the church. We, who were alienated from God and dead in sin, are the subjects of God's new creation. We have, in the words of Ephesians, put on the new humanity. And it is meaningful to talk in this context about destruction, for we have put off and crucified the old. But what is destroyed is not human being, but instead the power of sin that corrupts human beings. The new creation is not the cessation of one life and the beginning of a new life, but the transformation of human life that has been marred by sin. The new self in Christ is the old self of sin transformed. Accordingly, the new heavens and new earth are not to be thought of as utterly new and without connection to the present world. They are instead the present world transformed, as the culminating act of the new creation. This is the point that Paul made in Romans 8—not that the world will be destroyed, but that it "will be set free from its bondage to decay and will obtain the freedom of the glory of the children of God" (8:21). To care for God's creation, then, is to anticipate the consummation of the new creation and to participate in that new creation.

CARING FOR CREATION UNDER THE CONDITION OF FINITUDE

The church's care for the created world is performed under the condition of finitude. The finite character of our care has several implications. First, care is conditioned by the limitations of human understanding. Although we may fault previous generations for their lack of foresight in environmental matters, such lack is practically inevitable. Even when we do exercise foresight, our inability to foresee the full consequences of actions is a substantial problem. It results in uncertainty regarding the means of obtaining desired ends. Although many agree on the importance of developing alternative sources of energy, there is little agreement on which alternative sources are most promising and feasible. At least part of the problem here is our inability to predict accurately how well these sources will work and whether the consequences of their use justify their development. The finitude of understanding also appears in debates over scientific theories that bear on environmental concerns. As in all human affairs, environmental strategies are marked by this sort of limitation. Take, for example, global warming. The fact that this theory has not found universal acceptance is due in part to human obstinacy and in part to economic interests. But it is due in part also to the fact that the science and measurements underlying the theory are complex and open to varying interpretations. No doubt a consensus on this subject will be reached—we hope before it is too late—but it lies in the nature of environmental matters that their solution requires the results of the physical sciences. As is well known, the scientific community is often not able to reach conclusions before the political community requires those conclusions.

Another aspect of the finitude of our care is that we inevitably face conflicts of goods that admit of no easy resolution. The most pressing such conflict today is between the need to preserve and protect the natural world and the need of developing countries to provide basic goods for their populations. The understandable desire of these countries to alleviate poverty and reach the level of affluence already obtained by the developed countries means an increasing strain on the earth's resources and capacity to absorb pollution. The developed countries' laudable desire to preserve and protect the natural world is, not surprising, not always warmly received by developing countries. Some sort of accommodation will eventually be reached, but no resolution will be able to satisfy both demands optimally. A compromise is required.

The problem of the conflict of goods appears also in the fact that, necessarily, we have to make distinctions in our relations with the natural world. By now, most of us feel revulsion at the killing of primates and such mammals as whales. But few feel anxiety over intentional human destruction of harmful, disease-bearing insects. We are increasingly nervous about overusing the resources of the earth, but presumably no one would have serious objections to overusing the resources of Mercury or one of Saturn's moons. In making these sorts of distinctions, we inevitably use criteria that define the importance of things in terms of their relation to us. Primates and whales have some human-like characteristics, such as language, in rudimentary form. Bugs and bacteria do not. We depend on the earth and therefore are concerned for its well-being and that of the life on it. But we do not, so far as we know, depend on Pluto and it harbors no life. I am not saying that our judgments in these matters are misguided. I am just calling attention to the fact that our actions and policies inevitably arise from the perspective that we occupy. Although we may enlarge our perspective, we necessarily think from the perspective that we occupy. Stated differently, we do not possess a transcendent moral and epistemological standpoint. Calling attention to the perspectival character of our judgments is just another way of pointing to their finitude.

Finally, the finitude of our care is seen in the fact that it takes place within a larger cosmic reality in which chance events may well nullify the effects of our care. Current scientific theory indicates that at least twice in earth's past there have been mass extinctions, possibly caused by collisions with comets or asteroids. Scientists estimate that upwards of 90 percent of species were made extinct in these events. It is entirely possible that a future collision will take place. Unless we have by then developed technology capable of averting the collision, we can expect a similar level of extinction, and, since we are at the top of the food chain, we will be most vulnerable. But even if such a collision is averted, there are other natural disasters—volcanic activity, recurring ice ages, changes in the earth's magnetic field—capable of unimaginable alteration of life on earth. Almost none of these could be prevented by technology. Ultimately (although this event is billions of years in the future) our sun will finally have converted the last of its hydrogen into helium. Then will follow the final phases of the sun's life as a source of energy, in the course of which the earth will become utterly uninhabitable. So, in caring for God's creation, we should be under no illusion that our work is permanent. In our caring we labor under the greatest of limitations—the fact that our work can be voided at any moment by events utterly beyond our control. This fact, of course, is no excuse for laziness or a rapacious attitude. After all, we should still exercise and feed our bodies even though we know we will die. Accordingly, we are still responsible for ensuring, to the best of our ability, a resourceful earth for future generations and we are still responsible to God. But it is characteristic of our care that it occurs under the inevitability of the earth's eventual destruction.

The Practice of Caring for Creation in Community

The communal dimension of caring for creation rests on the premise that at least a part of our environmental problems results from humankind's tendency to think about the created world in overly individualistic ways, whether that means the individualism of the single person or of the single nation. Our thinking tends to focus on our immediate context: my individual self and its needs, my family, my immediate community, and so on. We find it all too difficult to take into account the needs of social realities with no direct connection to us as well as the needs of future generations. In part, this tendency is a manifestation of human selfishness—the tendency to achieve our own good even if it means diminishing others' good. In part, this tendency results from lack of legal structures. That is, in the absence of treaties or global agencies with enforcement powers, one nation (or other political entity) may undertake policies that harm others. In part, it results from lack of knowledge, as in the decades during which industries were unwittingly contributing to acid rain and affecting regions far beyond their own. At the heart of the problem is a lack of broad moral horizon and a persistent incapacity to see the consequences of our actions beyond our immediate circumstances.

What is the Christian community's role in this matter? Unlike such intra-church practices as baptism and worship, the care of creation is not the sort of thing that can be adequately addressed strictly within and by the church. Environmental problems are of such a magnitude that, in most cases, only large-scale, international, and corporate solutions are viable. What is needed is legislation, changes to corporate policies, and international agreements. No congregation and no denomination is in a position to effect a resolution of any environmental problem. But it is no criticism of the church to make this observation. The church's primary task is not to solve the world's problems, but instead to nurture believers in the faith and to bear witness to the gospel.

But this twofold task of bearing witness and nurturing is not without relevance to the care of creation. The church uses its tools of formative discipline to shape itself into a community that is sensitive to God's call to care for the world and to live moderately, with justice and wisdom. Through its educational efforts and other formative means, it forms Christian disciples who are mindful of the fact that the world is created by God and mindful as well of humankind's place in the created world. However, it is to be expected that this formative process will be a lengthy one. After all, our society as a whole and the church in particular have become aware of environmental problems only in the last forty or so years. The sorts of lessons that are required if believers are to be formed into people who care for creation will doubtless take a long time to become ingrained. Consequently, an extended commitment to nurturing and formation is needed if these lessons are to be internalized and expressed in customary modes of behavior.

In addition to its nurturing function, the church is called on to bear witness to the gospel. It performs this function in two main ways. The first is by being a community that cares for creation and that lives moderately, with wisdom and justice. This means that the church, at both the congregational and denominational levels, should engage in practices that are environmentally responsible. In this way, the church can model for the world what care for creation looks like in practice. To the extent that the church is faithful in these practices, it proclaims to the world the importance of responding to God's call. Further, by incorporating sound practices into its policies and routines, it ingrains, at least in a small way, in its members caring patterns of behavior. The second way in which the church bears witness is in the form of public declarations. A notable example of this is the pastoral letter by Roman Catholic bishops in the regions around the Columbia River. This letter was based on extensive study of the environmental problems associated with the river and with the economic contribution of the river. Conversations took place with scientists as well as with local inhabitants who were most likely to suffer from environmental problems and who would be most affected by proposed solutions. The result is a theological statement about creation and about the theological significance of attempts to remedy particular environmental problems. Although no one supposes that this sort of document will alone solve the range of environmental problems, it functions effectively as the church's witness to the gospel.

The Practice of Caring for Creation in a Fallen World

Our care for the created world occurs as well in a fallen world. The power of sin manifests itself in two ways. First, Christian disciples must struggle to practice moderation, wisdom, and justice. They do not come naturally to us but must be matters of constant attention and effort. Second, as already mentioned, we find ourselves embedded in social and economic practices that are, practically speaking, unavoidable but that are also destructive of the environment.

First, because our redemption is not yet completed, moderation, wisdom, and justice must be learned and then, by practice, made a part of us. But because the church exists in a fallen world, it is difficult to acquire these virtues as well as all too easy to lapse from them into profligacy, foolishness, and injustice. These negative qualities are subtly encouraged by the fallen world, which continues to exercise its effect on us by socializing us into patterns of consumption and into expectations of affluence that are at odds with moderation. This is why the church must be a community in which these virtues are exemplified, taught, and nurtured.

Second, even if Christian disciples were to perfect moderation and the other virtues, the church would still unavoidably participate in fallen structures—social, large-scale patterns of consumption that result in pollution and degradation of habitats. Unless the church is going to opt out of modern society altogether, it can hardly help participating in the extensive use of resources characteristic of our society. Modern church life is hardly conceivable without modern modes and volumes of communication, construction, and transportation. Individual believers must travel from home to work and the pattern of city building in the post–World War II era means that the distances traveled continue to increase, bringing increased use of fuels and increased pollution.

Although activities such as communication and travel are not sinful if they are considered with respect to their purpose, their effect on the environment is not negligible. It is, in fact, a part of humankind's overall use of the earth that has had, in some respects, a devastating effect on the environment. The church alone is not the cause of humankind's environmental problems and it is not the sole solution. But it can hardly help being—unintentionally—a part of the problem, and therein lies its unwilling participation in the fallen world. Thus is the church's care for creation partly vitiated by the enduring effects of sin. That is why a part of the church's proclamation and witness must be to the vision of God's kingdom in which a harmony between humankind's legitimate needs and the resources of the earth is achieved.

Caring for Creation and Participation in God

In spite of our participation in the fallen world, the Christian life is a participation in the trinitarian life of God. This means that our care for the created world is grounded in God's life and made possible by our participation in that life.

The trinitarian life of God is a life of movement: from the Father through the Son to the Spirit and back to the Father. This movement is repeated in God's relation to the world. All things in the world come from God the Father through Jesus Christ (in the Spirit) (1 Corinthians 8:6). The culmination of this movement toward creatures is the incarnation and its sequel, the giving of the Holy Spirit. In the incarnation, God identifies with the created world (in its representative, humankind), even to the extent of experiencing death. In the giving of the Spirit, God comes to be present to us in the most intimate way possible. The movement back to God the Father consists of praise given by the created world, both human and nonhuman (Psalm 149). In this praise, creation follows the lead of Jesus Christ, whose prayer was that the name of God might be holy (Matthew 6:9) and who, in the eschatological consummation of all things, will deliver the kingdom to God the Father, so that God may be all in all (1 Corinthians 15:24-28). To speak of God's care for creation is to speak of this movement whereby God comes to identity with the created world. This is why it is not a surprise that John's Gospel links God's love for the world with the sending of the Son into the world.

Consequently, our care for creation is our participation in the divine identification with the world. As the body of Christ, the church is a continuation of God's coming to creation and identifying with creation through the event of the new creation. The church continues the outward, newly creating movement of God. It is thus both a sign of the kingdom of God and, eschatologically, the embodiment of that kingdom. It is also the vanguard of creation's return to God through praise. In its praise of the Father through Jesus in the Spirit, the church offers vocally the praise of God that all creation offers silently. The church thus speaks for creation.

Particular modes of care are implied by these observations. If the church is truly the embodied continuation of God's new creation, then it must be mindful of its acts and of its effects on the object of that new creation—both the human and nonhuman worlds. Destruction of God's creation is, from this perspective, contradictory. Of course, this does not imply that the created world is not available for human use. Biological life within the world involves killing and eating. As organic beings who participate in that world, we participate in the process of killing and eating. But our use of the world will be marked by moderation and wisdom and conducted with the aim of achieving justice.

Likewise, if we see the created world as a chorus offering praise to God, with humankind taking the vocal part, then we will be ill-disposed to adopt a rapacious attitude toward the world, seeing it merely as an instrument for the satisfaction of our needs and desires. On the contrary, we will seek to preserve the diversity of the world, on the strength of the conviction that the world's diversity contributes beauty to the chorus of praise that the world offers to God.

Concluding Meditative Prayer

We praise you, Lord and Spirit of creation, who created all things and by whose will they exist. With every created thing we praise your wisdom and your goodness. Blessed are those who love the world as you love the world and care as you care. We confess to you, our Lord, our selfishness and our shortsightedness. We acknowledge our sloth in the task of caring for your creation. Preserve us safe from the spirit of greed and acquisition, from the temptation to exploit and destroy, and from being heedless of the beauty of your creation. Make us mindful of our place in creation and of our dependence on the world you have made. Give us eyes to see the world as you see it. Give us the spirit of thankfulness, and sanctify for us the good things of creation for our benefit and sustenance. We pray that you would hasten the final deliverance, when creation itself will be set free from its bondage to decay, when it will obtain the freedom of the glory of God's children. We pray that until then you would make us fit servants of your redemptive work. We pray as well for those who do not know you and do not know this world as your creation. May they come to entrust themselves to you, the faithful creator.

You, our God, who creates and creates anew, we praise.
>   We praise the Father, from whom and for whom are all things,
>   through the Son, through whom are all things and in whom all holds together,
>   in the Spirit, the Spirit of life, in whom all creation has fellowship with the Father and the Son.

We praise the holy Trinity, Father, Son, and Spirit, the beginning and end of creation.

Sources Consulted and Recommended

Anderson, Bernhard W. "Creation and the Noachic Covenant." In *From Creation to New Creation: Old Testament Perspectives*. Overtures to Biblical Theology. Minneapolis: Fortress Press, 1994.

————. "Human Dominion over Nature." In *From Creation to New Creation: Old Testament Perspectives*. Overtures to Biblical Theology. Minneapolis: Fortress Press, 1994.

————. "Relation between the Human and Nonhuman Creation in the Biblical Primeval History." In *From Creation to New Creation: Old Testament Perspectives*. Overtures to Biblical Theology. Minneapolis: Fortress Press, 1994.

Barr, James. "Man and Nature: The Ecological Controversy and the Old Testament." In *Ecology and Religion in History*. Edited by David Spring and Eileen Spring. New York: Harper & Row, 1974.

Bauckham, Richard. "Stewardship and Relationship." In *The Care of Creation: Focusing Concern and Action*. Edited by R. J. Berry. Leicester, England: Inter-Varsity Press, 2000.

Berry, R. J., ed. *The Care of Creation: Focusing Concern and Action*. Leicester, England: Inter-Varsity Press, 2000.

"The Columbia River Watershed: Caring for Creation and the Common Good. An

International Pastoral Letter by the Catholic Bishops of the Region." 2001. http://www.columbiariver.org/main_pages/Watershed/WORD/english.doc

Carroll, John T. "Creation and Apocalypse." In *God Who Creates: Essays in Honor of W. Sibley Towner*. Edited by William P. Brown and S. Dean McBride, Jr. Grand Rapids: William B. Eerdmans Publishing Co., 2000.

Derr, Thomas Sieger. *Ecology and Human Liberation: A Theological Critique of the Use and Abuse of Our Birthright*. Geneva: World Council of Churches, 1973.

Fowler, Robert Booth. *The Greening of Protestant Thought*. Chapel Hill, NC: The University of North Carolina Press, 1995.

Fretheim, Terence E. "Nature's Praise of God in the Psalms." *Creation* 3 (1987): 16-30.

Harrison, Peter. "Subduing the Earth: Genesis 1, Early Modern Science, and the Exploitation of Nature." *Journal of Religion* 79, no. 1 (1999): 86-109.

Hessel, Dieter T. ed. *After Nature's Revolt: Eco-Justice and Theology*. Minneapolis: Fortress Press, 1992.

Malchow, Bruce V. "Contrasting Views of Nature in the Hebrew Bible." *Dialog* 26 (1987): 40-43.

McFague, Sallie. *Super, Natural Christians: How We Should Love Nature*. Minneapolis: Fortress Press, 1997.

Santmire, H. Paul. "Healing the Protestant Mind: Beyond the Theology of Human Dominion." In *After Nature's Revolt: Eco-Justice and Theology*. Edited by Dieter T. Hessel. Minneapolis: Fortress Press, 1992.

Simkins, Ronald A. *Creator and Creation: Nature in the Worldview of Ancient Israel*. Peabody, MA: Hendrickson Publishers, 1994.

Tucker, Gene M. "The Peaceable Kingdom and a Covenant with the Wild Animals." In *God Who Creates: Essays in Honor of W. Sibley Towner*. Edited by William P. Brown and S. Dean McBride, Jr. Grand Rapids: William B. Eerdmans Publishing Co., 2000.

CONCLUSION

The distinctive features of Christian spirituality are essential practices and the theology that underlies them. Among those practices are those that I have described in this book: baptism, faith, worship, discipline, virtues, generosity and justice, and care of the created world. Others could be listed. The distinctively Christian theology that underlies these practices is multilayered. It presupposes the Bible's teaching about creation and redemption. It builds on its teaching about holiness and righteousness. It takes with full seriousness the devastating effects and pervasiveness of sin. It also takes fully seriously the possibilities of God's grace and the eschatological reality of the kingdom of God. Moreover, it sees grace as the new life available to us as we participate in God's trinitarian life. It is a theology that supports the emphasis on embodied practices that is needed today. It connects those practices to the Christian faith by drawing attention to the dual ethical impulses of the Christian life, the impulse toward participating in the world and the impulse toward transcending the world. Additionally, it does justice to the embodied nature of those practices and to the doctrine of creation by framing them within the limits of our essential finitude. Finally, it locates those practices in the corporate life of the church.

There are several implications of this theology. Some are quite obvious to anyone who accepts the theses and analysis that I have proposed. For example, it should be obvious that the church must have diligent regard for the way in which it embodies or fails to embody the Christian faith. Likewise, there will be little controversy about the proposal that we nurture the church's communal life because of its indispensability to living the Christian life authentically.

But there are other implications as well. For one, my analysis may be of help to clergy who labor in various sorts of chaplaincy and who, probably more than anyone today, work in the interstices of church and world. We live in very confusing times. On one hand, the wall of separation between church and state is more contentious than ever, as debates about mangers and the ten commandments in public places testify. On the other hand, the recent governmental emphasis on faith-based social programs means that clergy are today working in a wide range of governmental and quasi-governmental agencies for expressly religious purposes. In part this openness is due to the ideological slant of the current president, but in part it is due to what many in the health, welfare, and therapeutic communities are recognizing as the beneficial effects of religious devotion and practices. Of course, this openness is not restricted by confessional identities. If, for example, health experts come to believe that prayer is physiologically beneficial, it will likely matter little to them whether the prayer is Christian or Buddhist. Nonetheless, those in chaplaincy roles find themselves in the position of being publicly supported and sanctioned dispensers of the means of social well-being.

It is legitimate for chaplains to fill this role, in spite of what I have said about the importance of distinctively Christian practices and theology. It is legitimate because, as I have noted, Christians are called upon to transcend the world but not reject it. Practically, this means that, for example, Christian virtue transcends the public virtue of our culture and, where necessary, stands in prophetic judgment over it. But Christian virtue does not necessarily mean the rejection of public virtues and the practices of other religions. If honesty is good, then it is good whether proposed by Christians, Hindus, or a secular government, although Christians will believe that there is probably more to be said about honesty than others will say. If, in the course of grief or addiction counseling, it proves effective to urge people to seek out a higher source, then the Christian chaplain will take his or her place alongside people of other religions, although he or she will be convinced that the gospel has something essential to add to this counsel that other religions are perhaps not saying.

To use the words of Thomas Aquinas, grace perfects but does not contradict nature. Of course, Thomas knew that human nature had been distorted by sin, so he was not claiming that we can simply identify human behavior with graced behavior. But he was saying that, in spite of sin, human nature is capable of a certain measure of virtue and wholeness and that human society even outside the church can be structured so as to actualize this limited degree of virtue and wholeness.

Clergy who are chaplains are one way the church ministers to the public. Whether hospital, prison, police, or armed services personnel, chaplains are one of the public faces of the church; and theology should be another. One reason why it is not is that, in our cultural situation today, there is, as I have noted, a tacit public agreement that we will leave matters of religion to individual choice and inclination. Public debates about the merits and demerits of religion are rare and seem to constitute a breach of our social code. Individuals who prove to be too zealous in trying to convince their friends and neighbors about their religious beliefs are generally regarded as uncivil. In this atmosphere, publicly contending for the truth of the Christian faith is almost impossible because there are so few public venues at which such contending could take place.

Nonetheless, theology is a function of the church, and if the church is ethically to participate in the world, then its theology must as well. There are various forms that this can take. One is the apologetic task—defending the church's beliefs against wrongful attacks and arguing for the coherence of Christian belief. There are today any number of misconceptions about the Christian faith and Christian history, many of them lingering howlers from eighteenth-century rationalist attacks on the church or garbled versions of distant historical events. They appear in newspapers, radio, and more technical forums. The church needs those who are eloquent, conciliatory, and patient to respond to these attacks. Such response in itself probably will not gain many converts, but there is something to be said for setting the record straight.

Another form in which theology could be a public face of the church lies in presenting the Christian faith affirmatively to the non-Christian public. What is called for here is supplementing the church's practical witness with a verbal witness. The church's intellectual leaders (a group larger than its professional theologians) have the responsibility of presenting the Christian faith to the public in ways that are logically coherent and rhetorically compelling. The difficulty of this task is not coherent presentation, but rather communicating compellingly, a talent that not all theologians have, especially when we consider the importance of communicating to a public whose interest in theology is negligible and whose book-reading habits are declining. Nonetheless, if the church in America is to carry out its missionary task, it has to do more than provide a witness by practicing the faith. Public, verbal presentations of the gospel in a variety of media are necessary. This, of course, implies that theologians representing the church are cooperating with God in the redemption of the world and that in this way the church participates in the world even while ethically transcending it.

This discussion of the church's public face introduces another implication of my analysis of corporate spirituality. This implication bears on the relation between, in H. Richard Niebuhr's phrase, Christ and culture. This relationship has become more pressing than ever in view of the post-Christian character of American religion. As a result, fresh thinking about this relationship is needed. The problem is that, ever since Niebuhr, theologians have outdone themselves in trying to identify which type of relation that Niebuhr outlined best represents the authentically Christian view. The types are: (1) Christ above culture (exemplified by Thomas Aquinas); (2) Christ the transformer of culture (exemplified by the Reformed tradition); (3) Christ and culture in paradox (expounded by Martin Luther); (4) Christ against culture (exemplified by the Anabaptist tradition); and (5) the Christ of culture (exemplified by liberal theology). The leading candidates are almost always Christ the transformer of culture (most theologians choosing this one) and Christ against culture (the minority of theologians).

Grasping the dialectics of world-participation and world-transcendence enables us to go beyond a simple choice among these types and to see the partial truth of each type. In this way we come closer to Niebuhr's purpose in proposing these types. In stating that Christ is above culture, we affirm with Thomas Aquinas that grace perfects nature and that human virtues and goods are ecstatic in that they are grounded in God. We acknowledge the goodness of the created world while recognizing its incompleteness apart from grace and the toll that sin has taken upon it. We confess the goodness of the world in which we necessarily participate while proclaiming the need to transcend the world in its fallen state. In stating that Christ is the transformer of culture, we repeat the affirmations of "Christ above culture" but add that the impulse to participate in the world drives us to prepare the world for the realization of God's kingdom and, as far as is possible, to make the world an anticipation of that kingdom. The transforming motif reminds us not only that God is the *telos* of creation, but also that our calling to participation is a calling to cooperate with God's work of redemption. The truth of the "Christ of culture" type is its vision of the transformation of human culture to such an extent that the kingdom of God is fully incarnated in human society. In other words, this position represents the maximum actualization of the impulse toward world-participation with no impulse toward transcending the world. The power of this type lies in its eschatological hope. The danger is that we will adopt this position before the eschatological consummation and will fail to remember the distortions of sin. The partial truth of the "Christ against culture" type is its nagging reminder of the importance of nurturing the impulse toward world-transcendence. If the Christ of culture is a Christ that is thoroughly immanent and not at all transcendent, then the Christ against culture is all transcendence with little or no participation in the world. Although the "Christ against culture" type is not sufficient for the Christian life, we risk the vitality of the church if we ignore its truth. Finally, to assert that Christ and culture are paradoxically related is to assert that it is one and the same church with its members that both participates in the world and ethically strives to transcend the world. The "Christ against culture" type encourages us to think of the church as that which has rejected the world and regards many or most forms of participation with suspicion. To say that Christ and culture are paradoxically related is to say that the church must somehow participate in and transcend the world. It is not that sinners participate and saints transcend. It is the church and its members that must do justice to both impulses.

The necessity of this task lies in the trinitarian life of God. If paganism represented the truth about God, then we would be tempted to stifle the impulse toward transcendence and to identify our world with God's will. This is because we would see God mainly in terms of the divine participation in the world. If Gnosticism or Deism represented the truth, then we would face the opposite temptation—minimizing the participatory impulse and exalting transcendence. This is because these movements had little patience for talk about God's participation in the world. But because God is the Trinity—Jesus Christ, whom the Father sent into the world in the power of the Spirit—we confess that God transcends the world and also that God participates in the world, even to the point of incarnation. Moreover, we do not believe in two gods or parts of God, one that participates in the world, the other transcending the world. On the contrary, it is one and the same God who, without confusion or contradiction, fully participates and fully transcends. The Christian life is the attempt to mimic the divine harmony of participation and transcendence within the limitations of finitude and under the condition of sin.

A final implication of this analysis is the reminder that if the Christian life is, as a result of its eschatological character, a tensed life—a life tensed between the past and the future in the razor thin present of hope and despair—then it is also a graced life. It is graced because it is a communion in God's life. To say that it is a graced life is to say, first, that we receive it as a gift as we are drawn, through the Spirit, into the fellowship between the Father and the Son. It is to say, second, that it is conducted through the power of God. Admittedly, this is not a strictly empirical matter. We cannot isolate God's power in our lives and make it a subject of study. God works in us as we work. But without God's working in us, our deeds would remain utterly mundane. With God's working, we offer back to God the life that we receive from God, even in its finite and sinful condition. In this act of worship and consecration, we complete the cycle of creation, in which all things come from God and return, in due course, to God.

SCRIPTURE INDEX

Index of Names and Topics